COUNTERINSURGENCY IN CRISIS

Columbia Studies in Terrorism and Irregular Warfare

COLUMBIA STUDIES IN TERRORISM
AND IRREGULAR WARFARE
Bruce Hoffman, Series Editor

This series seeks to fill a conspicuous gap in the burgeoning literature on terrorism, guerrilla warfare, and insurgency. The series adheres to the highest standards of scholarship and discourse and publishes books that elucidate the strategy, operations, means, motivations, and effects posed by terrorist, guerrilla, and insurgent organizations and movements. It thereby provides a solid and increasingly expanding foundation of knowledge on these subjects for students, established scholars, and informed reading audiences alike.

Ami Pedahzur, *The Israeli Secret Services and the Struggle Against Terrorism*
Ami Pedahzur and Arie Perliger, *Jewish Terrorism in Israel*
Lorenzo Vidino, *The New Muslim Brotherhood in the West*
Erica Chenoweth and Maria J. Stephan, *Why Civil Resistance Works:
    The Strategic Logic of Nonviolent Resistance*
William C. Banks, *New Battlefields/Old Laws: Critical Debates on
    Asymmetric Warfare*
Blake W. Mobley, *Terrorism and Counterintelligence: How Terrorist Groups
    Elude Detection*
Guido Steinberg, *German Jihad: On the Internationalization of
    Islamist Terrorism*
Michael W. S. Ryan, *The Deep Battle: Decoding Al-Qaeda's Strategy
    Against America*

DAVID H. UCKO
AND ROBERT EGNELL

COUNTERINSURGENCY IN CRISIS

Britain and the Challenges of
Modern Warfare

Columbia University Press / New York

Columbia University Press
Publishers Since 1893
New York   Chichester, West Sussex
cup.columbia.edu

Copyright © 2013 David H. Ucko and Robert Egnell
All rights reserved

Library of Congress Cataloging-in-Publication Data
Ucko, David H.
    Counterinsurgency in crisis : Britain and the challenges of modern warfare /
David H. Ucko and Robert Egnell.
        pages   cm.
    Includes bibliographical references and index.
    ISBN 978-0-231-16426-9 (cloth : alk. paper) — ISBN 978-0-231-53541-0 (ebook).
    1. Counterinsurgency—Great Britain. 2. Counterinsurgency—Iraq—Basra. 3.
Counterinsurgency—Afghanistan—Helmand. 4. Iraq War, 2003–2011—Participa-
tion, British. 5. Afghan War, 2001—Participation, British. 6. Great Britain—History,
Military—21st century. I. Egnell, Robert. II. Title.

    U241.U255   2013
    355'.0218o941—dc23

Columbia University Press books are printed on permanent and durable acid-free paper.
This book is printed on paper with recycled content.
Printed in the United States of America

c 10 9 8 7 6 5 4 3 2 1

JACKET DESIGN: James Perales
JACKET IMAGE: Copyright © 2013 Corbis

References to websites (URLs) were accurate at the time of writing.
Neither the author nor Columbia University Press is responsible for URLs that may
have expired or changed since the manuscript was prepared.

CONTENTS

Foreword by Colin S. Gray   vii

Preface   xiii

Acknowledgments   xvii

Abbreviations   xxi

INTRODUCTION: RETHINKING COUNTERINSURGENCY

1

1. UNTANGLING THE BRITISH
COUNTERINSURGENCY LEGACY

19

2. THE BRITISH IN BASRA

45

3. ACT II: BRITISH COUNTERINSURGENCY
IN HELMAND

75

CONTENTS

4. "A HORSE AND TANK MOMENT"
109

5. WHITHER BRITISH COUNTERINSURGENCY?
145

Notes 167
Bibliography 187
Index 205

FOREWORD

Colin S. Gray

This book is not a comfortable read for a British strategist like myself. David Ucko and Robert Egnell are scholarly and measured in their treatment of the British experience with counterinsurgency, but they are all the more lethal as a consequence. British strategic effectiveness through counterinsurgency endeavors in the 2000s has been distinctly unimpressive. Indeed, it has been so unimpressive that the investigator is all but spoiled for choice in allocating blame. Although *Counterinsurgency in Crisis* should be read primarily as a careful study of the British experience of counterinsurgency in the 2000s in Iraq and Afghanistan, it speaks volumes to subjects with wide meaning. Specifically, the authors have much to say of high importance about our understanding and misunderstanding of strategy in its relation to tactics. They also raise and discuss basic vital questions pertaining to the relationship between counterinsurgency and war. These topics can seem to be merely scholars' conceptual playthings, but one should not be fooled into making such a dismissive judgment. Strategic theory is about strategic practice, and conceptual understanding of what it is that we believe we are doing in counterinsurgency is critical for our performance and its consequences.

As a Briton, one may not find it agreeable to be told that one's national strategic performance in the 2000s can be characterized as an unpleasant combination of "swagger and unpreparedness," in the authors' tellingly apposite phrase. Unfortunately, these words are exactly right, painful though it is for me to agree with them. There are villains—or perhaps only incompetents—everywhere. The British public is rightly proud of the bravery shown by "our lads and lasses" in extremely difficult circumstances. But the generally negative rating given in Britain today to the protracted counterinsurgency (and attempted "stabilization") experience in the 2000s is not yet suffused with appropriate understanding of why things went so badly wrong for British forces in both Iraq and Afghanistan. This book explains graphically the contextual challenges that the British state sought to meet, but it leaves the reader in no doubt whatsoever that many of the British counterinsurgency troubles in the 2000s were truly self-inflicted.

Counterinsurgency in Crisis is a genuinely important book in its ability to deal fairly but uncompromisingly with two protracted cases of counterinsurgency in both conceptual and historical context. Some of the British problem undoubtedly was particular to Britain, but much was not. This excellent study can be read as an audit of counterinsurgency effort that happens to be focused on Britain. One learns here about counterinsurgency, not just about Britain and counterinsurgency. The shortlist of villains responsible for the lack of quality in British strategic performance is well populated. Accepting the risk of apparent overstatement, I need to cite recent British weakness at every level of endeavor: vision of desired identity and role (culture), foreign policy, strategy, and tactical military competence. Ucko and Egnell reveal high British ambition for a continuing global role as loyal first lieutenant to Uncle Sam but also show British inability to think strategically with any rigor about what such a role demands. The fundamental structure and logic of strategy provide the conceptual forensic tools most readily suited to economical dissection of the British problem with counterinsurgency in the 2000s. To be plain,

- Britain was proud of its believed ability to "punch above its weight" in the world, particularly as an ally in the "special relationship" with the United States (a romanticized status invented by Winston Churchill)—overconfident in its ability to "muddle through" and behave adaptively to whatever came along, even when British assets were desperately short.

- British foreign policy ambition has not adjusted fully to the country's reduced circumstances.
- Grand and military strategy have largely been missing as direction for British action. In notable part, this absence is attributable to the fact that the classic logical structure of strategic reasoning (ends, ways, and means—effected in the dim light of some dubious assumptions) simply has not been applied in official decision making and subsequent behavior.
- The British military has been fatally short of suitable strategic sense from the top, of appropriate operational direction, and of tactical skills (as well of the numbers of people and the equipment necessary for contemporary conflicts).

The picture is a grisly one, though this shortlisted summary may inadvertently mislead the reader by failing to emphasize the most deadly sin of all: the failure to commit to interventionary action with a robustly viable political story. War and its warfare (by definition) are done with violence, but they are *about* politics. Carl von Clausewitz continues to be right.[1] It is entirely possible to lay most of the blame for the Western insurgency imbroglios of Iraq and Afghanistan on the United States as alliance/coalition leader, but that does not exonerate Britain.

I have written harshly here, but not with exaggeration. The story outlined is admittedly unvarnished, but, alas, it is not seriously contestable. For understandable reasons of loyalty and human empathy, this uncontroversial negative view of the recent British experience with counterinsurgency has yet to be assimilated politically in Britain, even though it is certainly understood in detail, isolated element by isolated element. David Ucko and Robert Egnell perform a signal necessary service by writing a book that is compelling in its layered detailing of British political, strategic, and tactical weakness. It aids comprehension of the full scope and scale of national strategic failure. On the positive side, however, they provide evidence that should help reform.

Beyond the book's British focus, the authors compel readers to pay attention to fundamental questions about insurgency, *ab extensio* counterinsurgency, and intervention in foreign(ers') conflicts. War and its warfare are really most sensibly to be approached conceptually and practically as a single unified category of human political nastiness. The reading of this volume rewards efforts to secure an intellectual grip on the understanding of contemporary and prospectively future war. Armed forces need to be led by people with strategic sense who understand what strategy is, why it matters, and how to do it. This is not to offer an irrelevant counsel of perfection. Rather, it is to claim only that when one considers going to war or at least conducting some warfare (however we choose to characterize it for political and legal reasons), one must think and behave in a manner alert to the implications of the logical structure of ends, ways, and means. Furthermore, indeed more basic still, we should honor Clausewitz in our deeds by insisting on the political viability of the intended consequences of the violence we expect to perpetrate.

A principal virtue of historical education is its ability to inoculate against capture by novelty. A strategic studies community heavily peopled by social and physical scientists has had serious difficulty thinking holistically about war and warfare as a subject that changes its character but not its nature in the great stream of time. What Britain was doing in the 2000s in Iraq and Afghanistan was not counterinsurgency as a new set of challenges requiring new strategic theory. Instead, the new challenge comprised dynamic variants of the all too familiar beast known broadly as war and including necessarily some threat and use of military force (violence) in warfare. It should not be an epiphany to recognize that the more lethal weaknesses in the British efforts in Iraq and Afghanistan generically were entirely familiar from experience in past conflicts. The British story of these two conflicts reveals yet again the difficulty of playing a subordinate role in a coalition or alliance (e.g., Britain in World War I in 1914–1917, World War II in 1944–1945, and Korea in 1950–1953), the absolute necessity for a good enough clear political purpose acceptable to all vital players, and a national military instrument that can generate the strategic effectiveness required to meet national objectives, be they great or small.

It is entirely appropriate to focus on the particular needs of strategic effectiveness in specific conflicts. After all, we know for certain that no two wars (or conflicts) are quite the same. However, when one looks closely at individual cases, as do Ucko and Egnell, one finds that nearly all the greater faults examined here could apply to any war or conflict, not specifically to those identified as having the British character of counterinsurgency. On the tactical level, Iraq and Afghanistan have of course been distinctive. But, more properly viewed simply as modern wars, they are far from distinctive. What I take from our bitter experience of the 2000s is a growing conviction that "war" and its warfare need to be understood and approached as a single broad category of more or less organized human behavior that contains a wide variety of particular cases. Our professional military needs direction by competent strategy and to that end has to be trained and equipped so as to be adaptable to the unique demand of particular challenges as they arise. However, much of the needful competence and capability is generic to the enduring nature of the activity of war.

The British failure in Basra and Helmand was essentially but not solely strategic. False assumptions, unclear or impossible political ends, impracticable ways, and inadequate means wrought damage in the 2000s for Britain, but when have such liabilities ever yielded a favorable outcome?

Counterinsurgency in Crisis is a "milestone" book that should have lasting value. It pulls no punches, but it is not a political work in the obvious sense that applies thus far to nearly all the works that have sought to reveal reasons for contemporary counterinsurgency troubles. In short, the book is deeply political, but only as it needs to be in its proper (Clausewitzian) appreciation of the purpose of war. Anyone who wants to understand why counterinsurgency in Iraq and Afghanistan proved so difficult to do competently cannot do better than by reading it.

PREFACE

Long considered the masters of counterinsurgency, the British military encountered significant problems in Iraq and Afghanistan when confronted with insurgent violence. Its efforts to apply the counterinsurgency principles and doctrine of previous campaigns reveal critical disconnects in how counterinsurgency is today planned and prosecuted.

In this book we provide a detailed account of the British military operations in Basra and Helmand. These experiences are counterposed to the British legacy of counterinsurgency so as to identify the contribution and limitations of traditional principles within the contemporary strategic environment. What emerges from this analysis is a troubling gap between ambitions and resources, intent and commitment.

On the basis of this analysis, we also offer an assessment of British military institutional adaptation in response to operations gone awry. Given the effectiveness of insurgent tactics, the frequency of operations aimed at building local capacity, and the danger of weak and failing states acting as havens for hostile groups, the military must acquire new skills to confront irregular threats in future wars. This book offers an inside view of how the British military has responded to this challenge, how it has realigned priorities and policy all against a backdrop of a financial crisis.

The discussion leads to the fundamental question of Britain's role in the world—how it has adjusted its horizons and expeditionary ambitions, or balanced the upsets of recent campaigns with a self-image as a major player in global affairs. Much will depend on assuming a more modest role and of treating the wars of the future on their own terms.

STRUCTURE AND ARGUMENT IN BRIEF

Given the number of books and journal articles already devoted to the colonial and postcolonial British experiences with counterinsurgency, this book will not engage once more with this rich yet highly checkered history. Instead, our first concern is with the historiography of the British counterinsurgency legacy—namely, its construction through generations of academic scholarship, memoirs, and storytelling. Chapter 1 examines this historiography and makes two key arguments: first, that the reading of past campaigns has tended to be informed by a selective and superficial analysis of historical events that fails to capture the variation in British counterinsurgency practice; and, second, that the strategic and operational contexts have changed dramatically since the heyday of colonial policing and withdrawal. Making comparisons and drawing lessons from past campaigns must therefore be done with utmost attention to the key differences in context, aims, resources, and tactical options. These factors are not accounted for in the necessarily pithy principles derived from the associated campaigns, which nonetheless continue to inform our contemporary counterinsurgency doctrine. In this sense, the common recollection of the British experience can easily become ahistorical and sloganeering, with purported best practices recycled and restated with scant attention to the contextual factors that once enabled their application. The underlying argument here is that the British military that invaded Iraq in 2003 operated on a false interpretation of its own counterinsurgency legacy.

It follows from this treatment of the British counterinsurgency legacy that much of its confidence with these types of operations was ill founded. To illustrate this point and to demonstrate the full complexity of contemporary counterinsurgency, chapters 2 and 3 assess British operations in Basra and Helmand. What emerges from these case studies is a clear picture of a military struggling to adapt to unfamiliar settings and challenges, under unclear political direction and typically with insufficient resources at hand. The analysis does not seek to rub salt into the wounds of the British armed forces, but rather to identify the requirements for operational and strategic effectiveness in the field as well as the difficulties they impose on the armed forces of today, given their structure, orientation, and training.

In light of the clear capability gaps exposed through the recent conduct of counterinsurgency, how has the British government and its Ministry of Defense (MoD) responded? How has the military sought to address these deficiencies, help its deployed soldiers, and prepare institutionally for future campaigns of similar or greater complexity? Chapter 4 deals with these questions. The assessment reveals a troubling combination of institutional innovation and inertia whereby change is often apparent but only rarely sufficiently deep-running. Despite daily, brutal reminders of the challenges of conducting war in Iraq and Afghanistan and the MoD's own forecast for a "future character of conflict" presenting similar difficulties, it is not clear at this point that the institution has reacted accordingly in terms of either its priorities and resource allocation or its understanding of war.[1]

To cap off this analysis, the concluding chapter examines what recent experiences in Basra and Helmand mean for the future of British counterinsurgency. These campaigns were bruising experiences for Britain: politically for its government, economically for its people, and personally for those who deployed and lost friends and relatives in the field. Given defense cuts, the recent memory of operations gone awry, and widespread public disaffection for protracted, costly, and bloody interventions, the question is whether British counterinsurgency truly has a future. The common tendency is to draw just the one lesson—namely, to define Britain out of future similar engagements, a posture reminiscent of the US attempt to avoid counterinsurgency in the aftermath of the Vietnam War. Yet if the challenges encountered in Afghanistan and Iraq are not unique to counterinsurgency, but typical of most land-based operations conducted in foreign countries in different cultures, languages, and settings, it will be critical for Britain to continue to learn from its recent experience with counter-insurgency, at least if it hopes to retain its global role and expeditionary reach. The challenge may be to find a more modest means of contributing to future operations and, in that manner, a new British role in maintaining international peace and security.

ACKNOWLEDGMENTS

Writing a book is always a far more collaborative effort than its cover page suggests. We owe debts of gratitude to many people—friends, relatives, colleagues, and practitioners who have over the course of several years assisted us with interviews, advice, critique, and encouragement.

Most of the individuals interviewed for this book wanted to remain anonymous and cannot be credited by name for their rich contributions and generosity with both time and effort. Among those we can thank, we would like to single out Brig. Ben Barry and Col. (ret) Richard Iron for their continuous engagement with us as authors and for commenting on draft chapters. Their help and input have resulted in a final manuscript of far higher quality than what would otherwise have been possible.

Research for this book started in 2008, and over the course of several years many people at many institutions have played key parts in making the final product possible. David Ucko thanks Wade Markell at the RAND Corporation for involving him on a project that led to the initial research into the British campaign in Basra; Mats Berdal at King's College London for shaping his thinking about war-to-peace transitions and the nature of military intervention; Thomas A. Marks at the College of International Security Affairs, National Defense University (NDU), for sharing his unique perspectives on insurgency and counterinsurgency and for commenting on earlier drafts of the manuscript; Frank Hoffman at the Institute for National Strategic Studies, NDU, for the many long conversations about counterinsurgency, both British and otherwise; and Ryan Evans for the many "off-site" meetings to discuss the book and the theses underpinning it. Robert Egnell thanks Daniele Riggio at the Public Diplomacy Division at NATO headquarters for providing the opportunity to conduct research in Afghanistan during a Tour of Opinion Leaders; and Stuart Griffin at King's College London for involving him in a special issue of *International Affairs* on the impact of Afghanistan on British and US defense thinking.

We extend particular recognition to the International Institute for Strategic Studies in London, which provided institutional and research support during the preliminary phase of writing this book. Nicholas Redman deserves particular mention for his comments on our work, but we also thank Caitlin Brannan for her help in setting up the conference "British Counterinsurgency: Past, Present, and Future," which we held at the institute in December 2010. With this conference, we were able to gather in one room many of the key players in the debate on British counterinsurgency and engage them in a full-day discussion of our research. We again want to recognize the key assistance and support of Brig. Ben Barry, without whom the event would have been far smaller and far less rewarding. Of course, the conference would not even have happened had it not been for the support from the Swedish Armed Forces, who agreed to fund the event in full through the Expeditionary Capabilities project and thereby contributed substantively to our research project.

Throughout the writing of the book, we have benefited from the advice and contributions of many academics and practitioners. There are too many to thank by name—and many, again, want to remain anonymous—but we would be remiss if we did not thank those who have played a particularly notable role: Alex Alderson, David Betz, Warren Chin, Christopher Dandeker, Theo Farrell, Stuart Griffin, Frank Ledwidge, Paul Newton, Kenneth Payne, and Matthew Smith. For their comments on previous drafts and research assistance, we also recognize Jillian Anthony, Clement Christensen, and David O'Donnell.

We likewise extend our gratitude to Bruce Hoffman, who not only believed in the project but also saw its potential as a book in the Columbia University Press Studies in Terrorism and Irregular Warfare series. We are also grateful to the excellent team at the press who supported us through the final phases of this project and made sure that the manuscript reached its maximum potential.

Finally, our families have once again provided us with the time and support necessary to complete a book. David thanks his parents, Hans and Agneta; his siblings, Daniel and Hanna; and his brother-in-law, Alexander, for their encouragement, companionship, and sense of humor. Of course, special thanks go to Kate for her love and support—and for taking extra care of our daughter, Magdalena, all those times I was "in the middle of a sentence." Robert thanks his entire family, but a special thank you goes to Ditte: there is no way of exaggerating the importance of your effort and support to make our wonderful family and busy lives function.

With all this, it remains to be said that all faults and errors in the book are entirely our own. It should also be specified that the views expressed in this book are also our own and do not reflect the official policy or position of our respective employers, be it Georgetown University, the National Defense University, the US Department of Defense, or the US government.

ABBREVIATIONS

ACC	Afghan COIN Centre
AKX	Army Knowledge Exchange
ANSF	Afghan National Security Forces
ARAG	Advanced Research and Assessment Group
CPA	Coalition Provisional Authority
CULAD	cultural adviser
DCSU	Defence Cultural Specialist Unit
DfID	Department for International Development
DRC	Democratic Republic of the Congo
EOD	explosive ordnance disposal
FDT	Force Development and Training Command
FRES	Future Rapid Effects System
IEMF	Interim Emergency Multinational Force
ISAF	International Security Assistance Force
LWC	Land Warfare Centre
LXC	Lesson Exploitation Centre
MND-SE	Multinational Division–Southeast
MND-South	Multinational Division–South
MoD	UK Ministry of Defence
MOG	Mobile Operations Group

NTC	National Transitional Council
OEF	Operation Enduring Freedom
ORHA	Office of Reconstruction and Humanitarian Assistance
OMLT	Operational Mentoring and Liaison Team
OPTAG	Operational Training and Advisory Group
PCRU	Post-Conflict Reconstruction Unit
PRT	Provincial Reconstruction Team
RMA	revolution in military affairs
RUF	Revolutionary United Front
SCIRI	Supreme Council for the Islamic Revolution in Iraq
SDSR	*Strategic Defence and Security Review*
UN	United Nations
UOR	Urgent Operational Requirements

COUNTERINSURGENCY
IN CRISIS

INTRODUCTION: RETHINKING COUNTERINSURGENCY

BOTH IN IRAQ and Afghanistan, the British armed forces have confronted violent nonstate actors that employ deception and intimidation to resist government control. These groups intermingle with the civilian population, imaginatively offset their conventional military weaknesses, and engage in criminal activity, coercion, and outreach to maintain their local influence. Although the campaigns in these two countries differ in important respects from the colonial struggles that gave rise to the term, they both gradually came to be viewed as "counterinsurgencies." The term seemed appropriate because even though the armed opposition did not always seek an insurrection, the tasks typical of counterinsurgency appeared to provide the beginnings of an appropriate response: the creation of local security, the alleviation of those grievances thought to be fueling the violence, and the gradual development of the central government's legitimacy, along with its ability to take over following an eventual transition to local control.

For the British armed forces, the encounter with counterinsurgency had a special significance. By virtue of its history and tradition, the British military had a particular legacy with counterinsurgency. Specifically, it was argued both inside and outside the organization that the experience of imperial conquest, policing, and withdrawal as well as with the Troubles in Northern Ireland had provided the British military with a unique capability to understand and manage political violence and defeat insurgency movements. This historical legacy is also responsible for many of the principles and theory that fill counterinsurgency field manuals and key texts produced throughout the West, not just in the United Kingdom. Indeed, once the instability of "postwar" Iraq had manifested itself, it was chiefly the *British* experience with counterinsurgency that provided the foundation for later elaborations of how to respond. As such, there were high expectations that, compared to their US counterparts deployed farther north in Iraq, the British forces deployed to the southern provinces would face fewer problems in "keeping the peace" based on their historical mastery of these types of operations. Initial operations appeared to confirm such expectations, but a much more complex and troubling reality soon emerged as British forces proved unable to prevent Basra's slide into criminality, insecurity, and lawlessness.

In Afghanistan, following the deployment to Helmand in 2006, British troops again ran into serious difficulties owing to confusion regarding the purpose of the mission, a flawed intelligence picture, deficiencies in troop levels, as well as a number of operational and tactical mistakes. British troops were again surprised by the robustness of the armed opposition and struggled to devise and implement a strategy that could bridge the limited means at hand with grandiose ends sought in a highly unstable province. Over the following five years, matters improved substantially, but it took increased troop levels, operational adaptation and relearning of counterinsurgency principles, as well as a massive reinforcement of US Marines to turn the tide.

The outcome in both campaigns related to extrinsic factors as well as to the British conduct of operations: in Iraq, Britain was a junior coalition partner with limited say, and in Afghanistan there was precious little that British troops could do to address the central government's lack of legitimacy, NATO's shortage of deployable troops, and Pakistan's reluctance to support fully the US-driven counterinsurgency effort. Nevertheless, closer scrutiny reveals that there was also something worryingly wrong with the British government's own ability to plan, prepare for, and conduct these counterinsurgency campaigns: a failure to understand the nature of the war, to engage with local actors and forces, and to devise and implement a workable campaign plan. The weaknesses were political as much as they were institutional and operational. The British government can be faulted politically for its low level of commitment to ongoing campaigns and for the failure to provide adequate resources or political guidance that could be implemented in the field; the British armed forces and other government agencies were ill prepared institutionally for the challenges of expeditionary stabilization and reconstruction, which translated operationally into a lack of familiarity with the tasks now called for and a slowness to recognize the incipient signs of insurgency and possible failure.

The aim of this book is to increase the understanding of contemporary British counterinsurgency as well as to assess its future in light of the troubled campaigns in Basra and Helmand. Informed by these cases, the book addresses four central questions:

1. What accounts for the British military's operational frustration in both Iraq and Afghanistan?
2. Are the principles derived from historical British counterinsurgency campaigns still valid?
3. What measures have the British government and particularly its armed forces taken to redress the shortcomings exposed in theater?
4. What are the implications of the operations in Iraq and Afghanistan for Britain's role in international peace and security?

Although focused on the British conduct of military operations, the study has far broader relevance. First, the British legacy with counterinsurgency has strongly informed the dominant understanding of this term today, most notably within the US military. If the prevailing understanding of the British legacy is problematic or the associated theory bogus, the implications for other militaries emulating the British approach will be far-reaching. The question, really, is whether the experiences of colonial policing and of later withdrawal are still relevant for contemporary operations of state building. Are today's armed forces engaged in operations that can usefully be described as "counterinsurgencies," or is that conceptual framework detrimental to our understanding of conflict and our effectiveness in achieving set political aims?

Second, the campaigns in Iraq and Afghanistan can in many ways be seen as representative of third-party interventions in foreign polities, whether they be termed "counterinsurgencies" or not. From the language and cultural barriers to the difficulties of facing irregular armed forces and of operating among foreign populations or alongside weak or altogether absent local partners, the challenges seen in Afghanistan and Iraq reflect not only those of counterinsurgency, but those of intervention and war as well. In that sense, the British experience in these two campaigns is greatly informative for other Western states bent on intervention, whether it is done to end a war, to build peace, or "simply" to create certain political conditions on the ground through the use of military force. Regardless of what we call these endeavors, many of the skills and capabilities called for in Basra and in Helmand will in all likelihood be needed again.

It follows that the lessons drawn from these operations will concern a spectrum of land operations far broader than just counterinsurgency. Specifically, the British case study reveals the pitfalls of military intervention in foreign countries, the requirements for strategic effectiveness, and the perennial difficulties of learning from past experience. Despite a decade of war fighting in Iraq and Afghanistan, it is questionable whether the right lessons have been noted, never mind learned. Do those actors intent on armed intervention truly understand the modern battlefield, and how far have they come in developing the capabilities so desperately needed in this environment? Most forcefully, what does the British experience tell us about the Western capacity for strategic thinking, and have these lessons been fully internalized? For those countries in the West that see themselves as expeditionary actors, the opportunity to learn from the British experience is matched in magnitude only by the failure to do so.

On these grounds, this study is perhaps of particular relevance to the United States, which has based its counterinsurgency doctrine on the British approach to these operations and which maintains, even after its campaigns in Afghanistan and Iraq, a desire to exert itself militarily across the globe. The challenge here is how to maintain expeditionary ambitions without entangling oneself in countering drawn-out, bloody insurgencies. Although operating on a smaller budget, with a smaller force, and with a less global agenda, Britain faces an entirely similar conundrum. For other powers seeking to resolve this quandary, the British experiences in theater and the case of British learning and adapting can once more provide a helpful precedent in identifying lessons to be learned and finding new ways of managing the security of this world.

FRAMING THE STUDY

WHAT IS COUNTERINSURGENCY?

Any study of counterinsurgency must establish the criteria by which separate campaigns across time and space are brought together under this particular rubric. What is it, in other words, that unites various operations said to belong to this category? The question is germane because counterinsurgency is often perceived to be a fluid concept that is entirely dependent on context. As counterinsurgency expert David Kilcullen points out in his seminal tome on the topic, "There is no such thing as a 'standard' counterinsurgency. . . . [T]he set of counterinsurgency measures adopted depends on the character of the insurgency."[1] From an analytical standpoint, this fluidity makes it difficult to pin down the exact nature of counterinsurgency and to distinguish it from other types of approaches or campaigns. In the absence of such delineations, is *counterinsurgency* even a valid or meaningful term? How do we *know* that the campaign in Basra or the one in Helmand was a counterinsurgency campaign, and how will we recognize future such campaigns if and when they appear?

Faced with this semantic hurdle, the first recourse is to definitions. The British Army defines *counterinsurgency* as "those military, law enforcement, political, economic, psychological and civic actions taken to defeat insurgency, while addressing the root causes." It defines *insurgency* as "organised, violent subversion used to effect or prevent political control, as a challenge to established authority." Contrary to conventional wisdom, the British Army does not view insurgency as necessarily geared toward the overthrow of government; instead, it clarifies that it can have "many aims, the most common of which are: to gain control of territory, seek resolution of a grievance or seek the overthrow of the existing authority."[2]

When these definitions are taken to their logical conclusion, counterinsurgency emerges as any activity that purports to counter organized, violent attempts to obstruct the established authorities from asserting their control and that also addresses the root causes behind the conflict. This is a helpful start, but many difficulties immediately surface. Who were the "established authorities" in Basra of 2003 or of 2006, and who were the "established authorities" in Helmand of 2006 or of 2009? Second, what do we call counterinsurgencies where root causes are not adequately addressed, either as a matter of policy or as a failure thereof? Who identifies root causes, and are these causes, even where properly determined, central to the cycle of violence once it has fully taken hold?[3] Furthermore, because both definitions are so inclusive, they do not help us determine where counterinsurgency begins, where it ends, and how it relates to other similar activities known by different names.

Given the sui generis nature of most campaigns, the contested nature of most terms, and the ambiguity and overlap of their respective definitions, it seems unlikely that greater intellectual investment in semantics will ultimately achieve the sought after exactitude. To gain a slightly more specific understanding of the problem and help settle the criteria for inclusion, it may help to *describe* these types of campaigns rather than to define them—to study them based on their shared characteristics rather than by what they were called. On this basis, the operations of concern to this study share three characteristics:

1. The deployment of foreign and/or local security forces among a civilian population;
2. The use of military force as a subset of a broader program of military and nonmilitary reform aimed at addressing the causative factors of violence; and
3. An insecure operating environment in which counterinsurgency forces, their allies, or the population are regularly targeted.

The combination of these three characteristics unites Britain's historical counterinsurgency campaigns, its experiences in Iraq and Afghanistan, and, most likely, its future land operations. Interestingly, these three attributes also tend to feature in what are termed "stability operations," "robust peacekeeping," and "counterguerrilla wars," and there is certainly no reason to exclude these types of engagements merely because they have not, often by mere happenstance, earned the label *counterinsurgency*. However termed, a narrow understanding of the operations under scrutiny based on these three attributes makes it at least possible to form apposite and insightful historical parallels between cases and to comment on the likely challenges of operations to come. By implication, it should also be clear that the focus of this study extends far beyond what is *called* "counterinsurgency" and touches upon what we perceive as typical, rather than atypical, complexities of third-party intervention, in particular those involving ground troops.

WHY COUNTERINSURGENCY?

The types of operations of concern to us having been defined, the next question is what makes counterinsurgency so important to this particular challenge. This question is pertinent given the dissent surrounding the term, its practice, and doctrine.[4] Simply put, the modest yet at the same time crucial value of counterinsurgency lies in the challenge it poses to the many preconceptions about war that have tended to dominate Western strategic thinking. Specifically, in its principles, enumerated in most field manuals and key texts on the topic, counterinsurgency provides a corrective to the view of war as militarily decisive, apolitical, and wholly distinct from peace. Although the latter reductive view of war is most closely associated with US strategic thinking, the widespread Western use of terms such as *conventional* and *traditional* to describe state-on-state war and *unconventional* and *irregular* to describe insurgency and terrorism belies a more pervasive bias as to how wars are expected to unfold.[5]

How do counterinsurgency principles improve on this normative understanding of war? In essence, they hint at the challenging and at times counterintuitive nature of the modern, populated, and intensely political battlefield. Several lists of counterinsurgency principles are currently in circulation, but a quick examination of five main principles helps make the point: political primacy, close civil–military cooperation, intelligence, minimum force, and flexibility.[6] These five principles have remained consistent throughout the centuries and underpin not only the British counterinsurgency legacy, but also the main field manuals and theoretical texts on the topic.[7]

The principle of *political primacy* serves as a reminder that the main aim in counterinsurgency is not to kill and capture insurgents but to address the causative factors of violence. As the grievance and conditions from which insurgents draw their strength are usually social or political or economic in nature, it follows that defeating the insurgent group will typically require more than a merely military approach. Indeed, David Galula's assertion in 1964 that "counterinsurgency is 80 percent political action and only 20 percent military" is still commonly heard in discussion of counterinsurgency today,[8] even though this ratio hardly reflects the division of labor in either Iraq or Afghanistan. The principle of political primacy also highlights the need for clear political aims to inform all military activities. In the context of British counterinsurgency, this notion is subsumed by that of "military aid to civil power," which subordinates military activity to political strategy rather than the reverse.[9] Indeed, as the most visible and potentially inflammatory instrument of power, the military has a particular responsibility to do its part with a keen awareness of the intensely political context in which it is also operating.

The principle of maintaining *unity of command* and close *civil–military cooperation* is closely linked to that of political primacy. The committee system developed during the Malayan Emergency of 1948–1960 is emblematic of this principle: this system was a network of interagency committees operating at the federal, state, and district levels to help implement the campaign plan, coordinate action, and enable communication between the relevant services and agencies. Malaya stands out for an additional reason: for two critical years of this campaign, Gen. Sir Gerald Templer acted as both the high commissioner and the director of operations, resulting in a single unified chain of command integrating both civilian and military means. This pragmatic solution to the problem of civil–military coordination has not been replicated since then, but the principle of "unity of command" remains.[10]

Another principle of counterinsurgency concerns the crucial role of *intelligence*.[11] Indeed, the section on counterinsurgency in the 2001 *British Army*

Field Manual describes good intelligence as "one of the greatest battle-winning factors."[12] Counterinsurgency theory tends to emphasize human intelligence sources, given the need to understand the local environment and its structures. It further stresses that the soldier on the ground is often the best gatherer of intelligence, given his or her daily contact with the local population.[13] Thus, some counterinsurgency authors have emphasized that "in counterinsurgency the traditional top-down flow of intelligence is reversed. Much depends on an intelligence organization adapting to this change—building the picture from routine information."[14]

The principles of civil–military cooperation and intelligence-led operations also relate closely to the principle of using only the *minimum amount of force necessary to achieve military and political objectives*. As the 1923 British Army manual *Duties in Aid of Civil Power* puts it, what is important is "not the annihilation of an enemy but the suppression of a temporary disorder, and therefore the degree of force to be employed must be directed to that which is necessary to restore order and must never exceed it."[15] Such instruction relates also to the principle of political primacy and is commonly tied to the notion of "winning the hearts and minds" of the local population rather than narrowly going after the enemy with no consideration of the broader context. Often maligned but seldom very well understood, this phrase is commonly thought to have originated with Gen. Templer, who noted that for the British to win in Malaya, "the answer lies not in pouring more soldiers into the jungle but rests in the hearts and minds of the Malayan people."[16] Taking this notion further, Frank Kitson, Templer's contemporary, stressed the potentially counterproductive impact of employing indiscriminate force because it might alienate those civilians affected by it and imperil the flow of human intelligence. Instead, Kitson emphasized the need to maintain the perceived *legitimacy* of the military force and of the political structures it is there to support.[17] In order to apply this principle in practice, operations need to be "intelligence led," which allows force to be used precisely and with better appreciation for its strategic effects, both direct and secondary.

The final principle of British counterinsurgency of relevance here is *operational flexibility and adaptation*. This principle emphasizes the need for soldiers, irrespective of rank, to innovate continuously in line with the unique and evolving challenges of each campaign.[18] Within the British context, this principle was formalized in the 1957 document *Keeping the Peace (Duties in Support of Civil Power)*, which stated that "there is no place for a rigid mind. . . . Although the principles of war generally remain the same, the ability to adapt and improvise is essential."[19] With regard to these five principles, therefore, the exhortation is typically to "break any of these rules sooner than do anything outright barbarous."[20]

To the casual observer, these counterinsurgency principles will appear largely self-evident—and not just as regards counterinsurgency. For instance, there is nothing particularly controversial about the need for good intelligence, and it is also clear that where adversary and civilian look alike and intermingle, obtaining good intelligence will require a special understanding of and with the local population. It is similarly difficult to find fault with the notion that a greater understanding of the environment, its people and structures, will present external actors with more and better options or that controlling and influencing key populations will first require that they are adequately isolated from others' intimidation, threats, and coercion. As to the focus on the legitimacy of the intervention itself and of the actors it seeks to support, this is a fairly obvious corollary of the need to establish political and military control over select populations. Although many of these principles seem banal, they nonetheless appear necessary in illustrating the unique logic of counterinsurgency and its distinctiveness from the "conventional" types of war for which most Western militaries train and prepare. For these military institutions, beholden to the utility of force as a stand-alone solution to security threats, the counterinsurgency principles represent a powerful antithesis.

Further, careful consideration of the principles and the challenge of their application helps prepare soldiers for the likely difficulties encountered in theater. Gen. (ret.) Sir John Kiszely, former director of the British Defence Academy, provides a compelling summation of these challenges: troops must possess the ability to "apply soft power as well as hard . . . ; work in partnership with multinational, multiagency organizations, civilian as well as military . . . ; master information operations and engage successfully with the media; conduct persuasive dialogue with local leaders . . . ; mentally out-maneuver a wily and ruthless enemy; and, perhaps most often overlooked, measure progress appropriately." As Kiszely adds, these competences require an understanding of "the political context; the legal, moral and ethical complexities; culture and religion; how societies work; what constitutes good governance; the relationship between one's own armed forces and society; the notion of human security; the concept of legitimacy; the limitations on the utility of force; the psychology of one's opponents and the rest of the population."[21]

This list of challenges and requirements goes some way toward explaining the checkered track record of counterinsurgency campaigns—endeavors that are typically costly in both blood and treasure. Indeed, it is important to note that counterinsurgency will always be notoriously difficult no matter how good the theory might be. It is relatively easy to derive priority tasks from past operations, yet knowing how to sequence, prioritize between, and implement these tasks represents a far more challenging proposition. It should not be a surprise, therefore, that though past campaigns reveal the *general* validity of a number of broad principles, the campaigns themselves were not always so successful.

Some argue that the limited success experienced in counterinsurgency is reason enough to reject it as a failed doctrine—an understandable yet overly hasty conclusion. Indeed, such a line of argument belies an expectation that military doctrine provide silver-bullet solutions to the problems of military intervention. Instead, the theory and principles of counterinsurgency provide mere guideposts for how to formulate a response to a problem that will itself never be easily solved. And although such guidance may be very helpful in the design and execution of an effective *campaign plan*, that plan itself, as the theory clearly states, must be adapted to specific circumstances; certainly, it must be closely tailored to the causative factors of violence, which will in each case be unique.

This last point is frequently missed in current discussions of counterinsurgency. Counterinsurgency doctrine and principles provide an idea of what questions to ask and how to approach the difficult task of countering an insurgency, but as Frank G. Hoffman has noted, "Best practice is not best strategy."[22] To be effective, counterinsurgents must go beyond what they can read in a field manual or glean from the canonical texts; they must adapt the premises and principles of counterinsurgency to meet specific political goals—or, put differently, marry these operational concepts to a viable and well-resourced strategy. "Strategy," Eliot Cohen writes, "is the art of choice that binds means with objectives. It is the highest level of thinking about war, and it involves priorities (we will devote resources here, even if that means starving operations there), sequencing (we will do this first, then that) and a theory of victory (we will succeed for the following reasons)."[23] A counterinsurgency field manual is plainly unable to address these difficult questions or to resolve the attendant trade-offs, yet, importantly, it may provide valuable guidance and insight when it comes to tying carefully defined strategic aims to the design of operations.

Another tempting yet overly hasty reaction to the challenges inherent to counterinsurgency is to seek not to conduct such operations in the future. Only a complete cessation of military activity abroad would ensure such an outcome (and even then there is still the chance of confronting similar difficulties domestically).[24] For those powers that maintain an expeditionary profile or the perceived need to intervene in conflicts abroad, refusing to study and prepare for counterinsurgency will not in itself reduce the need for the associated skills and capabilities. Indeed, because the operational difficulties associated with counterinsurgency are unlikely to disappear, we would then need a new concept to grapple with these endemic challenges. Rather than treat counterinsurgency as a dead end on the basis of operations gone awry, a better approach would be to *deepen* our study of this topic and of war writ large so as to make better decisions in the future—in terms of when and how but also *whether* to intervene.[25]

On that note, it should be recalled that counterinsurgency doctrine, as operationally oriented theory, does not encourage foolhardy campaigns to stabilize war-torn countries or to defeat insurgencies wherever they may rear their heads. If anything, a strong note of caution regarding the requirements of such interventions can be parsed from the field manuals and main texts. It can even be argued that it has been the lack of awareness of such doctrine and texts that has necessitated their rediscovery: witness the gradual introduction of counterinsurgency principles and practices following the invasions of Afghanistan in 2001 and Iraq in 2003, but also much earlier following the initial failures to grapple with incipient insurgencies in Malaya and Northern Ireland, to use only British examples.[26] When, as in these cases, a commitment is made to assist an insurgency-threatened government, the theory and principles of counterinsurgency can provide useful guidance in meeting this strategic end, but that end is always decided upon and defined at a higher level and will itself be more or less realistic. No amount of counterinsurgency wisdom can compensate for an unworkable strategy, and it is fair to say that the theory is better at raising the right questions than in providing the answers.

LEARNING AND ADAPTING

One of the key principles of counterinsurgency is the exhortation to "learn and adapt" to new circumstances—to innovate and find new answers based on a careful assessment of ground realities. Because learning is a key theme in this book, it is worth discussing what is meant by this term when it is applied to organizations rather than to individuals. This question is particularly germane in the British context in that the British Army has often been characterized as a "learning institution," which in turn, it is said, accounts for its remarkably successful track record with counterinsurgency.

This question of learning and adaptation has given rise to an extensive debate among scholars, policymakers, and practitioners. Even just within the military or strategic studies communities, entire bookshelves can be filled with works discussing the exact mechanisms by which military organizations adopt new ways of interpreting and responding to their environment.[27] Scholars are torn on the definition of learning, its relationship to adaptation, and the role of innovation in either process. What change is revolutionary, and what is merely evolutionary?[28] To add further complexity, there is also a distinction to be made between top-down learning, or change imposed on the organization by inspired leaders or elites, and bottom-up adaptation, or change derived "from the spontaneous interactions between military people, technology and particular tactical circumstances," often during wartime.[29]

For the purposes of this study, it is not necessary to enter too deeply into the discussion of military organizational learning, but two clarifications must nonetheless be made. First, the distinction between bottom-up adaptation and top-down learning is critical to the British engagement with counter-insurgency throughout history and therefore merits some elaboration. Bottom-up adaptation is here defined as changes in tactics, techniques, and procedures implemented on the ground and through contact with an unfamiliar operating environment, whereas top-down learning involves the institutionalization of these practices through changes in training, doctrine, education, and force structure. The learning provides a foundation of knowledge, but adaptation allows the troops in theater to mold the prescribed approach to particular circumstances.

In its long history with counterinsurgency, the British military has found it difficult to internalize the lessons drawn from previous campaigns and to prepare for future such contingencies. As a result, whenever the British military has been faced with an insurgency or similar challenge, it has had to rely on quick adaptation on the ground to overcome the initial lack of knowledge and ability. In this process of adaptation, the individual memory of previous notionally similar operations has sometimes raised the learning curve, but to institutionalize this wisdom has proved a different proposition altogether.[30] This pattern illustrates the importance of bottom-up adaptation: as Michael Howard famously and perhaps somewhat facetiously put it, "When *everybody* starts wrong, the advantage goes to the side which can most quickly adjust itself to the new and unfamiliar environment and learn from our [*sic*] mistakes."[31]

At the same time, the British experience also points to the importance of institutionalizing what is learned in operation so as to prepare for future nominally similar engagements. Adaptation thus fills the inevitable gap between what is learned and what is experienced, but the learning is indispensable in making this gap as small as possible. This need for learning and preparation is perhaps particularly severe today. In the past, the slower timelines, minimal media penetration, and greater domestic patience with foreign entanglements allowed for a longer period of adaptation to recognize the problem and devise a solution. Today, the time in which to show progress has shrunk to the degree that some analysts speak of the "Golden Hour" of postconflict stabilization, or the first twelve months of an operation in which leaders must demonstrate some degree of improvement to both the domestic and the local populations.[32] Media penetration and unrealistic expectations of quick progress may account for the apparent contraction of time. Another notable difference with counterinsurgency operations of years gone by is the fact that Britain no longer operates alone but contributes as part of a broader coalition, which makes it more difficult to learn "at your own pace" or, alternatively, to withdraw when conditions go awry. In short, proper analysis of required capabilities and their institutionalization within the relevant arms of government are necessary to shrink the gap between expectations and reality. They are also an intellectual responsibility because the first and foremost challenge for the statesman as well for as the commander is to understand the nature of the task being embarked upon.[33] In the words of US Army general H. R. McMaster, "You are never going to get it right before the war, but the key is to not be so wrong that you can't adapt once the complexity of the problem is revealed to you."[34]

A NOTE ON POLITICAL WILL

Success in counterinsurgency, as in any protracted military campaign, depends on the political will of the governments and nations involved. In assessing past and ongoing counterinsurgency campaigns, there is thus a tendency to ascribe suboptimal outcomes on the ground to the lack of political will back home. The military, after all, is only an instrument of national power, and if it is not used effectively or adequately maintained, the fault must surely lie with the workman rather than with the tools. This rightfully raises the question of whether it is at all relevant to study particular strategies in relation to operational outcomes or whether we are merely chasing the shadows of a larger problem—namely, the level of commitment underlying the campaign as a whole. The argument, simply put, is, whatever the tactical triumphs or setbacks, success or failure in any theater is always determined by political will.[35]

Political will is clearly an important factor in war, but to posit it as the singularly decisive factor is all too limiting, even paralyzing. How does one measure political will? In the absence of some gauge or objective indicator of political will, the main sign of it lacking will be the lack of progress in theater. Yet such analysis relies on a circular logic and quickly becomes tautological: failed operations reflect inadequate will, whereas successful ones, ipso facto, were those where the government was truly invested. Political will is thereby a catch-all and purely retrospective argument that is impossible to disprove, but therefore also analytically meaningless.

The more interesting question than whether there was sufficient political will or not is how the government at a strategic level and the military at an operational level grappled with the campaign's requirements and challenges—a question that lies at the heart of our study. As it turns out, fluctuations at the strategic and political level often reflect the course of events on the ground as well as domestic developments—elections, crises, other military entanglements—along with electoral interest and understanding of foreign affairs.[36] As Jeremy Black has noted, "To talk of American or French interests or policy, as if these are clear-cut and long-lasting, is to ignore the nature of politics and the character of recent history."[37]

Further, although a strategic mistake can be seen in the failure to match aims with appropriate resources, at the operational and tactical level it is still the commander's duty to decide how best to employ force to the greatest possible effect. As military studies from the dawn of time have illustrated, it is therefore not only possible but also fruitful to discuss operational and tactical competence of military organizations regardless of political will. Indeed, military performance and government decision making are inextricably intertwined and can rarely be neatly separated for analytical purposes.

★ ★ ★

With the Iraq campaign already several years old and the British government preparing to withdraw its troops from Afghanistan, many observers might comment that the time to discuss counterinsurgency is now over. Such a conclusion is seemingly strengthened by the recent cuts to the British defense budget, which would appear to turn the page on large-scale stabilization operations. Yet although it is true that we are unlikely to see "another Iraq" or "another Afghanistan" in the immediate future, this study of contemporary British counterinsurgency is still relevant for four main reasons.

First, there is merit in uncovering what happened in these two campaigns in order to expose the relevant lessons and identify areas both of strength and of weakness. Doing so is in part a first stab at establishing a historical record of recent military operations, but also an attempt to distill these experiences into "findings" for future consideration. The record-keeping function of academic inquiries such as this one is particularly salient to the context of British military campaigns in that open communication and transparency are readily circumscribed in this area—be it through political sensibilities or institutional censure.

Second, even within the narrow confines of what is termed "counterinsurgency," the two campaigns in Basra and Helmand are instructive as contemporary case studies. From the high reliance on coalitions to the limited public support and high media penetration, these two cases provide a glimpse of the operational challenges and opportunities that mark counterinsurgency today and, it is likely, in the future. For Britain, this inquiry is particularly relevant given its legacy with counterinsurgency and attempt to maintain a global expeditionary profile. For the rest of the world, the application of principles and theory to a new strategic setting should force a radical rethink of what it means to conduct counterinsurgency today and whether the strategic lessons of the early to mid–twentieth century—counterinsurgency's heyday—still apply.

Third, if we view counterinsurgency not only through the prism of the campaigns in Afghanistan and Iraq, but also as one possibility among a range of missions comprising similar and largely predictable challenges, it follows that the lessons derived from the recent experience with counterinsurgency will also be relevant to a far broader set of actors conducting a wider range of tasks. These challenges, as noted earlier, include the conduct of operations among civilians, the creation of sustainable political conditions, and the encounter with adversaries employing guile, subversion, and irregular forms of violence. Critically, these are challenges that will in all likelihood continue to mark interventions conducted in foreign lands, particularly those designed to protect key allies, defeat specific threats, or create a new and sustainable political order.

Finally, in part because of the difficulties faced in recent operations—in Iraq and Afghanistan principally—there is now a burgeoning academic literature on institutional and organizational learning. The sentiment underpinning this literature is clear: the structures of state are not always adequately configured to deal with the security problems faced, and there is a need to learn, to do better, and to be better prepared for the next eventuality. Although well intentioned and no doubt correct, the exhortations to learn, to adapt, and to innovate can often appear facile and somewhat misleading in their simplicity. It is therefore helpful to consider how this process plays itself out in real life, given institutional politics and limited budgets. The study of how Britain, principally its MoD and armed forces, but also its other government agencies, has "learned" from ten years of operational experience provides a rich case and an indication of the difficulties that supporters of reform face in carrying through on their visions.

The moment is for many reasons ripe to rethink counterinsurgency and British counterinsurgency theory, to learn from its experiences on the ground, and to consider, on the basis of this record, what can be done.

1

UNTANGLING THE BRITISH
COUNTERINSURGENCY LEGACY

A S BASRA FELL on April 6, 2003, the British Army quickly adjusted from a combat mindset to one of peace-support operations. Leaning on their experiences with peacekeeping in the Balkans, troops marked the end of "major combat operations" and the onset of "postconflict operations" by swiftly removing their flak jackets and replacing their helmets with berets so as to convey a more benign posture.[1] Despite the contextual differences between Iraq's Shia-dominated South, where British troops were operating, and the Sunni-dominated American area of responsibility, many interpreted the relative stability in Basra following the invasion as a product of the British Army's particular approach there: its appreciation of the campaign's political and economic dimensions and its firm but friendly manner of conducting tactical operations.[2] To the House of Commons in its "initial assessment" of the campaign, the British approach to postconflict operations had been "highly successful and [had] deservedly drawn high praise from many commentators." It went on to suggest that British historical experience and the many lessons learned—most recently in Northern Ireland, but also half a century ago in Malaya and Aden—had made the difference.[3]

The House of Commons report exemplified the somewhat self-congratulatory tone that marked many assessments of British "postwar" operations. In many cases, the celebration of the "British approach" contrasted with concern about the heavy-handed conduct of operations by the US military farther north in Iraq. The House of Commons, for example, "urge[d] [the] MoD to use its influence to affect MNF-I's posture and approach,"[4] and Gen. Mike Jackson, then the chief of the general staff, commented that "we must be able to fight with the Americans. That does not mean we must be able to fight as the Americans."[5] Concern was also evident in a leaked Foreign & Commonwealth Office memo that criticized US operations in Fallujah and Najaf in April 2004 for undermining local support for the coalition and, on this basis, recommended a redoubling of "efforts to ensure a sensible and sensitive US approach to military operations."[6]

Following such direction, a number of British officers spent both time and energy providing their American partners largely unsolicited counsel on counterinsurgency, much of which was based on British doctrine and its operational experience in Malaya back in the 1950s.[7] The publication in late 2005 of British brigadier Nigel Aylwin-Foster's damning account of US operations brought the backstage whispers and hushed advice into the open. Published in the US Army journal *Military Review* and picked up on by the mainstream media in both the United Kingdom and the United States, the article became a highly visible broadside against the Americans' apparent failure to understand the challenge of insurgency in Iraq.[8] Although Aylwin-Foster was quick to point out that no "arrogant exercise in national comparisons" had been intended,[9] his nationality and timing thrust his article to the forefront of a more general and far less bashful critique—one that in Britain was rooted in its own seemingly superior understanding of the situation.

Criticism of the initial US approach to operations in Iraq was in many ways justified. Even so, the early comparisons also displayed great confidence in Britain's own competence with counterinsurgency. Any attempt to explain this confidence—where it all came from—must begin with the narrative that the British military and government brought with it as it invaded and then occupied southern Iraq. This narrative was based on previous counterinsurgency campaigns and the theories derived from such engagements and implied a particularly British ability in these types of settings.

This chapter addresses these two areas by examining the dominant understanding of the British legacy with counterinsurgency at the turn of the twenty-first century. Two all too often unquestioned aspects of this narrative are its historical accuracy and, as important, its relevance to a strategic setting quite unlike that of prior campaigns. By examining these two areas, the chapter explains why the optimism behind this narrative was so misleading.

We argue here that at the onset of operations in Iraq and Afghanistan, the prevailing understanding of the British counterinsurgency legacy was informed by a selective and superficial reading of past operations. Too few of those participating in the current operations had studied the historical campaigns on which the legacy rested, and most relied, at best, on the easily digestible "counterinsurgency principles" to which the earlier campaigns had given rise. These principles were then repeated until they gradually became slogans, lacking context, and substituting for historical knowledge. This limited understanding encouraged a simplistic view of insurgency as a fairly manageable problem so long as certain tactical provisos were followed—such as the need to "win hearts and minds." In the end, such bare-boned familiarity with Britain's own historical campaigns would mean very little in the absence of capability and a viable strategy.

Nothing here should suggest that Britain's rich history with counterinsurgency is irrelevant to more recent and even future campaigns. Indeed, the wide selection of cases and experiences is arguably the greatest aspect of the British military's legacy with counterinsurgency today. As asserted by counterinsurgency expert Thomas Mockaitis in the mid-1990s, the United Kingdom "has much to teach a world increasingly challenged by the problem of internal war."[10] However, it does not follow that the British Army has an almost natural talent for counterinsurgency as a result of these historical experiences. Indeed, the difficulty of replicating past successes pushes important questions to the fore: Do these problems reflect an inability to implement historical principles, or are the principles themselves outdated or simply wrong? Also, what does the British legacy tell us about the nature of institutional memory—or the value of prior experience with specific types of missions? These questions are fundamental because they challenge the prevailing understanding of counterinsurgency and of a specifically British "model" or "approach"; they also signal the need to rethink how best to prepare for these notoriously challenging types of campaigns. For these reasons, among others, the relevance of this topic spreads far beyond the United Kingdom and its recent wars.

THE BRITISH COUNTERINSURGENCY LEGACY: ORIGIN AND NATURE

It is difficult to pin down exactly when the narrative of an enhanced British capability with counterinsurgency took root. There is a broad and varied literature on individual counterinsurgency campaigns written by former soldiers, journalists, and academics. A notable yet smaller range of literature seeks to distill methods and principles from these experiences, and, historically, some of these works have served as proto-doctrine for a military institution then reluctant to write its own.[11] It has been far rarer for academics and practitioners to put down in writing the notion of British superiority in these types of operations. So where did this narrative come from? Or, going deeper, does it even exist?

That the narrative exists and that it is a British fabrication are often accepted at face value, yet these propositions are difficult to prove. Much like any urban legend, the narrative builds on an oral rather than written tradition, which makes it difficult to trace its genealogy in the literature.[12] Indeed, until very recently, allusions to a superior and timeless British capability for counterinsurgency were most commonly made as a matter of course, not as hypotheses to be proved academically. Even so, there is sufficient evidence even in the literature to indicate both the narrative's existence and its prevalence. Witness, for example, a prominent British historian's allusion in 1986 to the "characteristic British mode of response to public security challenges, one which may well be labeled the 'British way,' a pragmatic, limited application of traditional legal doctrines."[13] An eminent British academic, counterinsurgency scholar, and former soldier similarly wrote in 1998 of the "intuitive professional character" of the British Army that "has for some time reflected the needs of smaller operations," also known as "small wars."[14] In 2001, the same authority explicated on the "British institutional wisdom" in counterinsurgency, presented as deriving "from Robert Thompson's classic articulation of doctrine in the 1960s."[15] Also in 2001, the army issued doctrine for counter-insurgency in which it suggested that "the experience of numerous 'small wars' ha[d] provided the British Army with a unique insight into this demanding form of conflict."[16] The earlier 1995 manual on "operations other than war" had similarly claimed that the "long experience of dealing with civil populations, both benign and hostile," had contributed to the army's "current military poli-cies" toward similar challenges.[17] Common to these and other statements is the notion of a timeless endowment built on a track record of notable success.

This narrative rests primarily on the sheer frequency of British military engagements with counterinsurgency. As noted by Gen. Sir Mike Jackson, former chief of the general staff, there "is a sense of a real historical thread in this type of operation for the British Armed Forces." The thread, he adds, "most certainly did not begin with Malaya, or even the period after World War II. . . . [W]e can go back at least a couple of centuries to Ireland, to India a century and a half ago, to Africa at about the same time, and, indeed, to Iraq almost a century ago."[18] This assessment is quite correct: through its colonial experience—of acquiring and then withdrawing from empire—Great Britain has frequently engaged in missions that might today be termed "counterin-surgencies," "stability operations," or even "peace operations."

Yet the narrative is not built on experience alone, but also on the British performance in these endeavors. This perception of this performance as on the whole successful rests most commonly—and quite precariously—on just two cases: the Malayan Emergency and the Troubles in Northern Ireland. Indeed, despite allusions to historical depth in some of the commentary on British counterinsurgency, it is these two cases that receive the most cover-age and that most immediately spring to mind whenever British prowess in counterinsurgency is discussed.[19] Malaya, in this context, provides us with an example of how counterinsurgency principles can be successfully applied and therefore serves as the original blueprint for both doctrine and theory. Northern Ireland is the place where these principles were refined to suit a more constrained political and legal environment, something that makes this case particularly germane to contemporary settings in which military activi-ties are under heightened scrutiny from human rights groups and global media. As Alexander Alderson has argued, "Northern Ireland inevitably shaped the Army's view of counterinsurgency best practice: an emphasis on intelligence, restraint and minimum force, training and adaptation, and civil–military cooperation."[20]

The Malaya and Northern Ireland campaigns have great educational value, but the narrow focus on just these two cases turned them into a synecdoche for the British counterinsurgency experience as a whole. Because both of these experiences are usually framed as "wins" for the counterinsurgents, this selective use of history encouraged a view of British counterinsurgency experiences as on the whole successful—a gross and rarely stated generalization, of course, but one that has helped set the British record apart from those of the French, the Portuguese, and the Americans.[21] As such, the narrative of British counterinsurgency depends at once on the sheer frequency of experiences yet also on the exclusion of many of them from consideration.

Another factor underpinning the perception of unrivalled British success in this area is the unfortunate tendency to conflate British counterinsurgency practice with its theory. As scholars and military analysts sought to understand what went right in Malaya or in Northern Ireland, the British discourse on counterinsurgency increasingly came to be marked by various principles, slogans, and themes: "hearts and minds," "unity of command," "police primacy," and so on. The problem arose when in some treatments of British counterinsurgency these *prescriptive* terms and notions were confused with *descriptions* of how British forces would comport themselves in theater. "The effect," as Hew Strachan has noted, "was to suggest that the British army conducted its minor conflicts with greater consistency than was actually the case."[22] This suggestion stems from a misreading of the main texts: as David French perceptively notes, Robert Thompson's seminal work *Defeating Communist Insurgency* was never intended to be read as a "historical treatise" on British operations, but as a "didactic book in which he tried to emphasize what future counter-insurgent operators should do if they wanted success."[23] This misreading has had a significant impact on the general perception of Britain's prowess with counterinsurgency.

If British academics and soldiers laid the foundations for this narrative, American commentary gave it a major boost—particularly following the invasion of Iraq in 2003. As the US military struggled with the postinvasion rise in violence and the difficulty of administering occupational duties, many academics, officers, and officials looked to Britain's history with counterinsurgency for guidance. A major factor here was the publication and spectacular success of John Nagl's book *Counterinsurgency Lessons from Malaya and Vietnam*, which contrasted various counterproductive American practices during the Vietnam War with the gradual formulation of a winning strategy in Malaya by a British military willing to learn and adapt. To US officers and civilians seeking a way out of Iraq, Nagl's book appeared to provide a time-tested way forward so long as the British model could be applied. By 2005, the book had been reissued in paperback,[24] gained a foreword by Gen. Peter J. Schoomaker, then the US Army chief of staff, and been distributed, on Schoomaker's insistence, to all four-star generals in the US Army. Around the same time, emissaries were deployed from Washington to London to glean from the British, to learn their special craft.[25] At worst, given the urgency of the situation in Iraq, there was a tendency to rummage through past campaigns for quick fixes and answers rather than to let this rich history frame the necessary questions.[26]

The rushed US embrace of the British legacy helped popularize a simplistic notion of British superiority in counterinsurgency. But the Americans were not alone in this effort. Swayed by the appearance of success in Basra and (it is likely) by the praise heaped upon the British military by their American counterparts, several British voices also kept the narrative alive. In the spring of 2004 and in 2005, one former soldier and well-placed academic spoke of the "particularly British approach to the question of low-intensity conflict"; he argued that "the British Army is a counterinsurgency army" whose "principal mission . . . since its very formation and for the greater part of its history . . . was to acquire and then to police imperial possessions."[27] A year later, another leading British academic and retired officer wrote of the "British approach to counterinsurgency" as codified in the main works on the topic and as adhering to the several principles underpinning its legacy. He also noted that "it is agreed that our history of low intensity operations does allow for a much easier transition to these from high intensity, as was witnessed in Basra in 2003."[28] As noted earlier, official government reviews of the British campaign in Basra were also keen to tie this latest of campaigns to the long and supposedly successful track record of British experiences in similar settings.

USING THE PAST: PERILS AND POSSIBILITIES

In Eric Hobsbawn's work on "invented traditions," he notes that one function of such traditions is "to establish continuity with a suitable historic past." The traditions can be "invented, constructed and formally instated" but may also emerge "in a less easily traceable manner within a brief and dateable period."[29] The relevance to the narrative of a British counterinsurgency legacy is clear: it too seeks to establish continuity with the past. But why should the past matter to the present, never mind the future? A more considered study of this question reveals that whereas there is indeed scope for transhistorical comparisons and learning, the key lies in using this history carefully, with an eye to context and without seeking to create myths. One critical error—an error that may be ascribed to the British military as it readied itself for Iraq—is to confuse past experience with counterinsurgency or knowledge of the relevant principles with an ability to master these types of operations, irrespective of political context or other circumstances. This error betrays an unquestioned and rather cursory understanding of the counterinsurgency experiences from which these principles are drawn—one that creates false confidence and grossly underestimates the complexity of third-party interventions then, now, and in years to come.

Two considerations should guide future efforts to learn from Britain's past.

1. How accurate is the prevailing reading of Britain's record with counterinsurgency? Rather than harvest "lessons" only from those campaigns that ended on relatively favorable terms, what can we learn from the historical failure to repeat such outcomes? This is in part a matter of appreciating variations between and, crucially, within specific campaigns, but also to discourage self-congratulatory myth making based on a partial record.

2. Is what worked in a different historical and strategic setting still relevant or useable today? Even among just the successful campaigns, the recol-

lection of these experiences must take into account the strategic and political contextual changes that may render some practices inapplicable or at least difficult to replicate.

A discussion of these two considerations can provide a fuller understanding of the utility of the traditional counterinsurgency principles and of the overarching British legacy with such operations. Such a reassessment is necessary because whereas there is plainly much to be learned from the past, a selective reading of history can have very dire consequences indeed.

THIS QUESTION OF ACCURACY

It is facile but nonetheless necessary to point out that among the comparatively successful British counterinsurgency campaigns that have contributed to Britain's legacy with such missions lies a number of far less notable cases in which British policy faltered or can even be said to have failed. Jonathan Gumz therefore criticizes the attempt to learn from past campaigns as ahistorical and parochial: the campaigns referred to in these efforts amount to "a bland cupboard from which to raid lessons learned which serve to confirm ideas already arrived at in the present."[30] With a specific focus on accuracy, this section discusses three aspects of the British record with counterinsurgency: the extent to which the British have a successful track record; whether the key cases were actually prosecuted as the traditional narrative would suggest; and whether the role of the British Army in these campaigns is accurately remembered.

As noted earlier, the main sources for historical lessons and principles have been the Malayan Emergency of 1948–1960 and the Troubles in Northern Ireland. That the outcome of the Malayan Emergency was successful is almost beyond debate. It would be possible to see the reconstitution of Communist irregular groups in the 1960s[31] and the momentary resurgence of ethnic violence in Kuala Lumpur in 1969 as evidence against the Emergency's success. Caroline Elkins goes further, stating that "repressive laws and undemocratic institutions, not peace and progress, were the primary bequest of the British to Malaya" and that the "Malaysian government's crackdown on dissent—including the suspension of due process and freedom of the press—is arguably the legacy of British repression."[32] But the opposite is equally if not more arguable: through British actions, the Malayan National Liberation Army was defeated, democratic elections were held, a multiethnic Malayan government was formed, and by mid-1960 the Emergency was declared over, with many former guerrillas becoming valued members of the newly independent state.[33] Moreover, one must be careful not to judge the outcome of the Emergency against rosy best-case scenarios, but in line with what was feasible in a country once fractured by ethnic enmity and war. Within the realm of human possibility, the results speak for themselves.

For all this, the lessons gleaned from this campaign all too seldom account for the enabling factors and operational advantages that contributed to its outcome. This campaign did not involve the challenges of urban operations, external support or sanctuary, or a more sophisticated guerrilla group capable of adapting to and circumventing British counterinsurgency practices. Raising these points should not force the pendulum the other way, so that the achievements in Malaya are needlessly belittled. However, it is necessary to point out that the transfer of lessons and principles from the particular case of Malaya to other essentially different and perhaps more complex contexts requires great caution. This lesson should have been made abundantly clear by the efforts of Robert Thompson, formerly the permanent secretary of defense for Malaya and close adviser to Gen. Sir Gerald Templer, to advise the United States on its effort in Vietnam. Although it might be argued that a good portion of his advice fell on deaf ears, it is equally true that the conditions were different and that the Malaya model, unless substantially changed, would not apply.[34]

The outcome of the conflict in Northern Ireland can also today be described as a success for the British government. In July 2005, following three decades of conflict, the Irish Republican Army Council announced an end to its armed campaign. Since then, the Provisional Irish Republican Army has ceased to exist in any meaningful sense. Northern Ireland remains part of the United Kingdom but is in many respects self-governed, while also being tied in some areas of policy to the influence and input of the Republic of Ireland. The role of the British counterinsurgency campaign in bringing about this outcome is the topic of a vast range of books and articles, many of which emphasize the army's sophisticated gathering and use of intelligence, its effective conduct of patrols and covert operations, and its application as part of a broader political strategy.

Yet here too there are contending ways of looking at the campaign—its conduct and legacy. That it took three decades for the Troubles to reach a political solution may be seen simply as reflecting the frustratingly long time-lines of irregular conflicts, but it might also be argued that there were as many mistakes and lost opportunities in this campaign as there were successes. The initial period of army operations, until the introduction of "police primacy," certainly echoes many of the errors committed in the initial phase of the Malayan campaign: the lack of intelligence, the excessive use of force, and the uncertain or altogether absent political guidance from the home govern-ment in London.[35] Another critical perspective concerns the great advantages afforded Britain in this particular setting: the geographical proximity, lack of linguistic or cultural barriers, and the familiarity of the troops with the urban terrain. These advantages facilitated the collection of intelligence, for which the campaign is now known. Given these advantages, is a thirty-year timeline still an adequate standard for success, and, if so, what precedent does it set for achieving "success" in campaigns farther afield—in Afghanistan, for example, or Iraq?

Clearly, the task of finding counterinsurgency successes is bedeviled by questions of context and variation.[36] The best that may be said is that the out-comes in Malaya and Northern Ireland ultimately met British strategic objec-tives and that some techniques and methods applied during each campaign denote both great sophistication and skill. Yet to go from this statement to making declarative judgments about British counterinsurgency capabilities across time and space is clearly an ambitious leap. Not only does this leap blur the complexity of the successful operations on which such assessments are based, but it also excludes from consideration all those cases where, by a simi-larly reductive logic, Britain "lost," be it in Aden, Afghanistan, India, Pales-tine, or even the United States of America in 1781. The suggestion here is not that a successful counterinsurgency campaign would have saved the British Empire or been an advisable course of action—when the British government opted to withdraw, it was oftentimes due to political calculation, in many cases a very good one at that.[37] The point, based on this mixed record, is that it is very difficult and therefore largely unadvisable to speak monolithically or undifferentiatedly about the British performance in counterinsurgency in and across different cases. The notion of such a legacy or a narrative of success belies critical variation both *between* and *within* individual campaigns. It also encourages simplistic tallies of "wins," "losses," and "draws" when the outcome in each case relates to a range of factors far broader than whatever counterinsurgency methods might have been applied at the time.

Beyond the outcome, the second bone of contention surrounding past campaigns, Malaya in particular, is whether the prosecution of these campaigns was really quite as it is remembered. In an authoritative reinterpretation of "the British way in counter-insurgency," David French has investigated the extent to which "the ways the British practised counter-insurgency between 1945 and 1967 actually conformed to the 'ideal-type' as defined by Thompson and refined by subsequent analysts." What he finds is that there is a substantial divergence between theory and practice. Most notably, French argues that the British, rather than emphasize winning "hearts and minds," actually "employed a wide variety of coercive techniques to intimidate the civilian population into throwing their support behind the government rather than behind the insurgents."[38] Paul Dixon and Andrew Mumford similarly argue that our understanding of past counterinsurgency successes may be flawed and that the operations of colonial withdrawal were actually far more violent and coercive than the literature would imply.[39]

It is true that the contemporary remembrance of past British counterinsurgency efforts tends to emphasize the tactical behaviors grouped under the rubric of "winning hearts and minds." Today, this phrase refers to three distinct activities: the use of military units and funds to conduct and enable humanitarian and development activities; the establishment of sound relations with the local population through cultural respect and adherence to the principle of the "minimum use of force"; and, finally, the use of information and psychological operations to gain influence and legitimacy.[40] The phrase "hearts and minds" therefore tends to evoke the "soft" and humanitarian aspects of operations. This connotation is problematic because it distances the term from its original meaning. Greater historical awareness reveals a far less utilitarian understanding of the phrase, one that blends co-option with a fair degree of coercion or at least control: "When we speak about 'hearts and minds,' we are not talking about being nice to the natives, but about giving them a firm smack of government. 'Hearts and minds' denoted authority, not appeasement. Of course, political and social reform might accompany firm government."[41]

This delicate fusing of coercion and co-option into an integrated strategy is all too often misunderstood. The key to the strategy is, of course, to employ both in a way that alienates insurgent leaders from their followers, all while persuading the latter that their interests are better served by siding with the government. However, within academia and the popular treatments of past campaigns, there is a tendency to take one side or the other: either to hone in on and overemphasize the benign aspects of past operations or to equate these operations with bloodshed and war crimes that border on genocide.[42] The former quite rightly (though at times with no great sense of balance) seeks to portray what was truly exceptional, at least from a comparative perspective, about *some* phases of *some* British campaigns. The notion of addressing the causes of violence, of building legitimacy, and of integrating social, economic, and political concerns into war planning and execution are so alien to the mindset of most militaries that these aspects of past campaigns have typically been lifted, underlined, and emphasized, sometimes to the extent of skewing the overall understanding of what happened. As a result, the opposite tendency—to emphasize the brutality of past campaigns—emerged very much as a corrective to this first wave of literature but arguably read too much into the equally regular instances of brutality, which are easily found in Britain's rich history with counterinsurgency. Both arguments have helped refine our understanding of past campaigns, but both are also flawed if their meaning is to comment on an overall "British approach," whether a particularly benign or brutal one at that. Given the broad swathes of territory and the many decades that make up the British counterinsurgency experience, it is difficult to find just *one* answer to this question; instead, it is important to move beyond these totalizing notions in favor of a richer understanding that is sensitive to specific cases and to variation within each. The British approach, in toto, was neither exceedingly brutal nor exceedingly benign.

The implication for the British military should be clear. We have already seen how the failure to pick up on variation encouraged a highly partial understanding of British competence in counterinsurgency.[43] When this partial understanding was further distorted through a false interpretation of "hearts and minds"—both its meaning and its prevalence—we arrive at a fundamentally flawed view of counterinsurgency as missions that the British have historically been good at, primarily through their use of accommodation and kind acts. Not only is this understanding built on a very selective tranche of history, but it also misrepresents even the limited history from which it purports to borrow. For inattentive scholars and practitioners of counterinsurgency, it can encourage the misleading notion that "nice guys finish first."

Missed here is an important question of how to employ violence and coercion in such a way that it does not become counterproductive to the political aims being sought. A closer examination of Malaya can in fact be highly instructive in this regard. It should be clear at this point that the British authorities in Malaya, as in any war, employed violence and coercion as part of their approach to operations. The concern here is not primarily with the more heinous yet isolated instances of brutality, such as the Batang Kali massacre of 1948, where British forces allegedly killed twenty-four unarmed civilians and burned down their houses. Such actions should by no means be forgotten, but they cannot be allowed to shape our understanding of the campaign as a whole. Our concern instead should be with more general practices, such as forced relocation or food-denial operations, which deliberately deprived insurgents of food so as to force their surrender. The question, then, is how these techniques could be used without either inflaming the Chinese population or delegitimizing the counterinsurgency effort and the structures it sought to bolster.

Two points stand out. First, many of the more coercive of approaches, although successful in isolating and weakening the insurgency, were also tied to an era where forces had greater latitude than they do today: global media scrutiny was more limited or could quite easily be shut down, and consideration of human rights was far less pronounced. When seeking to derive utility or "relevance" from comparatively successful historical case studies such as the Malayan Emergency, the focus should not be on replicating specific techniques and policies, but on achieving an equivalent effect. Thus, whereas forced relocation into "benign concentration camps" would be difficult to justify today, there is still great merit in attempting to separate the insurgents from the population from whom they draw their strength—hence, the use of berms, checkpoints, and other population-control measures in the US counterinsurgency operations in Iraq from 2006 onward. All while understanding past campaigns on their own merits, the drawing of lessons from such cases is better served by focusing on principle rather than on practice—particularly given changes in context and in what is therefore possible.

Second, alongside the more coercive techniques employed by the British forces in Malaya, the campaign also stands out for the constraints placed on the use of force, primarily from 1950 onward. Although coercion was used to establish control and to pursue the Malayan National Liberation Army, the strategy also emphasized the need for co-option as a road toward victory. The weight placed on co-option was neither consistent throughout the campaign nor unrivalled by other considerations, but it remains historically notable, particularly given the era (something that becomes quite clear when British policy in Malaya is compared to that developed contemporaneously in Kenya).[44] Thus, although the policy of forced relocation cannot be conducted without substantial harm to the local population, it belongs to the story that many members of this population were at the time "squatters" who had been without long-standing ties to their place of residence and that they were, in the "New Villages," given political, social, and legal rights and opportunities that had previously been unavailable to them.[45] And although the British military used blackmail and food-denial operations to glean intelligence from the Malayan National Liberation Army, it also purposefully refrained from torture and aerial bombardment and instead keenly sought out the backing of those who could be swayed to support its side. The implication for British forces and others seeking to learn from the Malayan Emergency is that coercion will always play a role in military operations, but that there are ways to use force that contribute to rather than undermine strategic objectives. This understanding of coercion gives rise to the common counterinsurgency technique of combining "sticks and carrots," and the campaign in Malaya provides an apt yet historically bound illustration of how this can be done.

Beyond the level of violence and the methods employed to achieve the tactical aims, another difficulty with the legacy's accuracy is that it tends to exaggerate the role of the British Army in past counterinsurgency campaigns. Most accounts are written by military officers or academics with a specific interest in military history, and perhaps for this reason they tend to deal predominantly or even exclusively with the role of the armed forces. Within the British military and, perhaps even more so, within its political leadership, this reading of past campaigns led to overconfidence about what the army can achieve on its own. Counterinsurgency then comes to be seen as a primarily military activity, obscuring the need for civilian partners and a political strategy to inform all activity.

A deeper historical understanding of past counterinsurgency successes reveals that the prosecution of such a mission, rather than involving just the army, relied on broad array of actors. Still within the security domain, these actors include locally recruited security forces such as the Iban Scouts in Malaya and, perhaps most important, national police forces, home guards, and other paramilitary outfits trained and controlled by the British.[46] I. A. Rigden, Frank Kitson, and many scholars of past campaigns highlight the importance of the police in particular.[47] Indeed, in the past, the police units have generally been the main "tools" of the counterinsurgency effort. In Malaya, for example, a total of 250,000 men had by 1953 been recruited into various constabulary, police, and self-defense units. In contrast, in the contemporary context, raising the standard, number, and accountability of local police forces represents a consistent and significant challenge not just in counterinsurgency operations, but also in other efforts to stabilize war-torn lands.

Going further, the historiography of British counterinsurgency tends to underplay, in favor of the military aspects, the role of civilian infrastructure and partners to carry out what is typically lumped together as the "nonmilitary" lines of effort—reconstruction activities, the provision of basic services, and the establishment of governance. These activities were in the past carried out by host-nation structures working together with colonial administrations, who commonly had years, if not decades, of experience within the particular political and cultural context. Their diminutive role in the historiography underplays the significance of their absence in today's counterinsurgency campaigns.

Finally, the focus on the military operations of past campaigns can easily obscure the fact that they required a political strategy to be meaningful. Whereas there is no shortage of books and articles on the evolution of military tactics in Malaya, one criminally underresearched element of the campaign is the way in which the British leadership in the country coaxed and convinced the Malayan elite to accept the inclusion of the ethnic Chinese population as part of the new nation. Because the ethnic tension between these two minorities and the disenfranchisement of the ethnic-Chinese lay at the root of the conflict, this political and social hurdle had to be overcome for the Emergency to be concluded as remembered today. Furthermore, no amount of tactical and operational skill on the part of the British military would have compensated for failures at the strategic level. Put simply, "had the British simply refused to leave, we would most likely be talking about a misguided British defeat—yet another Aden."[48] This point has significant implications also for military history as an area of study; as Jeremy Black puts it, where issues of winning over a population or of fomenting legitimacy are concerned, it is critical that "military history becomes an aspect of total history; not to 'demilitarize' it, but because the operational aspect of war is best studied in terms of the multiple political, social and cultural context that gave, and give, it meaning."[49]

RELEVANCE OVER TIME AND SPACE

Putting aside the various challenges to the accuracy of the British counterinsurgency legacy, we must ask whether that legacy, to the extent that it holds, is at all relevant today. Key changes have occurred from the supposed heyday of British counterinsurgency in the mid–twentieth century. Not only has the strategic context and Britain's international role evolved dramatically since the campaigns in defense of the British colonies, but so has the domestic British political and military context, which provided the foundation for earlier successes. Given notable change in these areas, which are fundamental to the conduct of counterinsurgency, a touch of modesty—even caution—is required before lessons from the past are lifted and made to apply to the campaigns of today and tomorrow.

First, counterinsurgency is not situated in the same strategic context as before. Invading or intervening in a foreign country to assist an insurgency-threatened ally or to impose a new regime, as in Iraq and Afghanistan, represents a very different endeavor from achieving an organized and politically acceptable withdrawal from a colony (Malaya) and from suppressing uprisings for national liberation against the established governments (Kenya, Algeria). The difference is that whereas Britain previously fought to *retain control* of or at least to *leave* its colonies on somewhat honorable terms, intervening governments today must usually do just that—*intervene*. Fighting your way in and asserting control bring a broader set of challenges ranging from domestic commitment to theater familiarity and the necessarily limited timeline. Winning the hearts and minds of the local population in order to remove support for an insurgency group preaching change is also very different from intervening to impose such change and fomenting local support for it. The contradiction is perhaps clearest in Afghanistan, where for many years the international community sought to form a democratically elected central government, a liberal economy, and social equality and justice. Although counterinsurgency was historically and by definition conservative, in a context such as Afghanistan it is the counterinsurgents who are the revolutionaries.

This contrast leads to a second difference in the nature of counterinsurgency today. In the past, counterinsurgency operations took place as "internal" challenges within the realms of the empire; today, operations are typically conducted by coalitions and in support of a legally sovereign state. In the place of the leverage that comes with colonial control, we are left with weak yet entirely independent host-nation governments that are either unable or unwilling to follow Whitehall writ.[50] Despite these obstacles, contemporary counterinsurgency theory still presumes a large-enough harmony of interest between intervening and host-nation governments, and the ability of intervening states to deploy a civilian presence large and capable enough to compensate for whatever weaknesses are found in-state. Practice provides a more sobering perspective: in Iraq, the institutions either collapsed through war or were dismantled through coalition decree, leading to the infiltration of various sectarian elements into positions of central political power and a government whose interests at times ran counter to those of the intervening coalition. In Afghanistan, the counterinsurgency campaign confronts a deeply dysfunctional state bureaucracy and a NATO headquarters that lacks the capacity and resources to run anything but the security aspects of operations. In both campaigns, difficulties with the host-nation government were compounded by differences among coalition partners as to approach, commitment, and contributions.

The nature of insurgency has also changed. Although it is easy to overstate differences between then and now, some key changes have occurred in the way insurgencies can operate. It is easier today for movements of different persuasion and type to communicate and cooperate across borders. John Mackinlay introduces the idea of the "insurgent archipelago" in order to highlight horizontally ordered, informal patterns of insurgents spread out transnationally, with no formal command structures or territorial basis, making them difficult to reach through a nationally based military campaign.[51] The information technology revolution has also provided insurgents with entirely new and efficient means of resistance in the struggle for hearts and minds. Whereas the British authorities in Malaya managed to clamp down on newspapers and other forms of media, today's insurgents are difficult to silence or to isolate from their target audience. Indeed, the expansion in ways and means of communication has increased the returns on what the anarchists of the early twentieth century called "propaganda of the deed."[52] Social media and the capability of finding an audience have allowed some groups to compensate for whatever they are lacking in capability with a powerful narrative.[53]

Beyond the changes in insurgency and counterinsurgency, the countries engaged in these struggles are also in a vastly different position than before. For Britain, its political and military capabilities for expeditionary operations have subsided significantly since the mid–twentieth century. It is obvious to note that the empire no longer exists, but the implications of its absence are less readily grasped. First, the colonial resources and structures that were in place within the empire are no more: instead of colonial administrators, most notably the Colonial Office, we are left with the "comprehensive approach," a mere rhetorical device that purports to mobilize a massive interdepartmental bureaucracy, much of which is domestically focused, for the purpose of coordinated campaigns conducted abroad. Beyond the jargon, few Western states have invested in civilian expeditionary capabilities, which leaves the military perilously isolated whenever it is deployed.

The military too has changed. The British military was never particularly devoted to counterinsurgency from an institutional standpoint, but it did benefit from a rich history with such missions and from its soldiers' individual experiences and memories. Given the nature of the colonial system, the British Army also had long-standing experience with the countries in which it was operating, was used to protracted conflicts far from home, and deployed its troops on operational tours of two years that provided at least a minimum level of local understanding as well as frequent experience of partnering with local institutions. With the end of empire, the opportunity to practice these skills vanished. Although this change should have forced a serious reconsideration of what British forces would be able to accomplish abroad, there is little evidence of such a reevaluation.

Instead, the British military has persisted in having a predominantly "conventional" view of war, as reflected in its force structure, culture, and education. During the Cold War, the prospect of a conventional, armored, and possibly nuclear confrontation across the Central Front might have warranted this prioritization (even then, though, the disinterest in counterinsurgency appeared more cultural than calculated). Following the Cold War, little changed: like most armed forces around the world, the British military was slow to respond to the strategic shift and never truly moved away from its focus on state-on-state combat. The 1991 Options for Change review of the British military made some significant cuts but failed to revisit critically the fundamental assumptions informing the structure or orientation of the armed forces. The 1998 *Strategic Defence Review* purported to bring a radical agenda of change: it emphasized expeditionary action, downplayed national defense, and highlighted the increased need to "help prevent or shape crises further away."[54] Yet despite a greater focus rhetorically on "flexibility and deployability,"[55] the end result was continuity. Not only did the *Strategic Defence Review* ring-fence many Cold War–era procurement projects, but it also persisted with a defense policy set in the immediate aftermath of the Cold War.[56]

Throughout the 1990s, the focus was overwhelmingly conventional in nature, meaning that the forces were still primarily trained and equipped for large-scale warfare on the European continent. To the extent that the decade's experience with peace-support operations in the Balkans and the Horn of Africa had made a mark, such challenges were still considered "containable and potentially resolvable within a state-centric framework and the national and international security arrangements developed during the Cold War."[57] As a result, by the time the British Army made its way to Iraq in 2003, it had "changed little in terms of structure, training focus and ethos from that which had stood ready to face the 3rd Shock Army on the plains of Westphalia during the Cold War."[58]

This was also a time when the British armed forces as well as many of their international counterparts were preoccupied with defense transformation based on a "revolution in military affairs," or RMA. With its roots in the US doctrine of Air–Land Battle, the RMA was a product of the perceived sense of technological superiority displayed during the Gulf War of 1991. It was an attempt to make use of this technology, much of it concerned with information dominance and communications, to transform armed forces into a network-centric self-synchronizing "system of systems," where control, communications, reconnaissance, electronic combat, and conventional firepower were to be wholly integrated.[59] Such a system would produce so-called dominant battle-space knowledge, meaning total awareness over the events on the battlefield and the ability to control such events through the combination of "sensors, deciders and shooters" in long-range, precision-guided, and intelligent munitions.[60]

Although the need to transform the armed forces to face new challenges following the Cold War was very real, the RMA school of transformation was still inherently steeped in state-on-state warfare and did not prove particularly helpful when applied to the counterinsurgency campaigns in Iraq and Afghanistan. More generally, the project belied an understanding of warfare as a targeting exercise won by the armed forces with the superior technology and critically underplayed the difficulty of turning military successes into political progress or of operating in a congested, cluttered environment. As a result, intellectual and resource investment in this "revolution" had the unfortunate effect of distracting the armed forces from the challenges of war as it would present itself in practice.

The culture and policies of the armed forces informed its training and education. For most of its recent history, the British Army has based its education and training on state-on-state, "conventional" warfare. In theory and as explained in 2004 by Brig. Simon Mayall, then the MoD's director of army resources and plans, the British train for major war while constantly staying ready for different forms of peace operations.[61] The apparent flexibility required for this system to work is a source of institutional pride, but it has never received the investment it needs to work. Instead, what dismissively used to be called "operations other than war" have typically been marginalized or lumped together, despite their respective nature and requirements.

For example, the focus on counterinsurgency in the British Army's Advanced Command and Staff Course decreased substantially in 1997. One term in five had previously been devoted to gaining "a detailed understanding of joint operations, peace-support operations and counter insurgency." Included in this term was a comprehensive three-week counterinsurgency module that included the counterparts from the Police Staff College. Come 1997, when the Joint Services Command and Staff College replaced the single-service academies, the time devoted to land warfare was reduced from three terms to one. The focus on counterinsurgency was similarly reduced so that it represented but one of three topics to be covered in a three-day module also allocated to "other operations."[62]

In doctrine as well, counterinsurgency came to be subsumed under the heading of peace operations. The 1995 document *Wider Peacekeeping* helped familiarize parts of the force with the specificities of these types of operations—an understandable priority given the decade's experiences in the Balkans and Somalia.[63] Yet the doctrine for peace operations not only remained fraught with conceptual difficulties[64] but also swallowed up whatever remained of Britain's legacy with counterinsurgency. Because neither represented "conventional war," these two types of operations were conflated and the differences between them and their distinct requirements were thereby lost.[65] Although the British Army did publish updated counterinsurgency doctrine in 1995,[66] as Alex Alderson explains, it was neither studied nor taught, and the subject therefore fell into decline.[67]

As a result of this neglect, by the time the army reached Iraq in 2003, it was not uncommon for British officers to be unable to "list the British COIN [counterinsurgency] principles, define their meaning, or discuss past British successes in a meaningful way." There was also little familiarity with the traditional texts on counterinsurgency, in large part because of the limited focus on this topic in institutions from Sandhurst to the Staff College.[68] In retrospect, the assumption of adaptation and flexibility would appear seriously flawed. Although certain basic skills and activities pertain to almost all military operations, Britain's own counterinsurgency doctrine has consistently noted the unique challenges of these types of campaigns—challenges that require specialized or distinct preparation: how to operate among civilians, against irregular nonstate armed groups, with indigenous forces, and so on. By grounding all military education and training in conventional combat, these "alternative" skills were ignored.[69]

All of this lost learning makes the British military very unlike that which participated in the counterinsurgency campaigns of yesteryears. The difference or gaps in knowledge and capability could not be remedied simply through appeals to Britain's past with counterinsurgency. Nor could they be balanced out by the army's regimental system, which some commentators framed as key in ensuring the flexibility required for counterinsurgency. To this view, the regiment, in contrast with the division, benefits from a strong identity and sense of community in that it recruits locally and experiences less turnover in terms of personnel.[70] It is also claimed that regiments enable an informal process of learning from history, as each captures the lessons from previous campaigns and passes them down to the younger generations. Whatever merits this system may once have proffered, it did not protect these units from the overriding institutional focus on conventional warfare. Indeed, due precisely to its informality, the learning enabled through the regimental system is less systematized and thorough as well as dangerously dependent on an ad hoc practice of information sharing.[71] For this system to have any bearing on a unit's counterinsurgency capabilities, it must either have continuous experience with such operations, to keep the familiarity alive, or view such engagements as important and prepare accordingly. In the British case, neither of these conditions obtained.

The suggestion here is not that the past is dead; in many ways, it is not even the past. However, the history must be treated with caution and care, particularly if it is to be lifted from its context and play a role in the present day or tomorrow. Where does this caveat leave traditional counterinsurgency theory and the associated principles? Perhaps counterinsurgency expert David Kilcullen gets it right when he asserts that "classical theory is necessary but not sufficient for success against contemporary insurgencies."[72]

When looked at differently, much comes down to what is expected from the classical theory. In distilled form, the principles of British counterinsurgency would seem largely timeless: given the nature of Western interventions today, it is difficult to argue against the importance of achieving a nuanced political understanding of the campaign, of operating under unified civil–military command, of using intelligence to distinguish civilians from insurgents, of isolating insurgents from the population, of using the minimum amount of force necessary to achieve set objectives, and of assuring and maintaining the perceived legitimacy of the counterinsurgency effort in the eyes of the populace. Most valuable, perhaps, is the exhortation to "adapt and learn" and to arrive at a tailored response rather than to fall back on template solutions. And yet the critical distinction must be made: these principles are guideposts, some of them more obvious than others, but they are insufficient in the absence of a viable strategy, adequate resources, and the skills and capabilities to apply them in the field. In all of these respects, the British military that invaded Iraq was seriously unprepared.

THE DANGER OF MYTHS

Although mentions of Malaya and Northern Ireland are now likely to invoke much skepticism—arguably both campaigns have been overhyped and oversold—there is great merit to our study of these and other historical wars. The key lies in understanding to what uses we can and cannot put these past campaigns—in other words, how we learn from history and how we treat the counterinsurgency theory and principles to which this history has given rise. The problem is that the British counterinsurgency legacy was misinterpreted as conferring an immutable advantage in these notoriously difficult types of operations, wherever and whenever they may arise. This interpretation of the British counterinsurgency legacy is deeply unhelpful. For the British military, it resulted in far too much faith being placed in its ability to master the challenges of insurgency by instinct, without investing in the necessary capabilities, skills, and understanding.

Four key misinterpretations on aggregate left the British military at once quietly confident in its ability yet entirely unprepared. First, to the degree that the British military was institutionally and individually aware of its historical experiences with counterinsurgency, it tended to overemphasize the comparatively successful campaigns at the expense of the rest. As a result, consideration of the British counterinsurgency legacy encouraged an institutional sense of complacency with such missions—it had, in the words of one former chief of the defense staff, become "too complacent" and "smug" about its past.[73]

Second, the recollection of even the successful experiences tended to be superficial, with slogans such as "hearts and minds" ceaselessly repeated yet seldom understood. Most notably, the exaggerated focus on the more "benign" aspects of past British counterinsurgency strategies resulted in a mistaken belief in a winning formula based on kindness, charity, and accommodation. Lost in this manner were critical insights into how co-option can be fused with coercion so as to meet strategic objectives. More generally, knowledge of the British principles of counterinsurgency, where extant, tended to be confused with an ability to put those principles into practice.

Third, invocations of past successes tended to underappreciate the radical contextual changes between then and now and therefore the need to rethink both ways and means. Most fundamental, the effects of the end of empire were not fully grasped, leaving the army with a false sense of confidence as to with whom it might work and what it could achieve abroad. On a more strategic level, too few realized the categorical changes between defending empire from nascent resistance movements and intervening in foreign countries to put in place new political systems.

Fourth, in part because of its sense of confidence with counterinsurgency, the British military either deliberately or unwittingly let its counterinsurgency-relevant capabilities fade, so much so that by the end of the 1990s counterinsurgency had become a peripheral concern, marginalized in both training and education. By 2003, when the British military invaded Iraq, individual memory of counterinsurgency was scarce, and the institution had failed to provide the needed preparation. It might be argued that the British military did what it was funded to do because counterinsurgency was not prioritized either at the political strategic level or by the military leadership. However, the failure to prepare for counterinsurgency is in fact a failure to prepare for war as it presents itself, given the challenges that are present in virtually all contemporary land operations. And as former chief of the defense staff Air Chief Marshal Sir Jock Stirrup has argued, "You're only as good as your next success, not your last one."[74]

This backdrop contextualizes the confidence and self-congratulatory tone that accompanied initial assessments of British operations in Iraq. The mentions of a "British approach" at the time harked back to historical experiences but were blind not only to what those experiences entailed and how much had changed in the world, at home, and within the British military since that day. Most fundamentally, they belied an expectation that operational approaches and best practices, even if properly implemented and understood, could substitute for a viable strategy.

2

THE BRITISH IN BASRA

With Heads Held High into the Abyss

PUBLIC AND MEDIA attention over the British role in the Iraq War has tended to converge primarily on Prime Minister Tony Blair's determination to involve the United Kingdom in the overthrow of Saddam Hussein. Even during the Iraq Inquiry held in the aftermath of the campaign, in 2009–2011, the stories grabbing the biggest headlines were those that dealt with the case for and lead-up to war. The bias is understandable given the financial, political, and human costs wrought by the decision to invade Iraq. Nevertheless, an equally controversial and urgent area of inquiry is the British effort *following* the invasion to "help create [the] conditions for a future, stable and law-abiding government of Iraq."[1] Indeed, for Britain's role in international peace and security, the conduct of operations in Iraq and the circumstances of the British withdrawal in 2009 are likely to have effects as far-reaching as the initial invasion of the country in 2003.

The campaign in southern Iraq signified the reencounter with counterinsurgency by a military force often lauded for its ability in this area. Long-exalted principles and know-how were put into practice, nowhere more conspicuously than in Basra. The issue was not that the British forces faced an insurgency when they entered southern Iraq, but rather that through their actions and lack thereof they helped foment one, if by insurgency we mean "organised, violent subversion used to effect or prevent political control, as a challenge to established authority."[2] This outcome—and the British difficulty in crafting an adequate response—has left many asking what happened to Britain's prowess in counterinsurgency. Others point to the threadbare civilian and political support for the military's efforts and question why the British Army was left to fight "with one hand tied behind its back." The lessons that the armed forces draw from this campaign and how they interpret it will inform not only the British military's future with counterinsurgency, but British civil–military relations as well.

British involvement in Saddam Hussein's overthrow was more broadly the culmination of Blair's "doctrine of international community." Articulated in Chicago during the Kosovo campaign in 1999, the doctrine envisaged a strong international role for the United Kingdom not just in guaranteeing its strategic interests, but in resolving humanitarian crises and combating gross violations of human rights.[3] Returning to Chicago ten years later, with his premiership behind him, Blair reflected on whether the campaigns in Iraq and Afghanistan had dented his doctrine: "Should we now revert to a more traditional foreign policy, less bold, more cautious; less idealistic, more pragmatic, more willing to tolerate the intolerable because of fear of the unpredictable consequences that intervention can bring?"[4] Blair's own response to this question was a bold reaffirmation of his original vision—it almost had to be—but the experiences in Iraq will weigh heavily on the minds of future British governments as they seek to formulate their own approach to British foreign policy. Much as the campaign has provided the military with reasons for reflection and reform, it has also shaped wider thinking about Britain's strategic ambitions.

Two broad lessons stand out: first, the British military's prowess with counterinsurgency is neither innate nor sufficient in the absence of a well-conceived and resourced strategy; and, second, the British government's failure to prepare for and adapt to the challenges encountered in Basra reveal a low understanding and prioritization of state building. Both lessons signal a need to raise the level of competence for these types of missions across government, but also for greater realism about what intervention can realistically achieve.

SETTING THE STAGE:
BRITISH INVOLVEMENT IN BASRA

The Basra governorate is located at the southernmost tip of Iraq and is flanked by Iran to the east and Kuwait to the south. The province covers an area of around nineteen thousand square kilometers and is home to a population of just less than two million, making it the seventh largest and, as of 2003, fifth most populated governorate in Iraq. The only Iraqi province with maritime access, Basra has traditionally benefited from strong international trade links, resulting in a historically vibrant economy as well as a high degree of social and ethnic diversity. The majority of Basra's population is Shia Muslims, which contributed to the province's often tense relations with the Saddam Hussein regime: revolts erupted in Basra in 1991 and 1999 and were both times crushed by the Baathist government. Going back further, Basra's residents have long emphasized their distinctness from the rest of the country and from Baghdad in particular, which is perceived as exploiting Basra's resources, especially its oil, without investing in its infrastructure or providing it with political representation and power. Despite these pressures toward greater autonomy, British and American planners anticipated a relatively uncomplicated occupation of Basra: it was expected that the Shia population would welcome the disposal of Saddam Hussein and look forward to a new golden era for Basra within a liberated Iraq.[5]

On March 21, 2003, following two days of air operations, the US-led coalition sent military ground forces across the border into Iraq. The US component was split between V Corps and the Marine Expeditionary Force, which were to perform a pincer maneuver across the country, directed at the capital. The intent for the British force, the Armoured Division, was to seize the oil-rich Faw Peninsula in southeastern Iraq so as to allow the US forces around the Rumaila oilfields and Az Zubayr to move farther north. The combat phase of the campaign was decidedly one-sided, with the coalition facing few problems in overpowering the resistance it faced. As US forces made solid progress on their "blitz to Baghdad," British forces engaged with Iraqi forces in the South and sought to shift to occupational duties as soon as security conditions would permit. By March 24, Basra International Airport was under UK control. On March 31, "a school reopen[ed] in Rumaylah, and markets and hospitals open[ed] in Az Zubayr," a town in the Basra governorate. On April 1, UK forces begin patrolling Az Zubayr, and five days later they entered and remained in Basra, facing little opposition. By this point, US troops were already in Baghdad, and by the end of the month President Bush would declare the major combat phase of the operation over.[6]

Following the invasion, it fell to the United Kingdom, with its 46,000 troops in theater, to assume transitional control over Basra Province and the country's three other southernmost provinces: Maysan, Dhi Qar, and al-Muthanna. Postinvasion operations in these provinces were in May 2003 given legal status through United Nations (UN) Security Council Resolution 1483, which recognized the United States and the United Kingdom, along with the other members of the coalition, as "occupying powers" and thereby rendered explicit their "specific authorities, responsibilities, and obligations under applicable international law."[7] To administer the duties of occupation, the US government formed the Office of Reconstruction and Humanitarian Assistance (ORHA), but this office was then quickly subsumed under the Coalition Provisional Authority (CPA). In contrast with ORHA's light footprint, the CPA assumed "executive, legislative and judicial authority" and was to serve as an ersatz government pending the development of local institutions to whom power and responsibility could be transferred.[8] To help meet its objectives, the CPA split Iraq administratively into four parts: the northern, predominantly Kurdish areas; Baghdad and the surrounding Sunni areas; the South Central Region; and the South Region, including Basra, which was put under the control of CPA South.

The CPA had an ambitious vision for Iraq, though the exact wording of the desired end state differed between declarations and as the situation on the ground evolved. CPA Regulation Number 1, issued in May 2003, laid out three fundamental tasks: "to exercise powers of government temporarily in order to provide for the effective administration of Iraq during the period of transitional administration, to restore conditions of security and stability, [and] to create conditions in which the Iraqi people can freely determine their own political future."[9] A strategic plan issued by the CPA later that year described the "ultimate goal" of the endeavor as "a unified and stable, democratic Iraq that provides effective and representative government for the Iraqi people; is underpinned by new and protected freedoms and a growing market economy; is able to defend itself but no longer poses a threat to its neighbors or international security."[10] The British interpretation of this vision differed slightly in that it deemphasized "democracy" in favor of "representative government."[11] Despite this difference, the envisaged transformation of Iraq was fundamental.

STRATEGIC MISCALCULATIONS

Prior to and in the year following the invasion, the notion that the campaign might evolve into a fully fledged counterinsurgency operation was far from war planners' minds. On paper, the transition to peace was to occur smoothly along three identified stages: "stability," in which a sufficiently secure environment would be established; "recovery," involving reconstruction and economic development; and "transition," the gradual handover of tasks and responsibilities to a "peaceful, self-governing Iraq."[12] Yet little thought and few resources had gone into staffing and implementing this plan. As far as actual planning was concerned, most of it focused on the measures needed to avert any humanitarian crisis that might be provoked by the war. This aim was certainly laudable, but it left coalition forces ill prepared for the likely effects of the country's central regime being overthrown or the duties thus imposed on the occupying powers.[13] From the beginning, therefore, a major disconnect existed between lofty political ambitions and adequate planning for a political transition. In general, it was assumed that the UN would accept a significant role in this transformation—an unlikely eventuality given the acrimony within the Security Council over the initial invasion.[14]

An underlying problem here, relating to the nature of the campaign as a coalition effort, was that the United Kingdom was a junior partner and had largely abdicated its planning responsibilities to the United States. As is now widely recognized, the US planning assumptions for the war were for the most part wrong—or at least overly optimistic. Despite extensive State Department, interagency, and military research into likely postwar scenarios, those who came to dominate war planning resisted serious consideration of what was to follow Saddam's removal. Instead, they persisted with what Gen. Tim Cross, the most senior British officer involved in the war planning, has described as a "paradigm": "the US plan was that 'we do not need a plan.' The Iraqi people, it was argued, would respond to the overthrow of Saddam Hussein with huge relief and a desire to establish democracy and we (the US) would downscale quickly and move on to the next issue."[15] This paradigm is reflected in US Central Command's official assumptions behind the invasion: "Opposition groups will work with us; . . . co-opted Iraqi units will occupy garrisons and not fight either US forces or other Iraqi units"; the US Department of State "will promote creation of broad-based, credible provisional government—prior to D-Day"; and the number of US troops in theater will be reduced to 5,000 by December 2003.[16]

The US errors in planning for the Iraq War are well established. Until the British Iraq Inquiry in 2009, it was less well known that a similar combination of disinterest and optimism had also marked UK deliberations on the war. In the Permanent Joint Headquarters, there was, according to Gen. Cross, a "reluctance to close with" the issue of postconflict planning: "the emphasis at this stage was ensuring that we—the UK Military [sic]—could sit alongside the US in the war fighting phases of the operation . . . ; longer term reconstruction was not seen as MoD business."[17] Problematically, neither was postwar planning occurring elsewhere across government. The Foreign Office was reluctant to get involved, preferring to defer to the military. The senior leadership of the Department for International Development (DfID) was personally opposed to the war and at best stayed out of or at worst obstructed the required interministerial planning. Across government, "there was an underlying belief that the US would quickly be able to bring whatever was necessary to bear."[18]

Reflecting Britain's lack of preparedness, the Foreign Office unit responsible for postwar planning was set up only three weeks before the invasion. A divisional plan for postconflict operations was issued fifteen days after Basra fell.[19] Until January 2003, moreover, coalition plans foresaw Britain entering

Iraq via southern Turkey; it was only when the Turkish government proved unable to secure parliamentary approval for this option that attention shifted southward.[20] As a result, little of the minimal postconflict planning that had occurred related specifically to the Iraqi South. The British troops who entered Basra had neither the plans nor the structures or resources needed to fulfill their occupational duties and satisfy their government's objective of transforming Iraq.

It was in this context that the British military's legacy with counterinsurgency was invoked. On the surface, faith in a specifically British approach to the difficult task of postconflict stabilization seemed vindicated. With an unanticipated environment in view, British troops adopted a soft and unobtrusive approach that appeared successful in containing postwar violence. To lend a local face to security operations, British forces stood up Iraqi security forces: within a week, they conducted joint patrols, and by July the Iraqi police were said to number 2,000.[21] The British soldiers, meanwhile, assumed a nonconfrontational stance so as to "normalize" the province: they wore berets rather than helmets to appear constabulary rather than military and eschewed checkpoints and curfews.[22] Where force was used, the emphasis was on discretion so as not to alienate the local population; through prior experience, British forces were said to be particularly comfortable with the notion of "smile, shoot, smile."[23]

British forces also swiftly empowered local political leaders so that the Iraqis could enjoy their newfound freedom. After only days in Basra, British forces appointed tribal leader Sheikh Muzahim al-Tamimi to head a thirty-member council that would administer the province. Meanwhile, the British Army complemented the efforts of its civilian partners to repair infrastructure and deliver basic services. It detailed staff to the coalition's regional authority (CPA South), had the Royal Engineers conduct limited reconstruction, and with civilian representatives oversaw quick-impact projects; 1 Armoured Division administered £10 million worth of such projects in the first six months.[24] Already on April 22, 2003, the UN declared the security climate in Basra to be "permissive," and most observers were hopeful about the province's continued "normalization." Indeed, the term *normalization* pervades early commentary on British activities in Basra, belying the heady assumption of there being a functioning "normal" to which the province, with minimal coalition input, could return.

PEACE OPERATIONS
OR COUNTERINSURGENCY?

During at least the first year of operations in Basra, many observers within the British government and armed services perceived the army's ability to lean on prior operational experience at unit and formation level as compensating for the lack of formal postwar planning.[25] To the MoD, Britain's "counter insurgency experience from Northern Ireland and the Balkans [had] enabled the British Army to make a positive start in Iraq."[26] Indeed, during this first year of the campaign, complacency developed around the notion of British soldiers in berets engaging with local community leaders, conducting reconstruction, and operating in a manner that US forces, with their harsher methods and cultural resistance to peace operations, struggled to understand. That the British forces formulated this response on the hoof and without strategic guidance also lent credence to the notion of a "British approach" passed down and refined over time.[27]

There are two problems with this interpretation. Not only did the initial calm in Basra relate only marginally to British operations there (the relatively stable environment related in large part to the local population's opposition to the Saddam Hussein regime), but the apparent tranquility was also largely illusory or at least superficial. In this early, critical period, errors of judgment resulted in the gradual takeover of Basra by sectarian militias, criminal networks, and other predatory actors, sowing the seeds for eventual British failure. British actions no doubt prevented a more immediate inflammation of the southern provinces, but they were a tactical solution to a strategic problem.

Three factors prevented the British military from adopting the principles of previous counterinsurgencies: the armed forces' misinterpretation of their own legacy, the absence of civilian support, and the lack of strategic guidance from Whitehall. Each factor also poses a particular challenge to Britain's future with counterinsurgency.

First, as we saw in the previous chapter, the British military, principally its army, had by 2003 forgotten the principles and practices of its counterinsurgency legacy. Instead, the British military's initial reaction was to lean on more recent experiences—in the Balkans as well as Northern Ireland, which by the 1990s had turned comparatively peaceful. With these campaigns fresh in their minds and informing expectations, the approach adopted in Basra was passive and shaped by the peacekeeping principles of "doing no harm," maintaining "neutrality," and applying only the "minimum use of force."[28] Whereas counterinsurgency doctrine, by contrast, presumes a contested environment in which security forces must establish control, British forces deliberately refrained from population-control measures. Whereas counterinsurgency theory posits presence and a firm monopoly on the use of force as prerequisites for influencing either hearts or minds, British troops adopted a low profile and assumed that doing so would lead to greater support for the occupation. Intended to "normalize" postwar Basra, this seemingly reflexive adherence to the principles of peace operations instead ceded the initiative.

The initial stability in Basra, relative to elsewhere in Iraq, appeared to validate the soft approach. Overlooked in this analysis was the fact that although violence was less acute, Basra was nonetheless engulfed by mass looting and criminality. Not only was the looting unanticipated, but it was also dealt with naively by senior commanders unwilling to defy the population that they had just liberated. Some even painted the chaos as an expression of liberty or as a long-awaited redistribution of wealth after decades of autocracy.[29] Iraq's new freedom was to be celebrated, not curtailed—and certainly not by British forces.

The measures taken by the British military to secure the province were by themselves insufficient. The concept of "smile, shoot, smile," although well intentioned, rested on assumptions lifted from the more peaceful settings of the 1990s: that the spoilers were few and finite; that eliminating them would guarantee security; and that the rest of the people, those being smiled at, would smile back unless unduly interfered with. In this situation, support was more likely to be gained through an active rather than passive stance—by securing infrastructure, establishing security, and preventing mass theft. Indeed, the sporadic patrols mounted by the British military had a clearly positive effect where and when they passed, but disorder ensued when they were out of sight.

The establishment of local security forces also belied unfamiliarity with this essential counterinsurgency task. In May 2003, the British military reconstituted a force of 900 unarmed Iraqi policemen and announced that this force was now the "functioning police": not only was it too weak, but as an institution the police had never provided public security—a task that had fallen to the army and intelligence sector.[30] Establishing competent security forces would require a concerted program of security-sector reform, something the British presence, short of expertise and support, did not turn to until the following year. In the meantime, although the army reforms were comparatively successful, police training lacked clear ownership, resources, and manpower.[31] To the degree that any progress was being made, it focused mainly on bringing up the numbers of the police so as to give an Iraqi gloss to combined operations.[32] Not only did the weakness of the police prolong the looting and lawlessness, but the rushed process of reconstituting this force also made it susceptible to infiltration by various militias.[33] Such infiltration undermined subsequent British efforts to raise the competence of the police force because the loyalties of those receiving training at the Az Zubayr police academy and in Jordan often lay elsewhere.

The second factor undermining the Basra campaign was the lack of attention paid to reconstruction and development activities in the province. Infrastructure in Basra had suffered neglect under Saddam, damage during the war, and further devastation during the looting. It required immediate redress. But the civilian presence in Basra was too small and ill resourced to carry out the interim functions of an occupying power. There were some early successes, such as the Emergency Infrastructure Plan, a civil–military effort to enable initial reconstruction. However, the distribution of funds through this project was haphazard, reflecting a general unpreparedness across the British civilian ministries for state-building activities.[34] Compounding this situation was the tardiness of guidance and financial support from CPA headquarters in Baghdad; the assumption was that the United Kingdom would manage and fund its own region.[35] In fact, until sustained riots occurred in August 2003, Whitehall allocated no funds specifically for reconstruction.[36] Yet the problem went beyond resources: as Warren Chin notes, "What [the CPA] needed was a head with experience of running a large municipal authority [and] . . . experts in the provision of public education, health, and management of utilities, but such expertise was virtually nonexistent."[37]

The army-administered quick-impact projects attempted to compensate for this capability gap, yet as a later MoD review would note, the armed forces lacked "the resources and expertise to play more than a limited role in other campaign strands—political, economic, social, legal and cultural."[38] Furthermore, many within the army's senior command begrudged the civilian tasks foisted upon them: the feeling was that with Saddam Hussein toppled, the military's job was largely done, and they ought now to be relieved by civilians, not the other way around.[39] In the meantime, garbage piled up, electricity outages were frequent, and problems with sewage and water caused an outbreak of cholera. These problems, along with the looting, turned the population against the occupying forces.

Fanning the discontent was the haphazard transfer of political control. To the British, influenced by the catchphrases of earlier peace operations, the idea of establishing "local ownership" no doubt seemed appropriate, but the politics and divisiveness of this process were underestimated. Britain's first man in Basra, al-Tamimi, and the council over which he presided had to be replaced after merely six weeks amid allegations of links to the Baath Party. A suggested successor was quickly rejected on the same grounds. Plans then changed as the CPA put a sudden end to devolution. Offices occupied by those previously empowered were vacated, and the CPA governorate coordinator was put at the helm.[40] Making coalition officials the de jure leaders of the province solved the problem of continuity, but it antagonized the local population, whose patience with the CPA was wearing thin.

Finally, errors on the ground were compounded by graver errors of strategy in London. The Blair government had set out several grand strategic objectives to be met in Iraq, but it was also painfully aware of the rancor back home over the war. Whether out of expedience or naivety, the brief lull following the ousting of Saddam Hussein was misinterpreted as heralding an ineluctable transition to peace and pounced upon to justify the early withdrawal of troops.[41] Reflecting this misreading, the British government began reducing its forces as early as May 2003, and within three months of the fall of Basra force levels had shrunk from a maximum of 46,000 to some 10,500.[42] For all their domestic appeal, these swift withdrawals made it impossible for coalition forces on the ground to provide any form of security for the local population, whose safety was now in the hands of hastily formed local security forces. Indeed, by late 2003, only a little more than 9,000 coalition soldiers remained for the approximately 4.6 million inhabitants of Multinational Division–Southeast (MND-SE)—a far cry from the tentative force ratios found to apply in previous counterinsurgencies.

Britain's inability to carry out its occupational duties or to transfer them to able host-nation institutions created capability gaps readily filled by others. Among the forces vying for power, two factions dominated: the Supreme Council for the Islamic Revolution in Iraq (SCIRI), formerly based in Iran, and its armed wing, the Badr Brigade; and Moqtada al-Sadr, a vocal opponent of the occupation and leader of the Jaish al-Mahdi (JAM) militia. Along with other aspirants, SCIRI and Sadr engaged in a struggle for political control over Basra. Although these militias seldom confronted coalition forces directly, they did insist on substantial freedom of action. One rare attempt by the British military to assert control, an effort to disarm the town of Majar al-Kabir in June 2003, resulted in the deaths of six British soldiers and was the last such action in the Southeast for some time. The operation reflected the lack of counterinsurgency-related and cultural training provided to the occupying forces: use of sniffer dogs, raids into private homes, and an attempt to confiscate weapons in what was still an insecure environment all but guaranteed a confrontation.[43]

Informed in part by these events, the CPA put off dealing with the militias. By and large, the CPA leadership in Baghdad "was sympathetic to the political parties who said their militias were an 'insurance policy' pending a political solution that would ensure their security against other groups."[44] Left in place, the militias competed with one another and made arrangements with the coalition that reflected their power and influence.[45] SCIRI was particularly adept at presenting itself as a friend of the coalition and accordingly was rewarded with political power. In Baghdad, SCIRI head Abdul Aziz al-Hakim was appointed to the Interim Governing Council; in the South, SCIRI members filled provincial governorships, council seats, and senior police posts, and members of the Badr Brigade became heads of intelligence and customs police in Basra.[46] Not only was the appearance of a common cause between the coalition and this Iranian-backed Islamist group largely illusory or transient, but SCIRI's elevation was also unconditional because it left the group's militia—swiftly renamed the Badr Organisation for Reconstruction—in place or integrated wholesale into the emerging security structures.

SCIRI's elevation in this manner can be seen as the first instance of "accommodation," a term that would come to describe Britain's future dealings with Basra's militias. Already at this juncture, it proved a highly problematic strategy, yet it allowed for what appeared to be an orderly transition to local actors and was therefore preferred to confrontation. The exception was Moqtada al-Sadr, whose rhetoric against the occupation and complicity in various acts of violence made him a persona non grata to the CPA. In other words, political power was doled out to those who purported to support the occupation, but with no real consideration of their local legitimacy, broader political agendas, or independent coercive capabilities.

Despite these significant setbacks, the British government long considered the operation in Basra as largely successful. To this view, the British military's passive stance represented a more respectful posture that had prevented undue confrontation. This interpretation was based on the lower number of fatalities in Basra than elsewhere in Iraq, a discrepancy that was only natural given Basra's ethnic composition and history, but that was nonetheless lauded by some as testament to an innate British capability to conduct counterinsurgency.[47] Not only did this argument misinterpret its own chosen metric, but the resultant appearance of a successful counterinsurgency also belied the creeping infiltration of extremist elements into Basra society.[48]

OPERATIONAL ADAPTATION AND STRATEGIC INERTIA

From a historical perspective, the fact that the operation in Basra got off on the wrong foot was hardly an anomaly; many prior campaigns, such as those in Malaya and Northern Ireland, had also begun badly. The difference is that in earlier campaigns initial missteps were acknowledged and corrected. This did not happen in Basra. In mid- to late 2005, a surge in violence in Basra signaled the limitations of British control in the province and prompted the British military to shift toward a more aggressive stance, involving raids, strikes, and confrontations. Yet this operational adaptation occurred without a concomitant shift in strategy, resources, or political support. Despite the severity of the challenges on the ground, the British government did not increase the military presence in the province or rethink what would be necessary to be strategically effective in this environment. Meanwhile, the deteriorating security conditions had prompted most civilian agencies to restrict their activities, and the programs still running were inadequately integrated with military efforts.[49] The understrength force was thus left to prosecute a ramped-up offensive on its own, without civilian partners and without their government's backing and guidance. Even where tactically adept, these operations could not bridge the fundamental mismatch between ends and means or the lack of an adequate strategy.

The British Army was also without host-nation partners, which were either weak or infiltrated. In November 2004, SCIRI's political grip on the province was strengthened, as Hasan al-Rashid, a SCIRI-affiliated Islamist, replaced the moderate Wael Abdel-Latif as governor. Yet SCIRI was far from uncontested. Sadr boasted a following among Basra's mass of urban dispossessed and a powerful militia in JAM. A third force, Hizb al-Fadhila al-Islamiya, also enjoyed support among Basra's poor and could draw on its control of the 15,000-strong Oil Protection Force for muscle and patronage.[50] In January 2005, Fadhila gained second place in the provincial elections and proceeded to claim the governorship (assumed by Muhammad al-Waeli).

The militias competed over three main assets: access to public institutions; control over security forces; and control and trafficking of oil.[51] Through coercion and public outreach, they arrived at a rough partition: Fadhila controlled the oil infrastructure; SCIRI the intelligence sector; Sadr the local police, port authority, and Facilities Protection Service (established to protect governorate infrastructure); and Hizballah (a minor force unrelated to its Lebanese namesake) the Customs Police Force. This power struggle undermined British efforts at security-sector reform and deprived the coalition of reliable host-nation security forces. By May 2005, the Basra police chief acknowledged that half his force belonged to militias and that only a quarter of his officers were trustworthy.[52] According to one militia leader, 80 percent of assassinations were by 2006 "committed by individuals wearing police uniforms."[53] Most problematic were the 200–300 members of the Serious Crimes Unit (SCU), which exerted influence over the rest of the police force and acted with impunity. More than anything, it was SCU's abduction of two British special-operations soldiers in September 2005 and their imprisonment in the Jamait police station that exposed the lack of British control and the deep inadequacies of the institutions to which that control had been ceded.

When in response to these conditions the British military escalated, it was thus without interagency and host-nation partners and with an under-strength force. The rescue operation mounted against SCU in October 2005 revealed the contradictions of the new, more aggressive stance. The operation was launched without explicit MoD authorization because officials in London worried about the political implications of a British attack on an Iraqi police unit, albeit a severely infiltrated one. Taking the initiative, British forces partially destroyed the police compound but were confronted by a mob throwing bombs and grenades at the evacuating soldiers. Although a confrontation with SCU was certainly overdue, the British force was too weak to reclaim any form of authority, particularly as attempts to do so antagonized the full range of forces that had already established themselves in the province, including the Iraqi institutions that the British military was ostensibly there to help. Nor did the British soldiers enjoy much popular support or legitimacy, given the United Kingdom's inability to address the local population's immediate grievances or provide public security.[54] Frustrated, these people were instead receptive to the militias' antioccupational rhetoric.

Whereas counterinsurgency doctrine frequently speaks of military forces providing the shield of security behind which political, economic, and social reforms can take place, the best that the undermanned and isolated British forces could hope for were costly and strictly short-term tactical gains.

Undeterred, the British military persevered with its tougher stance, resulting in confrontations with militias and increased attacks on British forces. Because the targeted actors were politically connected, Britain's relationship with Basra's leadership suffered. Beginning in September 2005, the governor organized rallies against the British forces, branding them a "destabilizing presence."[55] From October 2005 to May 2006, the provincial council suspended cooperation with the British military due to their arrests of corrupt police officers and their mishandling of Iraqi prisoners, as shown in a leaked video. With the British forces thus excluded, and the militias free to roam, reported homicides in Basra increased from fifteen in November 2005 to thirty in February 2006 and then to one hundred or more in the ensuing months.[56] Responding to the instability, Iraqi prime minister Nuri al-Maliki declared a state of emergency in Basra city in June 2006, but without coalition support the Iraqi troops dispatched to Basra were unable to do much.

Nor did the provincial council's decision to renew its cooperation with the British military in May 2006 bring greater stability since the remaining 7,000 UK troops had by now become marginal in the local contest for power. Attempts by a newly rotated British unit to regain the initiative provoked fierce resistance and daily attacks, resulting in several casualties. Perceiving itself as out of options, the British military limited its ground movements in summer 2006, arguing that its presence was causing rather than preventing violence.[57] Although this was in all likelihood true, the new stance also meant abandoning the objective of stabilizing the province.

It was paradoxically at this point that the British government breathed life into its civilian efforts in Basra. The UK Stabilisation Unit began work in 2006, and in April the United Kingdom established a Provincial Reconstruction Team (PRT)—an interagency effort to support local recovery and capability development. The initiatives were too little and too late; they also got off to poor starts, struggling with issues of size, mandate, and resources.[58] The PRT's influence was further constrained by its civilian staff's need for a military escort, given the security conditions. The working relationship was a long stretch from the unity of action and command that had characterized the Malayan campaign and been emphasized in counterinsurgency doctrine thereafter.

Of course, the situation in Basra differed substantially from Malaya. As Cambridge political scientist Glen Rangwala notes, "Thinking about counterinsurgency has taken as a foundational premise that there is either a constituted government which some seek to overthrow, or that a functioning government is in the process of being created."[59] Basra's government was provincial rather than national and was itself a battleground between competing militias. Nevertheless, it should be recalled that the US military was facing a very similar conundrum in other parts of the country—namely, the elevation of militia-wielding sectarians within government and their entrenchment in that position through elections. The difference for the United States was President George W. Bush's willingness, following the congressional elections of 2006, to use his remaining political capital to change strategy in early 2007. Popularized as the "surge," the new American approach featured an increase in troop levels in Baghdad and Anbar Province; a new force posture designed to establish a security presence throughout the city; and a range of nonmilitary measures designed to satisfy the political requirements for stability. US troops were henceforth to work with Iraqi partners at the state and local levels "to help Iraqis clear and secure neighborhoods, to help them protect the local population, and to help ensure that the Iraqi forces left behind are capable of providing the security that Baghdad needs."[60] Many factors went into the security gains seen over the following twelve months, but most analysts agree that the change in the US approach and strategy was critical in turning the tide.[61]

The UK government under Blair and later under Gordon Brown never elected to change course in this manner; there was no real appetite to increase the investment in Iraq or to conduct a surge of any kind. Perhaps nothing illustrates this reluctance better than Operation Salamanca, planned in the summer of 2006 by Lt. Gen. Sir Richard Shirreff—then the commander of MND-SE. Salamanca had been designed as a comprehensive civil–military surge operation to defeat the Mahdi Army in Basra, excise the death squads, and rebuild the city.[62] Given its level of ambition, the operation called for additional British manpower and Iraqi reinforcements. Yet in both London and Baghdad, the plan was badly received: back home, the plan appeared too disruptive and therefore risky, and to Prime Minister al-Maliki the targeting of the Mahdi Army risked support from Moqtada al-

Sadr, then a key political figure with significant clout. Following extensive cajoling, Shirreff persuaded his local and national Iraqi political partners to back the plan, but support from London would be more difficult to obtain. Apparently because of the deployment to Afghanistan, Shirreff's request for extra troops was downgraded to a mere two battalions, which would be available for just a few weeks.[63] The US military offered to provide one of its battalions instead, but as Lt. Gen. Shirreff explained in his evidence to the Iraq Inquiry, "The idea of American troops on the streets of Basra did not go down particularly well in London."[64] In the end, Salamanca did not see the light of day. Even though the British approach was patently failing, there was no desire to acknowledge this fact and react accordingly. Instead, cracks in the strategy were papered over in the hope that Basra's deterioration would go unnoticed or be ascribed to something else.

Given this political direction, one has to feel some degree of sympathy for the British troops on the ground: hemmed in by political sensitivities in both London and Baghdad, let down by poor military resourcing and preparation, lacking civilian and host-nation partners, yet asked to perpetuate a good-news story about the Iraqi South. To a large degree, this outcome was the logical culmination of the British—and American—failure to prepare and plan for the operation. It was also a direct function of the British government's failure to react to the challenges of the operation once they presented themselves. Whereas the United States was able to formulate a new campaign plan by the end of 2006, the British government intransigently pursued its strategy of transition, which increasingly began to look like an unconditional and messy retreat. The way the operation was handled in 2003–2006 casts a long shadow over Britain's future with counterinsurgency or any operation that is bloody and politically divisive but requires the sustained commitment of resources and troops over a potentially protracted period of time.

SPIN-DOCTORED RETREAT

The decision to get out was taken in late 2006.[65] This political backdrop explains the course of Operation Sinbad, a watered-down version of Salamanca but nonetheless a major effort to reclaim control of Basra. Launched in September 2006, the operation sought to confront the militias, establish security, enable a handover to loyal and trained Iraqi security forces, and kick-start Basra's economic reconstruction. It would see Iraqi and British troops launch search-and-cordon operations across the province while implementing quick-impact projects—actions that would be followed by twenty-eight days of increased patrolling, continued reconstruction, and investigation and reform of the local police force by a British transition team. Sinbad was the closest the British military in Basra had come to a comprehensive counter-insurgency operation, yet even though the six-month operation produced a brief lull in violence, the results were disheartening.

First, the operation was too brief to address the structural causes of instability. Indeed, since many of the militias in the provincial council were also represented in the national government, they were able to push Maliki to limit the British offensive. Just as profound, the UK government also showed no desire to build on Sinbad's tentative achievements.[66] Even during the offensive, the British consulate evacuated its headquarters at Basra Palace due to safety concerns; although the evacuation was presented as a "temporary measure [in] response to increased mortar attacks," the civilian staff never returned.[67] Then, on the day the operation ended, Blair announced the withdrawal of 1,600 British troops, leaving behind a reduced force of 5,500. Blair's position was that though Basra was "still a difficult and sometimes dangerous place," Operation Sinbad had created the conditions for a transfer of control and that "the next chapter in Basra's history can be written by Iraqis."[68] Reports have since suggested that only concerted US pressure averted a complete withdrawal at this time.[69] Sinbad was, in other words, "a last-ditch effort prior to a troop drawdown."[70]

Once initiated, the transition took less than a year. In early 2007, British forces were stationed at six main bases: the Old State Building, the Shatt-al-Arab Hotel, the Shaibah Logistics Base, the Provincial Joint Command Center, the Basra Palace, and the Contingency Operating Base at Basra Air Station. Over the next year in two phases, it would withdraw from all but the latter, gradually transferring control to the Iraqi security forces. The handovers were presented as enabling Basra's transition to "provincial Iraqi control," which required coalition forces to have left the city. Transition to provincial

Iraqi control, in turn, was the British ticket out, regardless of conditions on the ground.

The withdrawals were presented as a deliberate strategy to stabilize Basra. Noting that 80 percent of recorded attacks targeted UK forces, the British government and military command argued that withdrawing those forces would reduce the levels of violence. To Air Chief Marshal Sir Jock Stirrup, then the chief of defense staff, the British presence was "creating a spurious but tangible legitimacy for violence, and for Iranian interference in support of such violence," while also providing local politicians with a convenient scape-goat for all that was wrong in the governorate. To "free Basra from its cycle of violence," he explained, it was necessary to "withdraw our permanently based forces from Basra city, and to put the Iraqis in the lead there. In our view the Iraqis would then have to deal with the intra-Shia problem, and to confront the allied issue of Iranian involvement."[71]

If this strategy was ever sincere, it failed. The first round of British with-drawals did not stem the violence as expected but instead led to increased attacks against coalition forces throughout the summer, from a weekly aver-age of forty-five in April to from eighty to ninety for June and July.[72] Mor-tar attacks on the remaining bases occurred daily. Rather than placate, the withdrawals emboldened those interested in a complete British departure, who (especially JAM) now pushed home their advantage. Violence against Iraqi civilians also continued, with an average of thirty attacks per week.[73] Indeed, the main effect of the initial withdrawals was to stall further British efforts at security-sector reform: by July, the military transition teams based at Basra Air Station could "not go out on operations with the Iraqi Army units, because it was not possible to provide force protection."[74] These con-ditions also constrained British efforts at reconstruction and development, which had yielded minimal results despite the £744 million committed by August 2007.[75]

Against this backdrop, the notion that Britain's final departure from the city in autumn 2007 would "free Basra from its cycle of violence" seems insin-cere or grossly overoptimistic. Adherents to the notion placed much faith on a secret deal struck between British government representatives and Ahmed al-Fartusi, an imprisoned JAM leader, in August 2007. Promising a cessation of violence if British authorities left the city and released 120 JAM prisoners, Fartusi appeared to be providing a tempting exit strategy that would also help stabilize the province.[76] That the British government took the bait may not be surprising, but it betrayed a misunderstanding of local politics and causes of instability. Not only did this final act of accommodation overestimate the British role in fueling the violence, it also misread the motivations of the militias it left in place. Rather than representing a nationalistic struggle against occupying forces that would cease with their disappearance, the attacks against coalition forces were part of a larger power struggle in which the British military was merely an "illfitting [*sic*] brake."[77] As Colonel Richard Iron, then the mentor for the senior Iraqi Army commander in Basra, recalled, "When we moved out, lawlessness took over. . . . We thought if we moved out we would remove the source of the problem. But actually the Jaish al-Mahdi had been fighting us because we were the only obstacle to their total control."[78]

The British government never formally acknowledged the deal. Whether the withdrawal was unilateral or part of a bargain, the results were the same: attacks on coalition forces decreased, but the general level of violence did not.[79] This outcome was predictable: even by Britain's own criteria, Basra had not reached the standards for provincial Iraqi control, yet it was now in the hands of Iraqi security forces, whose readiness, standard of equipment, and factionalism represented significant problems.[80] Even Iraq's 10th Division, the training of which had been comparatively successful, was too weak and easily intimidated.[81] In theory, British troops still retained security responsibility pending the granting of provincial Iraqi control, yet with no British troops in the city and with local forces penetrated by militias, these guarantees meant little. Whatever his other motives, even Lt. Gen. Mohan al-Furayji, to whom command of Basra Operational Command was transferred, expressed little faith in a British reintervention: "The question is, are British forces ready to provide this help? . . . I do not think so."[82]

For all this, the British government still sought to put its withdrawal in a positive light. Acknowledging that casualty rates in Basra remained "broadly the same," MoD officials maintained that "this was in line with our assessment" and that the attacks would "reduce as the Iraqis, and the Iraqi Security Forces, grow in capability and confidence." That casualties had not increased, meanwhile, showed that "the [Iraqi security forces] are doing an effective job of maintaining control of the city without UK support."[83] In effect, the MoD suggested that the British forces had been irrelevant to the level of violence affecting Basra's population, which in a curious sense justified their withdrawal, particularly since their presence was causing both civilian damage and British fatalities. Indeed, many Iraqis, including some of its political leaders, also supported the retreat for these reasons.[84]

As a means of transferring control to local authority, however, Britain's withdrawal suffered from two flaws. First, the unchanged casualty rate did not denote progress. It may have been the case, as Prime Minister Gordon Brown noted, that "while the four southern provinces have around 20 per cent of the Iraqi people[,] they still account for less than 5 per cent of the overall violence in Iraq."[85] Even so, this quantitative measure belied a grim reality for the citizens of Basra, a city wracked by unemployment, insecurity, and crime, whose public institutions were weak and corrupt, and in which Islamist militias forcibly imposed Talibanesque mores on a vulnerable population. As al-Furayji later exclaimed, "The lawlessness is an insult to the Iraqi people and an insult to the Iraq government. It simply cannot be tolerated."[86]

Second, the unchanged casualty rate related less to the Iraqi security forces' effectiveness than to the temporary cease-fire called by Sadr in August 2007. This cease-fire did not arise from events in Basra, but in response to increased US pressure in Baghdad and JAM's growing recklessness, which was costing Sadr political support.[87] Renegade units were operating without direction from Sadr, targeting each other and civilians for war spoils even in Shia-dominated Basra. Following a firefight between the Mahdi Army and the Badr Organization in Karbala in August 2007, Sadr called the cease-fire in order to reform his movement and disassociate his loyal fighters from the criminal gangs operating under the Mahdi flag.[88] As a result, many Mahdi fighters stayed off the streets in September, immediately following the British withdrawal, which dampened levels of violence. Nonetheless, Basra remained highly insecure, particularly since the JAM units deemed renegade (and thereafter called "special groups") would later ignore Sadr's call for order.

On December 16, 2007, provincial Iraqi control was finally granted. For Britain, the move signaled a shift from "tactical" to "operational overwatch":

UK troops were no longer responsible for security but would continue to train local forces, provide an in extremis reintervention capability, and conduct combined countersmuggling operations outside the city. In practice, there was little difference between British duties before and after the transition. Nonetheless, the transfer signified the MoD's confidence that the criteria for Iraqi control had been met—criteria based on "the level of threat; . . . the capability of the Iraqi security forces to deal with the threat; the capability of the national and provincial governments; [and] the capability of Coalition forces to step in . . . as needed."[89]

None of these conditions obtained. Militias enjoyed strongholds in the city and could murder and target with impunity their political opponents and those violating their rules; in 2008, the killing of women deemed to have behaved irreligiously became a particular concern.[90] The Iraqi Police Service was infiltrated, and the Iraqi Army was too weak to guarantee security. In recognition of the 10th Division's deficiencies, it was replaced with Iraq's 14th Division, formed around the 5th Brigade, 10th Division, and staffed with personnel from elsewhere in the country. The new unit performed comparatively well, deploying to Basra's main squares and streets, but it was underequipped and undermanned to control the city. Nor could Basra's political institutions provide for its citizens. Unemployment soared,[91] the provincial council was infiltrated by extremist elements, and Iraq's central government did not recognize Basra's governor but operated in the province via the Baghdad-appointed police and military chiefs. British government assistance, meanwhile, was hampered by the ban on diplomats and development officials from entering the city, resulting in an awkward reliance on those Iraqis "willing to risk militia reprisal for meeting with foreigners at the airport."[92] Finally, the British troop presence now stood at 4,500, which made it difficult to sustain and protect the force itself should an intervention be required, particularly given the prevailing insecurity.[93]

Although transition to provincial Iraqi control was clearly premature, the issue was not a lack of time: instead, the handover ceremony, held under tight security, was the culmination of a deliberate strategy of "transition" that actively sought to isolate the dwindling number of British troops in the region. Given this "strategy," there was little these troops could do to improve the situation in Basra.

To an outsider, the transition would appear motivated by the recognition of failure in Basra, the lack of interest in coming up with and resourcing new options, and the possibility of a redemptive shift to Afghanistan instead. In its briefings, however, the British government and military celebrated its withdrawal: "we actually constructed what turned out to be a winning strategy," noted Air Chief Marshal Sir Jock Stirrup, then the chief of the defense staff, in his testimony to the Iraq Inquiry.[94] There were of course positives to be pointed at: the Iraqi security forces contained an eruption of violence by the Jund al-Samaa cult in early January 2008; the manning of Basra's Commando Battalions reached 80 percent, and they achieved initial operational capability to conduct counterterrorism operations; countersmuggling operations were becoming more effective; and police reforms got rid of hundreds of corrupt officers.[95] Yet as the International Crisis Group had noted in 2007, "What progress has occurred cannot conceal the most glaring failing of all: the inability to establish a legitimate and functioning provincial apparatus capable of redistributing resources, imposing respect for the rule of law and ensuring a peaceful transition at the local level."[96]

SALVATION: CHARGE OF THE KNIGHTS

The image of a successful British transition suffered with the launch of a major military operation by Maliki in March 2008 to reclaim Basra from the militias. The first phase of Operation Charge of the Knights was uncertain because coalition forces were caught unawares. The blueprint for the operation ironically had been drawn up by a British colonel, Richard Iron, in conjunction with Lt. Gen. Mohan al-Furayji, the Basra operations commander whom he was advising. Yet the timing of the operation was a surprise, so much so that it occurred while the British commander of MND-SE was on a mid-tour skiing holiday. Once in motion, the operation exposed the inadequacies of the UK-trained Iraqi security forces as two brigades of the 14th Division melted away and as few as one-third of Basra's police stood their ground.[97] With the later deployment of army reinforcements and of critical US and more modest yet still important UK supporting assets, the tide turned. Following a cease-fire agreed upon in Tehran (illustrating Iran's influence in the province and over JAM), the operation came to a close. But Maliki was careful to consolidate his gains: during the operation, the Iraqi Army involved local residents in reconstruction and neighborhood patrols, and 20,000 army troops remained in Basra afterward to patrol the city and occupy Iraq's only port so as to remove customs revenue from militia control.[98]

Charge of the Knights was a turning point for Basra, not least because it was conducted with Iraqi soldiers in the lead. The operation also owed much to Basra's becoming a "[c]orps main effort," which brought US forces and corps assets (attack helicopters and unmanned aerial vehicles in particular) into play. Finally, as a critical difference from Salamanca and Sinbad, Charge of the Knights unfolded so quickly and so unexpectedly that there was less chance for the British government and MoD back in London to interfere or set the conditions for British participation. The UK role was admittedly minor, but a careful examination still reveals important adaptation on the part of British soldiers and a promising vignette of what can be achieved when they are provided adequate resources and political latitude.

The first change concerned the advising of Iraqi security forces. Seeing an opportunity to play a role at a key moment, senior commanders committed British Military Transition Teams to accompany Iraqi Army units on operations rather than restrict their activities to isolated bases. Such participation had previously been beyond the teams' mandate, and a formal request to engage in this manner was only lodged retroactively, on April 1, 2008 (and approved by the MoD the following day). In support of this new approach, additional air controllers were brought into theater, along with communications-support personnel, medics, and interpreters.[99] The partnering continued after Charge of the Knights ended: the United Kingdom deployed some 1,000 personnel in Military Transition Teams to advise and assist local Iraqi Army units, and newly arrived US teams focused on the police force. Each UK team, consisting of twenty to thirty trainers and headed by a major or lieutenant colonel, also featured a small force-protection unit of around sixty troops, which allowed them to deploy alongside Iraqi units.[100] This close partnering enabled greater oversight and effectiveness and granted the Iraqi Army access to coalition intelligence, surveillance, and air assets, which it had previously lacked.

Second, following Charge of the Knights, the British military participated in the establishment of joint security stations throughout Basra, each of which brought together Iraqi police and army with military and police transition teams. The system had been successfully adopted elsewhere in the country as part of US counterinsurgency operations; in Basra, it was intended to "allow the IPS [Iraqi Police Service] to use the Iraqi Army as an 'enabler' and to enhance the counter-insurgency capabilities of the [Iraqi security forces]."[101] The point was to bring all relevant players together in one outpost and to establish a joint, permanent presence across the city. In a sense, this structural innovation was reminiscent of the "district war executive committees" established as part of the Malayan Emergency, which brought together civil, military, and police representatives at the local level.[102]

Third, with the security gains, the British government took new steps to encourage infrastructure development and economic recovery—mission components that had stalled up to this point. Representatives from UK DfID and other civilian agencies were again seen in the city, initiating projects to kick-start Basra's economy, boost investment, and enable reconstruction. The armed services also assumed a greater role in reconstruction, with the British Army forming interagency joint reconstruction action teams to help clear the city of rubbish and deliver essential services.[103] With an eye to longer-term growth, UK personnel also encouraged international investment in the resource-rich province, establishing the Basra Investment Commission and inviting businesses to assess its commercial potential.[104] Progress was slow, eliciting complaints over power outages and unemployment (much lower now, but still estimated at 30–50 percent). Even so, these problems were now being tackled, and, following Charge of the Knights, reports of investment deals, commercial activity, and reconstruction flourished.

The changed circumstances compelled Whitehall to formulate a new transition strategy for the remaining 4,500 British troops. They were to complete the training of the 14th Division, return Basra airport to civilian control, set the conditions for provincial elections, help boost economic development, and then leave. By February 2009, these tasks were deemed completed: control over the airport was transferred, provincial elections were held, unemployment had fallen to 17 percent, the port at Umm Qasr was experiencing increased trade, and the 14th Division was maturing. In the following months, the British force readied itself for a second transition, with the conditions on the ground entirely unlike those of its initial departure.

When we compare the British approach before and after Charge of the Knights, it is possible to say that Britain learned counterinsurgency during the course of the campaign. Senior commanders implemented new practices and were granted greater flexibility by their political leaders, and with this support the soldiers on the ground proved highly capable. The operation in Basra is in this sense reminiscent of previous British counterinsurgencies: the armed forces began on the wrong foot but then changed strategy, achieved comparative stability, and then withdrew. Yet this interpretation errs on two grounds, both of which highlight the difficulties faced by Britain in conducting counterinsurgency as it once did.

First, a significant US force remained in Basra following Charge of the Knights, which allowed the departing British troops to transfer their residual responsibilities to another coalition partner rather than to rely wholly on Iraq's own institutions; to Maj. Gen. Andy Salmon, this new approach meant that "we're not going to have a vacuum when the British forces redeploy."[105] In effect, at a ceremony on March 31, 2009, Maj. Gen. Salmon handed over his command of MND-SE to US Army major general Michael Oates, who assumed command of the newly formed MND-South. The British operation officially ended one month later, when the withdrawal of its forces, barring one to two hundred naval advisers, was complete. Meanwhile, a US Army brigade assumed coalition responsibilities in Basra, dispersing across five outposts in and around the city to ensure security, complete Iraqi security force training, and promote economic growth. By the end of summer 2009, an estimated 6,000 US troops were in Basra as part of MND-South, with responsibilities extending throughout the nine provinces south of Baghdad.

Second, the adaptation and accomplishments of the last stretch of the campaign do not prove correct the earlier British approach to operations, as some observers were eager to suggest. Maj. Gen. Barney White-Spunner's comment in July 2008, for example, that "our vindication . . . is in the [deployment] of the Iraqi Army now. . . . Look at the end product," is highly misleading in that it focuses narrowly on the outcome rather than on how it was achieved.[106] Similarly, it is difficult to accept Armed Forces Minister Bob Ainsworth's comment during a visit to Basra that it is "a testament to the success of the UK's transition strategy that Iraqis are solving Iraqi problems and Basra is now a secure city."[107] The desire to put a positive spin on this grueling campaign for the UK military as a whole and particularly for its individual soldiers is understandable but intellectually dishonest. Charge of the Knights did not build on a workable UK strategy in Basra but instead sought to address the effects of that strategy's many shortcomings. Empowered by the results of the US military's comprehensive counterinsurgency campaign in and around Baghdad, Maliki was able to compensate for the lack of a similarly robust effort in Basra. The British government's efforts since then have been commendable and demonstrate what its military is capable of when put to the right use and given the needed resources. Yet it should not be forgotten that this phase of operations relied on a level of security achieved by others and on the ability to transfer residual tasks to others—indeed, this type of cooperation is likely to be critical in British campaigns to come.

* * *

The campaign in Basra represented an initial blow to the notion of an innate British ability to conduct counterinsurgency. The soft approach assumed by British forces in Basra produced at best uneven results and ignored many of the counterinsurgency principles derived from Britain's earlier and nominally similar campaigns. In the first year of the campaign, the issue was not necessarily a failure to conduct counterinsurgency, but rather the encouragement—through actions taken and not taken—of political instability, crime, and violence. This failure was not in the first place that of the British troops, but of those institutions and senior leaders, both civilian and military, who failed to prepare for the fairly predictable challenges of building peace in the aftermath of war and who then refused to provide adequate support once these challenges had become clear.

This brings us to the realm of strategy. Here, it should be said, Britain was constrained by its status as a junior coalition member: decisions over currency, the economy, role of local security forces, and local governmental structures were all national-level issues to be settled in Baghdad but with stark consequences for the provinces. To some degree, the lack of strategic direction in Basra was therefore an outgrowth of the problems affecting the largely improvised US approach to "nation building." At the same time, the lack of study of the territory to be occupied, the quick reduction in forces after the invasion, the misunderstanding of the looting, and the minimal civilian resources and presence in Basra were all errors "made in the UK." These errors not only hampered subsequent operations but also revealed a failure to grasp the nature and requirements of these types of campaigns.

Even when the difficulties of the operation had surfaced, Whitehall never adjusted its basic approach. This lack of action left the military isolated: without civilian partners, adequate support, or host-nation partners, the undermanned force was expected to hold the line against a mounting threat. In this context, the escalated use of force seen in 2005–2006 unsurprisingly had limited utility since it lacked the enabling conditions that would give it meaning, principally a workable and resourced campaign plan. Counterinsurgency is not primarily a military activity, although the military has an important role to play in establishing the security required for progress. In this case, given the limited number of troops in theater, even this contribution to the campaign was far beyond Britain's grasp.

Two troubling but necessary conclusions must be drawn from this British reencounter with counterinsurgency. First, the British historical experiences with counterinsurgency did not translate in Basra into an innate or instinctive understanding of how to conduct such missions. The way in which the UK government stacked the odds against itself in the lead-up and early, critical phase of the Iraq War should dispel any notion of a state and military familiar with the challenges of conducting "wars among the people," to borrow the phrase famously coined by Gen. Rupert Smith.[108] Second, the campaign in Basra revealed the British government's difficulties in integrating civilian and military arms of government, in formulating a strategy or campaign plan, and in resourcing the operation as needed. These lessons touch upon the British armed forces' aptitude for modern wars, the viability of a "comprehensive approach," and Britain's future as an operational partner to the United States or as a strong European military power in its own right. They suggest a need to "learn counterinsurgency" rather than to rely on a past with such operations, yet they also suggest that Britain can no longer expect to conduct counterinsurgency as it once did. Indeed, these concerns should inform political thinking in Britain regarding its position in the world and, far more broadly, about the nature of military intervention in foreign polities.

The most promising aspects of the British engagement in Basra were the conduct and aftermath of Charge of the Knights, and perhaps this experience provides some indication of where the future of British counterinsurgency may lie. The period during and after Charge of the Knights offers promising evidence of a British ability to perform, given the necessary support and partners. Even though the achievements in this phase do not validate the approach to counterinsurgency taken beforehand, they hold valuable lessons regarding partnering and advisory work, combined operations with host-nation security forces, and the consolidation of security gains through effective engagement with local populations. All of these areas, as we shall see, require further study and investment for future contingencies.

3

ACT II: BRITISH COUNTERINSURGENCY IN HELMAND

I N SPRING 2006, at the height of violence and chaos in Basra, the British armed forces were presented with the added challenge of deploying also to Helmand Province in southern Afghanistan. The mission was integral to NATO's plan to extend its influence across the whole of the country because Helmand was a Taliban stronghold and, barring a small US PRT, a no-go area for the International Security Assistance Force (ISAF) and Afghan government. As in Basra, British troops quickly ran into serious difficulties owing to confusion regarding the purpose of the mission, a flawed intelligence picture, and deficiencies in troop levels as well as operational mistakes. By 2012, matters had improved substantially, but it took a slow process of tactical adaptation and the relearning of counterinsurgency principles as well as a massive reinforcement of US Marines to turn the tide. Even then, the tactical successes witnessed from 2010 to 2012 did not enable clear strategic gains owing largely to ISAF's inability to address continued shortcomings within two of the three pillars of its own campaign plan—namely, governance and development.[1]

This problematic outcome again puts into doubt the validity of the British counterinsurgency legacy and the British capacity to conduct and sustain large-scale counterinsurgency operations as it once did. It also poses some fundamental challenges to the contemporary interpretation and application of counterinsurgency principles. By analyzing the conduct of British operations in

Helmand between 2006 and 2012, this chapter provides an analysis of the difficulties faced by the United Kingdom when engaging in these types of missions.

SETTING THE STAGE

The British deployment to Helmand had a long prelude. British forces took part in the initial US-led intervention in Afghanistan following the terrorist attacks on New York and Washington, DC, on September 11, 2001. The first British troops were thus deployed in November 2001 as commandos from the Royal Marines helped secure Bagram Airfield. Soon thereafter, a 1,700-man British battle group, Task Force Jacana, was deployed as a contribution to the US-led Operation Enduring Freedom (OEF). The task was primarily to destroy terrorist infrastructure and interdict al-Qaeda movement in eastern Afghanistan. Wider British aims in 2001 included attacking al-Qaeda internationally, denying al-Qaeda its Afghan base, and preventing Afghanistan from again becoming a terrorist sanctuary—a goal that involved not only defeating the terrorist organization, but also removing the Taliban government from power.[2]

Following their initial contributions to the campaign against al-Qaeda and the Taliban, the British government led the negotiations within NATO and the UN to create ISAF. ISAF's initial purpose was to assist the Afghan Transitional Authority in creating and maintaining a safe and secure environment in Kabul and its surrounding areas.[3] The United Kingdom assumed the leadership of ISAF from December 2001 to June 2002, when the reins were handed over to Turkey. During these six months, the British government provided roughly 2,000 troops for ISAF command, maintained security in Kabul, and conducted limited training of the new Afghan National Army. Operation Herrick started as Turkey took command of ISAF in June 2002, yet at this stage the British contribution also scaled down to 300 troops, whose main mission was to provide security in Kabul.

For the first few years following the Taliban's initial collapse, ISAF's mandate did not extend beyond Kabul, which left the remainder of Afghanistan largely untouched. To address this problem, NATO formulated a plan to expand its mission, which was then included in UN Security Council Resolution 1510 of October 2003. The plan foresaw an expansion built around four stages. Stage 1 would entail a push to the north and was completed in October 2004. Stage 2, the expansion to the west, began in May 2005 and was completed in September. Stage 3, the taking of the South, was the most challenging part of the plan because it required capturing the Taliban strongholds of Helmand and Kandahar. It was launched in May 2006 and completed in July. The final stage was to the east, and its conclusion, in October 2006, signaled the formal completion of ISAF's expansion, supposedly across the entire country.[4] Yet while the allocation of Afghanistan's provinces to ISAF contributing nations and units was now complete, in many respects control remained elusive—not least in the more volatile areas such as Helmand Province. Measured in troop numbers, the deployments outside Kabul were also very limited. In many areas, the expansion signified only the creation of a PRT manned by a few hundred soldiers yet with the responsibility of covering vast areas and millions of people.[5]

During these years of expansion, the British force presence in Afghanistan grew. By 2003, it amounted to a battalion-strength deployment tasked with manning two PRTs in northern Afghanistan, in Mazar-e Sharif and Maymana, as well as with providing a rapid-reaction force for the area. In 2004, a Royal Air Force detachment of six Harriers was deployed to Kandahar in support of OEF. The decision to redeploy British assets to Helmand was at this point already being discussed as British officials pushed for the NATO expansion and as US officials were pressing their allies to increase their force contributions. According to Gen. Sir Richard Dannatt, chief of the general staff from 2006 to 2009, Prime Minister Tony Blair had refused an American request for the British Army to take over all the southern provinces as early as 2004. Instead, as NATO announced in December 2005, the British deployment would follow a slower timeline, to commence in 2006. As Gen. Dannatt explained later, "The assumption had to be that if the UK was going to increase its force levels in Afghanistan in 2006, then we would be substantively out of Iraq by then."[6] This assumption turned out to be seriously flawed.[7]

At this point, Helmand was a blind spot for the British and allied intelligence services. In the early years of the campaign, the province had seemed relatively calm, though mostly because it lay beyond ISAF and the Afghan government's reach. Before the British deployment, about 100 US Special Forces troops had been stationed in Helmand to hunt for remnants of al-Qaeda. They did not engage the local drug lords or Taliban leaders and had limited interaction with the local population. Behind the facade of relative calm, Helmand was nevertheless a true powder keg ready to explode at the first incautious touch.

Although support for the Taliban was very limited after 2001, the group was able to exploit popular grievances over the abusive and inherently corrupt governance within the province and thereby increase its influence. Specifically, the Taliban managed to tie itself to the local population by providing protection services and a functioning system of arbitration. Behind the scenes, it had also developed a symbiotic partnership with the local drug lords and warlords and was able to represent the voice of the farmers by condemning ISAF and US poppy-eradication programs.[8] By 2006, the Taliban was again an important force in the province, though, as Tom Coghlan explains, it "[sat] within and overlap[ped] with other tensions and drivers for instability"—tribal dynamics, poppy production, Islamist warlords, and corrupt governance at all levels.[9] These forces maintained an uneasy balance readily disturbed by any outside interference.

As planning began for the British deployment, the first decision was how to approach and understand this complex balance of power and work with its political leadership. Guided by the ideals of good governance, counternarcotics, and the turning of a new page in Afghanistan, a decision was made in Whitehall that the governor of Helmand, Sher Mohammed Akhundzada, would not be a suitable partner for what the British were hoping to accomplish.[10] The feeling was that he was too deeply entrenched in the drug trade as well as in the political balance between forces that NATO and the UN described as illegitimate. The British government therefore insisted upon Akhundzada's removal as a precondition for their deployment. In late 2005, Afghanistan's president Hamid Karzai complied and installed a new governor, Mohammad Daoud, an outsider to the province, with limited support and authority.

The change in leadership was to have significant unintended and adverse consequences. First, for all his faults, Akhundzada was an important figure in

President Karzai's struggle against the Taliban. Second, his dismissal deprived British planners of a valuable source of information on the province's tribal, political, and ethnic makeup.[11] Third, as he stepped down, he also stopped paying about 3,000 members of his militia, forcing them to look elsewhere for financial support and patronage. Not only were these men removed from the fight against the Taliban, but there is also evidence that many switched allegiance.[12] Although the effects of Akhundzada's removal were unintended, a more concerted study of the province prior to the deployment may have enabled more enlightened decision making. At the very least, given the relatively limited British footprint and its very sketchy intelligence picture, a less intrusive entry into Helmand might have been advisable until the force could be strengthened and its situational awareness improved.

Ready or not, in April 2006 the United Kingdom deployed its first unit into the province—a 500-strong battle group drawn from 16 Air Assault Brigade and tasked with "clearing, holding and building" on a number of key locations of central Helmand. The idea was for this "advance party" to set the conditions for initial reconstruction and development in these areas and thereby help the central government in Kabul establish its authority in the province. In the following months, the troop presence grew to 3,200. To complete their mission, the British forces established a main base—Camp Bastion, northwest of the Helmand provincial capital Lashkar Gah—and two forward operating bases: Robinson in the Helmand River valley and Price in Gereshk.[13] The idea was to implement traditional counterinsurgency methods and to concentrate forces in these locations, thereby creating a number of "ink spots" of stability and reconstruction that could then be expanded over time. This plan resonated with the idea of "New Villages" as applied in Malaya some fifty years earlier.

In practice, the strategy faltered—in part because the area of operations was far less secure than British planners had envisaged. The units were not prepared, manned, or equipped for what turned out to be a hornet's nest of Taliban fighters and drug lords, all of whom viewed the arrival of British troops as a threat to their interests. The Taliban had in fact prepared a spring offensive in anticipation of the British deployment,[14] and throughout the summer of 2006 it launched mortar and human-wave attacks on the widely dispersed

British positions. Retired US general Barry McCaffrey made an assessment of the Taliban in Helmand during a field trip in May 2006 that underlined their strength and power. He noted that there were "thousands of heavily armed Taliban . . . aggressive and smart in their tactics." The insurgents had secure base areas in Pakistan, operated in battalion-size units, and had "excellent weapons, new IED [improvised explosive device] technology, commercial communications gear and new field equipment," as well as "excellent tactical, camouflage and marksmanship training."[15] Taken by surprise, the British forces found themselves fighting for their lives during the entire summer of 2006.

STRATEGIC MISCALCULATIONS AND OPERATIONAL MISTAKES

The turn of events in Helmand following the British troop deployment reflects a deeply flawed strategic planning process. Interestingly, the decision and strategic rationale behind the deployment of troops to Helmand in 2006 did not spark nearly the same controversy or debate as the decision to invade Iraq in 2003, and yet the campaign has to date caused many more British casualties. Key areas to be examined in this case involve the underestimation of Taliban capability and the inadequate number of British troops deployed, as reflected in their inability to hold vital ground or demonstrate clear progress.[16] This section discusses four factors that led to this very suboptimal starting point: the confusion regarding British objectives; the lack of decent intelligence; the limited size of the force; and, finally, the decision that changed the very nature of the operation—the deployment of an already stretched force also to the northern parts of the province.[17]

Occurring against the backdrop of NATO's expansion beyond Kabul, the deployment to Helmand was mired in confusion as to the nature of the mission there. As Astri Suhrke asked in this same period, "Would it be just a robust form of PRT deployment, a reconstruction mission in a difficult security environment? What was the relationship to the American OEF? Was NATO going into full combat in Afghanistan?"[18] Part of the problem was a lack of certainty and consensus regarding the international aims in Afghanistan as a whole, which had over time led to three separate but increasingly related operations going on at the same time but with different missions: the American-led counterterrorist effort to hunt down any remaining al-Qaeda and Taliban fighters; the NATO-led ISAF operation with a mandate to provide security and to enable the third mission led by the UN and devoted to political and economic development. The issue of counternarcotics then came to overlap with these three missions—especially beginning in 2009. As Anatol Lieven has argued, "Each goal [was] set by powerful Western forces, and indeed real Western needs," yet the division of labor was unfortunate because the West "lack[ed] institutions and leaders capable of choosing between these goals, and coordinating a strategy in pursuit of the most desirable and achievable ones."[19]

Although never quite defined in a coordinated way, the international community's aims also changed over time. What was initially a spontaneous reaction aimed at the perpetrators of the September 11, 2001, attacks morphed, in the relatively calm years following the fall of the Taliban regime, into a state-building effort both to prevent al-Qaeda's return and to build a democratic Afghanistan. NATO allies disagreed on whether counterterrorism or state building ought to be the driving motivation for the overall mission, and these tensions only grew as the security situation deteriorated from 2004 onward, and the Taliban regained its strength. As the frequency of attacks on government and international targets increased, the language of development and state building shifted in favor of counterinsurgency, culminating in a formal change in strategy announced by President Barack Obama in 2009. At this point, with eight years on the war clock, the counterinsurgency campaign only had so much time to succeed, and so by 2011 the focus again shifted to one of "transition" and withdrawal as NATO troop contributors sought a way out. To enable some degree of success in this now decade-long endeavor, the ambitious language of state building and even of counterinsurgency gave way to the more limited aspirations of counterterrorism—completing a full circle, in other words, on the international involvement in Afghanistan.

The search for a way out by 2014 has placed in greater relief the tensions inherent to pursuing disparate aims. From a counterterrorist perspective, the aims will more or less have been met so long as a force remains that can prevent al-Qaeda from using the country for training and basing. However, from a development perspective, a withdrawal in 2014 risks reversing whatever limited progress has been achieved in terms of good governance, gender equality, and sustainable economic growth; indeed, such progress even risks becoming a point of negotiation in any "peace and reconciliation talks" with the Taliban.

Looking more specifically at the British government policies, the initial aim in the wake of the September 11 attacks was to support the United States in countering international terrorism and to maintain the "special relationship." On the one hand, both of these objectives pointed to the need to defeat al-Qaeda and topple the Taliban regime that had given it sanctuary. The notion of state building, on the other hand, was secondary and framed foremost as an indirect means of ensuring al-Qaeda's permanent exile from the country. As the MoD explained, "Britain's own security is at risk if we again allow Afghanistan to become a safe haven for terrorists. It is therefore vital to the UK that Afghanistan becomes a stable and secure state that is able to suppress violent extremism within its borders."[20] Hence, as noted by the House of Commons Foreign Affairs Committee in 2009, the United Kingdom moved "from its initial goal of supporting the US in countering international terrorism, far into the realms of counter-insurgency, counter-narcotics, protection of human rights, and state-building."[21]

Because state building was a means to an end rather than an end in itself, the appreciation of this task and commitment to what it would require were far from consistent.[22] The confusion of trying to do so many (difficult) tasks at one time also contributed to great uncertainty regarding the nature of the mission and British objectives. Why were British forces being sent to Helmand—as a means of countering al-Qaeda or to improve conditions for the local population? No clear or consistent answer was ever provided. Thus, it was also never quite resolved or explained what role the Helmand deployment would play within the larger British aims of counterterrorism in the region. The political leadership initially talked of a peace-support operation to support counternarcotics, whereas the brigade personnel worked under the assumption of a major counterinsurgency campaign.[23]

Contributing to the strategic confusion was the very limited and often contradictory understanding of Helmand and the strength of the Taliban there.

The intelligence agencies had warned that the Taliban were planning to target the British upon their deployment, and the predeployment planners from 16 Air Assault Brigade had also warned of a tense and potentially hostile reception for the British troops.[24] Despite these reports, Brig. Ed Butler, British national contingent commander in Afghanistan and later head of the Helmand Task Force, has since argued that he was told to plan for an essentially "permissive environment" in Helmand.[25] According to his subordinate, Col. Stuart Tootal, commander of 3 Battalion Parachute Regiment during the first tour to Helmand, the planning team from the Permanent Joint Headquarters was working under similar assumptions. From Tootal's perspective, "The mission was conceived as a peace support operation. Any use of force was seen as a last resort and actually having to hunt down the Taliban was not part of the mission. Instead our intended role was to provide security to protect the development and reconstruction efforts of the Provincial Reconstruction Team."[26]

In the midst of mixed messages, the political and military leadership chose to frame the operation as a peace-support operation, and in an interview on April 24, 2006, that has since gained a certain infamy, Secretary of Defense John Reid claimed that there were two inherently different missions in Afghanistan—an American mission involving counterterrorism and a British one that was about reconstruction: "If we came for three years here to accomplish our mission and had not fired one shot at the end of it we would be very happy indeed. If the American Operation Enduring Freedom came here to counter terrorism and seek them out and had not fired a shot in three years time they would be very unhappy and disappointed."[27] Although Reid later argued that he never expected that British troops would fire no shots, his words appear to reflect an official planning assumption that Taliban resistance would be limited and the deployment relatively peaceful. This assumption was also shared among Britain's coalition partners, who tended to present the expansion as an effort of reconstruction and stabilization. As an example, highly placed Canadian politicians opined that combat seemed an unlikely prospect.[28] It may be speculated that this framing helped the leading politicians of the time sell the military campaign to an increasingly war-weary domestic electorate. Nevertheless, the ensuing confusion regarding the strategic aims in Helmand in particular and in Afghanistan at large was never really resolved.

The third contentious aspect surrounding the deployment to Helmand was the early limitation on the number of troops. That the deployment coincided with a major ongoing commitment in Iraq did not help: as the House of Commons Defence Committee commented, it did not seem as if "the implications of the decision to move UK Armed Forces into the South of Afghanistan in early 2006 were fully thought through, in particular, the potential risk to UK Armed Forces personnel." Stemming in part and most seriously from the strategic confusion and limited intelligence, a disconnect appeared between the aims for the campaign and the resources provided to achieve them. Interestingly, the committee noted that the strategic miscalculations were not simply a problem for Whitehall but stemmed equally from the inadequate communications between the armed forces and its political leadership. The committee was disturbed by the fact that commanders on the ground had in 2006 told the defense secretary that they were content with the troop levels, equipment, and support they had received from London when it later emerged that clearly they were not. The committee concluded that senior military advisers should have used their professional judgment and given voice to their concerns. The failure to do so, the committee's report continues, perpetuated the problem of insufficient troop numbers, which in turn meant the British force could only ever secure a small section of Helmand by themselves. The committee's final critique of the political and military leadership is damning: "We view it as unacceptable that UK Forces were deployed in Helmand for three years, as a result of a failure of military and political coordination, without the necessary personnel and equipment to succeed in their Mission."[29]

OPERATIONAL MISTAKES

The British units that deployed to Helmand in spring 2006 were clearly dealt a poor hand. Looking back at the circumstances of the deployment, Brig. Ed Butler paints the mistakes made—in troop numbers and resources provided—as influenced by various political and financial considerations rather than by military judgment.[30] This interpretation of what went wrong will understandably resonate with members of the armed forces and has since given rise to a so-called stab-in-the-back theory that castigates politicians for failing to support the troops sent in harm's way. It should be noted, however, that although the resource problem was substantial, this sort of hurdle is something that all military commanders have to deal with. The challenge lies in adopting appropriate military activities in relation to the resources provided. This was not done during the early years of the British campaign in Helmand or—for that matter—within the larger NATO campaign in Afghanistan.

Indeed, mistakes were also made at the operational level, which compounded the strategic miscalculations discussed earlier. The first and principal operational error at the time of deployment was the decision to expand the British area of operations to include the northern as well as the central areas of the province. This shift in policy grew out of a desire to support the newly appointed provincial governor, Mohammad Daoud (and by extension President Karzai), in reestablishing control of Helmand's northern districts. The logic, Governor Daoud suggested, was that unless UK forces returned the North along with the center to government control, he, the new governor, would not be able to claim the necessary authority and political credibility in the province.[31] Daoud also expressed his disappointment in the British force sent to Helmand because he had expected 3,000 combat-ready troops rather than the force sent: rifle companies totaling about 650 men, supported by a large support component, all focused on reconstruction efforts rather than on offensive operations.[32] The governor made his frustration known very clearly at every opportunity and even threatened to throw the British out of the province unless they made their presence felt. He moreover had President Karzai reinforce the message.[33] Despite not having nearly the resources required for a deployment to northern Helmand, the British in the end succumbed to the local pressure and in May 2006 accepted the governor's argument. The result was a rapid change in tactics as British troops dispersed in company- and platoon-size units to be based in so-called platoon houses in Now Zad, Sangin, Musa Qaleh, and later Kajiki.

This decision was of great strategic significance because it changed the very nature of the mission and thereby completely derailed an already weak strategic plan. As the British military simply added the new districts to the already ambitious map of deployments, it forced its troops to disperse over

large parts of Helmand rather than focus on a limited number of key locations as originally planned. The House of Commons Defence Committee
later revisited this decision and found that it had originated with tactical-level
commanders and was supported by operational-level headquarters: "We consider it to be unlikely that this fundamental change to the operation was put
to Ministers for a decision as to whether to proceed. . . . As the change put
the lives of Armed Forces personnel at much greater risk, it should surely have
gone to the Cabinet for endorsement."[34]

The fact that Des Browne replaced John Reid as minister of defense on
May 5, 2006, makes it difficult to know where the decision took place: Reid
argued that he had only heard about it upon leaving office, and Browne that
he learned about it after the fact.[35] A parliamentary committee investigating
the matter concluded that in all likelihood the military leadership had not
properly informed the politicians involved. At the same time, it is far from
unthinkable that this piece of information got lost somewhere in the midst of
a ministerial transition, the overriding focus on Iraq, and the shocking level
of violence in Helmand that required those on the political level to deal with
British casualties on an almost daily basis.[36]

The deployment to northern Helmand ultimately indicates a weakness
of the civil–military system as it pertains to the creation and execution of
strategy. Without a sound strategy and clear political direction from London,
military leaders in the field found it almost impossible to withstand the pressure placed upon them by Governor Daoud. However, formulating a viable
and appropriately resourced strategy would also have required far better communication between commanders at the operational level and the political
and military leaders at the strategic level. Instead, in Helmand, the British
counterinsurgency principle of maintaining close civil–military cooperation
and unity of command was clearly violated.

Another factor complicating the early British efforts in Helmand was the
coincidence of the British deployment into the province and the US Operation Mountain Thrust, designed to preempt the Taliban spring offensive and
prepare the ground for NATO's expansion into Helmand and Kandahar. The
operation started in March 2006 with air strikes and peaked with sustained
ground assaults through search-and-destroy operations in June and July,

involving some 10,000 troops from the United States and NATO allies as well as a contingent from the Afghan National Army. It was the biggest coalition offensive since the invasion in 2001.[37] However, rather than having the intended effect of preparing the ground for the incoming troops, the operation antagonized the local population and made it more hostile to the newly arrived British troops. The operation was clearly a failure in itself, but British commanders compounded the error by committing its troops to these offensives. Despite already having to spread their troops in platoon houses throughout the province, where they were fighting for their lives, the British forces were thereby also expected to contribute troops to some of the offensive raids within Operation Mountain Thrust—putting further stress on the units and limiting the possibility of reinforcing the defensive positions throughout the province.[38]

By the end of the deployment in the summer of 2006, most British forces were thinly spread out in company- or platoon-size bases in both central and northern Helmand, making any serious attempt at population control, economic development, and good governance virtually impossible.[39] Widely dispersed and under fierce attack, the troops became fixed to defending their base locations. The large number of fixed positions in turn created problems in terms of logistics, medical evacuation, and air support because ISAF lacked the aerial resources to cover the large number of locations involved in combat.[40]

Some of the fiercest fighting took place in the town of Musa Qaleh, where British and Danish troops found themselves under siege during the summer of 2006. During the worst period, the troops fought off one hundred Taliban attacks in forty days. Despite the desperate situation, the troops clung to their positions until October 2006, when task force commander Brig. Ed Butler struck a deal with local tribal leaders. The controversial arrangement involved guarantees that the Taliban would be prevented from retaking Musa Qaleh in exchange for a British withdrawal from the town. In October, further relief was brought to the British troops as 3 Commando Brigade replaced 16 Brigade—a rotation that also added about 2,000 soldiers. Yet despite the arrangement with local leaders, with the British forces out of Musa Qaleh, the Taliban retook the town in early February 2007.[41]

The operational approach of 16 Brigade, especially the so-called platoon-house strategy involving small-unit posts across the province, can be described as nothing short of failure. During the first year in Helmand, the British forces spent most of their efforts on combat operations, which, because they were spread so thin, had at best only a transient effect on the insurgency controlling the province.[42] The fighting in the northern part of the province also spread the conflict geographically "as the more peaceful towns to the south that ought to have been models of secure development became host to disaffected Afghan families fleeing the fighting further north."[43] The British and their coalition partners were in fact holding very little territory at this early stage, which not only impeded but virtually made impossible any progress in the areas of economic development and governance—both essential aspects of ISAF's campaign plan and the British strategy. The lack of security and stability meant that the civilian organizations that were supposed to work on humanitarian relief, economic development, and governance issues simply could not gain access to the province.

As a result, the population of Helmand not only was forced to live in fear for their lives but was also without any representation or services provided by either the central or provincial governments. It proved very difficult to tie the government in Kabul to the people of Helmand or to foster the conditions deemed necessary to undermine Taliban propaganda and build legitimacy for the central government. In counterinsurgency terms, no "ink spots" of security were developed, so no political and economic progress could take place. Instead, traditional counterinsurgency principles of minimum force, tactical flexibility, and civil–military cooperation were disregarded in favor of traditional fighting. In the end, the severe fighting not only led to casualties among British troops and Afghan civilians, but also, as David Richards, the British general and then the commander of ISAF, later acknowledged, damaged the cause of establishing popular support and consent.[44] In fact, the British troop presence became an enemy of the Taliban and the local population alike.

Within the specific context of the deployment, this outcome is not all that surprising. Indeed, 16 Air Assault Brigade—the first unit to deploy to Helmand—was largely the victim of desperate and unforeseen circumstances in response to which it formed an improvised response. By the time the force had dispersed to the northern part of the province, the only adaptation possible, short of a major retreat, was to jettison the idea of peace-support operations in favor of offensive and defensive combat operations conducted for survival. Far more surprising is the failure of subsequent brigades to learn from this experience, particularly given the opportunity to lean on the recent experience in Basra—never mind the British military's reputation for swift adaptation in counterinsurgency environments.

Anthony King explains the failure to adapt as the product of the British military's organizational ideals, "conditioned by years of professional training, experience and peer pressure."[45] Because military training has focused on major combat operations and the traditional principles of war, the British units in Afghanistan reverted to this training in the absence of clearer plans. The adaptation aligns with the organization's doctrine and ethos and, as King further notes, "demonstrates [the units'] willingness to seize the initiative and engage with the enemy: to act."[46] Mark Etherington, who headed the British government's joint planning team for Afghanistan in 2005, also made note of this culturally engrained faith in action and firepower: "I think some in the military were just jolly keen to get stuck in—you know, to charge off over the Helmand desert in a stripped-down Land Rover with a 50cal machine-gun."[47] It might also have been the case, as Frank Ledwidge suggests, that unit commanders perceived the execution of a massive combat operation as the best way of making the tour count and of creating a good-news story for the brigade.[48] Whatever the explanation, when the operation in Afghanistan is examined, it is apparent that the principles of counterinsurgency did not come quite as naturally to the British Army as the more enthusiastic proponents of this legacy would suggest.

Organizational culture had a second effect on the conduct of operations. Indeed, within the general ethos of the British military organization, Anthony King highlights the more specific role of regimental culture in shaping how the deployed units operated and adapted.[49] Thus, it would be false to suggest that the first three brigades deploying to Helmand replicated the same, misguided approach. Instead, each took significant pride in its adaptation to the environment, but in each case such adaptation was based not on strategic aims or operational context, but on each brigade's respective regimental core competences.[50] For this reason, none of them engaged successfully with the difficult question of achieving strategic effect.

Faced with the consequences of poor strategic guidance and inadequate resources, the paratroopers of 16 Brigade dispersed and ended up spending the remainder of their tour in a desperate defense of their platoon houses. This unit's role historically has been to conduct operations behind enemy lines—for example, the taking and defending of bridgeheads without much support and using relatively small units. It is not hard to imagine the platoon houses as bridgeheads to be defended after a traditional parachute drop—an analogy that goes some way toward explaining how the paratroopers of 16 Brigade accepted being dispersed in this manner for so long. To extend the analogy somewhat, the addition of northern Helmand proved "a bridge too far."

When 3 Commando Brigade took over in November 2006, it introduced a very different concept of operations—or CONOPS, in military speak. The Royal Marines of 3 Commando had studied the challenges of the platoon-house strategy, which had prevented British forces from supporting reconstruction and development by constraining the forces to a number of fixed positions. They also brought more men as well as more and heavier equipment in order to deal with what was clearly a much harsher climate than initial planning assumptions had suggested. While 16 Brigade went "a bridge too far," the Royal Marines of the Commando Brigade sought to create more mobility for themselves by unlocking the fixed positions in the north of Helmand and engaging the enemy more directly across larger swathes of territory. Although there was clear merit to this idea, its implementation related more to the unit's cultural preferences and training than to the specific challenges on the ground.

The Royal Marines have a tradition of aggressive charges on islands or beaches in speedboats. In Helmand, they replicated the essence of such operations by creating Mobile Operations Groups (MOGs) and again making sweeping charges against the Taliban—although this time obviously not in speedboats. A commanding officer described the idea: "We evolved our tactics quite a lot; it was a case of fixed vs manoeuvre. Herrick 4 was fixed; it was platoon houses. We manned them but we sought to manoeuvre from them. We developed Mobile Operations Groups (MOGs): in Company groups, 200 strong with 13 Vikings, WMiKs, 21 Pinzgauers and 105 guns. It was a heavy company group package. The logistics were independent. It was like a

Long Range Desert Patrol. We would probe and then strike."[51] In the end, the MOG concept failed. Rather than drawing the Taliban into prepared "kill zones," as was the intention, it was most often the Taliban who, with a superior knowledge of the local terrain, managed to fight on their terms by instead drawing the British into such prepared "kill zones." As a result, soldiers from the Royal Marines would later describe MOG operations as "advance to ambush."[52] Quite apart from the risks involved, the concept of operations did not improve the dire security situation in Helmand or dismantle the platoon houses or allow for development and governance-related reforms.

The third brigade in Helmand was the 12th Mechanized Brigade, deployed in April 2007. Again, adaptation came to be focused squarely on its core competence—mechanized warfare. The brigade pursued an attrition campaign against the Taliban, involving several large-scale clearing operations. Although the idea of clearing ground to avoid the mistakes of the previous brigades could be viewed as effective adaptation, it did not enable the reconstruction, development, and governance reforms for which the clearing of terrain was intended and as emphasized in the campaign plan. The reason for this was that the 12th Brigade lacked the manpower to hold the territory it cleared or simply cleared more territory than it could hold. In other words, the operation continued to suffer from a combination of troop shortages and overstretch, which in this case was self-inflicted. When the British troops departed one "cleared" area, the Taliban returned, which caused the British task force commander to argue that the repeated sorties felt like "mowing the lawn"—after each mowing, the grass always grew back.[53] For the same reasons, the high-intensity clearing operations also did little to secure the population or to win their consent and support.

This discussion demonstrates how a combination of strategic and operational errors contributed to a failure to align ends and means and to provide a sustainable plan for operations in Helmand. The most serious mistakes were arguably those committed at the strategic level, where muddled thinking and a lack of frank civil–military communications resulted in an operation planned on unrealistic best-case scenarios and without serious contingency plans or resources. As Michael Clarke argues, "Throughout this period, from the beginning of 2005 until the late summer of 2006, when the UK clearly had a small war on its hands in Helmand province, the decision-making system seems to have operated in such a way that strategic appreciation rested everywhere and nowhere."[54] In essence, the security situation was much worse than anticipated, but even as the real nature of the operation became clear, little was done to close the gap between ambitions, resources, and the nature of the campaign. It was as if the government in London and the senior commanders in Afghanistan believed that by "staying the course" the war would eventually get back on message. Indeed, as Brig. Butler has noted, while the British soldiers were fighting for their lives, "London was very concerned that there was too much kinetic activity going on and too many soldiers were being injured and killed. . . . [The politicians] needed to see the evidence of reconstruction and development. They were fixed on this issue because that is what the government had presented to the British people."[55]

The British systems for strategic analysis and decision making clearly failed, but there are also notable lessons to be drawn from events at the operational level: the lack of voiced concern on the part of the military leadership (which also contributed to mistakes at the strategic level) and the inability from then on to make the most of the limited resources provided.[56] The end result was an operation with tactical activities and ambitions completely out of proportion to the end pursued or the nature of the campaign. This inauspicious start to the operation raises questions about the British ability to plan and mount counterinsurgency campaigns at this scale and to find operational expression for the key principles underlying its legacy with these types of efforts. At the very least, these years in Helmand should seriously challenge the notion of a superior British military ability to adapt to the nature of counterinsurgency campaigns or to punch above its weight.

WERE THE EARLY MISTAKES INEVITABLE?
LESSONS FROM IRAQ

The British had three difficult years in Basra under its belt by the time it deployed to Helmand. It should be expected that some valuable strategic and tactical lessons could be transferred from the bruising experience in Iraq to the new operational context of Helmand. In some cases, lessons were clearly noted and learned, but on the whole the outcome, even in these select cases, was far from optimal.

First, whereas close civil–military cooperation and whole-of-government planning were notably absent from the campaign in Iraq until its very final stages, the British government conducted comprehensive planning for Afghanistan that involved all relevant ministries, resulting in the Joint UK Plan for Helmand. Even so, this symbol of civil–military unity and mutual understanding did not fare well once it came to application. As Brig. Butler argued later, "What was not fully recognized, by some of our civilian counterparts, was that no plan survives contact with the enemy."[57] The point of contact in this instance was the requirement to coordinate a civil–military plan in an environment far more violent and against an adversary far stronger than previously realized.[58]

James Ferguson gives pause for thought when he notes that the British government's Afghan planning committee, which created the highly ambitious Joint UK Plan for Helmand, ignored concerns from 16 Brigade predeployment planners as well as the advice from the Post-Conflict Reconstruction Unit in London for "a more measured approach."[59] Regardless of attempts to plan or to voice concerns, in the shockingly violent context of Helmand the disconnect between political ends and military and civilian means became painfully obvious. The military units were left fighting to survive, and the civilian components again found themselves unable to operate and gain access to the province—all while the political leadership spoke the language of peace operations and counternarcotics.

A second lesson that should have been learned from Iraq concerns the importance of training and partnering with local forces—one of the early failures in Basra, yet critical, in the end, to Operation Charge of the Knights. The fielding of Operational Mentoring and Liaison Teams (OMLTs) in Helmand from the onset of operations would seem to indicate that this lesson had been internalized since these units had as their main purpose to train and mentor local Afghan forces.[60] However, the scale of the mentoring effort, in combination with the subpar state of the Afghan army and police in Helmand, meant that for three critical years the impact of the OMLTs remained wholly inadequate. It was not until the introduction of the US-led NATO Training Mission–Afghanistan that this problem was remedied and the effort of funding, mentoring, and training Afghan security forces received a more concerted level of attention.

Other and arguably more important strategic lessons should have been transferred from Iraq to Afghanistan but were missed or disregarded. The first relates to the Clausewitzean dictum that statesmen and commanders must "establish . . . the kind of war on which they are embarking; neither mistaking it for, nor trying to turn it into, something that is alien to its nature."[61] Doing so requires a combination of sound judgment and solid intelligence, which as we have seen was absent in Iraq and then in Afghanistan. Moreover, there is a danger of assuming to know or failing to consider the secondary and tertiary effects of deploying troops into a foreign country with the aim of changing the political situation there. It is easy to underestimate the speed with which the character of the conflict can change and, indeed, how quickly the security situation can deteriorate in a contested environment. The underestimation of the complexity of the situation in postinvasion Basra had deleterious effects on the remainder of the campaign. Repeating this mistake of underestimation in Helmand, based on very limited intelligence, compounded the error of Iraq and put even more lives at risk.

Similarly, one has to wonder why, given Iraq's object lesson in the dangers of undermanning a mission, the same error was repeated in Helmand. Related to this issue of troop numbers is the risk of seeking to do too much and thus creating overstretch. In Iraq, Britain struggled with four provinces under its control; in Helmand, although just the one province, the very same mistake was repeated. The implication, it would seem, is that seeking to maintain these large areas of operational responsibility is something that the British military is ill placed to do unless it is put on a war footing and the reserves are called up, as during the initial invasion of Iraq in 2003.

OPERATIONAL ADAPTATION, STRATEGIC INERTIA

The deployment of 52 Infantry Brigade in October 2007 saw the first signs of a more concerted British effort to apply the counterinsurgency principles underpinning its campaign plan. Based on a better understanding of the situation and the insurgency both in the field and in London, the British government started revising its strategy for Afghanistan. Following a review, a new plan, the Helmand Road Map, was approved in spring 2008. A novel aspect of the review was that it was largely a bottom-up product that allowed greater input from the field and was therefore more successful in reflecting the situation on the ground.[62] The plan expanded the role of governance and development, and rather than trying to cover the entire province, combat and security operations were restricted to smaller and more populated areas—the Afghan Development Zones—that coalition forces could actually hold.[63] Increased emphasis was again placed on the population as the focus of the campaign and on the importance of achieving legitimacy and support. In many ways, the plan was a return to the original "ink spot" strategy of 2006, with the important difference that the entire command chain—from the tactical level in the field to the political leadership in London—was now more involved in the planning process. The resulting road map included important lessons from the field, increased both military and civilian resources somewhat, and created a political narrative that better reflected the situation in Helmand than had the rhetoric of counternarcotics or peace operations in 2006. The change in approach was in many ways a significant improvement in achieving a more joined-up civil–military or "comprehensive" approach.[64]

As part of this shift in approach, 52 Brigade also sought to move away from the combat-oriented operations of previous brigades by building greater capabilities for so-called influence operations—activities focused on gaining legitimacy and support from the local population so as to marginalize the enemy. This shift led to such innovations as the company-level Nonkinetic Effects Teams and a new methodology, the Tactical Conflict Assessment Framework, used to assess the effectiveness of the military's civilian engagement.[65] With a view to improving its ability to implement the "comprehensive approach," the British-led PRT increased its civilian staff from twenty-five in 2007 to eighty in 2009. Staff structures and planning procedures were also changed. In 2008, a senior Foreign Office diplomat took command of a combined civil–military mission in Helmand, created through the merger of the British task force headquarters and the PRT. Changes in and increased emphasis on the development and governance-related aspects of operations was also notable in that the PRT in 2008 started deploying stabilization advisers to four different bases across Helmand. Newly established military stabilization support teams also supported the advisers.

These changes had the purpose of extending the reach and capability of the "civil effect"—another concept highlighting the new emphasis on gaining the trust of the local population by supporting good governance and enabling development and reconstruction.[66] In its search for local partners through whom to implement these programs, the British military propped up district and local leaders, providing them with resources for development activities and manpower for reconstruction projects. Underpinning the shift was the creation of the Stabilisation Unit in London, which had greater resources and responsibilities than its predecessor, the Post-Conflict Reconstruction Unit, and contributed to a more joined-up operational planning process across Whitehall.

The deployment of 52 Brigade in October 2007 clearly represented a shift in attitude and approaches—a shift that, according to Theo Farrell and Stuart Gordon, was later carried forward by 16 Air Assault Brigade and 3 Commando Brigade on their respective second tours.[67] However, the theoretical adherence to the traditional principles of counterinsurgency contrasted with their application, which deviated widely from the plan and from the methods that British doctrine champions. It was quite clear at this point that the British government and military spoke the language of counterinsurgency, but the prospect of applying it in the field proved to be a more difficult proposition altogether. Indeed, despite the positive changes discussed here, the British effort still lacked the resources—both military and civilian—needed to meet what were now more ambitious, though geographically circumscribed, ends.

Indeed, the Afghan Development Zones failed to make an impact because, as in previous years, the British effort lacked the military and civilian manpower to hold the ground that had been cleared or to recruit and employ indigenous forces for those tasks. As to the conduct of military operations, it was not at all clear that the many rotations and significant expansion in troop numbers, from 3,150 to 8,500, had fundamentally changed the practical conduct of operations and the campaign structure.[68] Although the number of personnel had increased, so had the areas over which control was to be asserted, which had the effect of extending a subpar approach over a larger territory. The result was that well into 2010 the British forces were still "mowing the lawn" through repeated raiding.[69] The two "recaptures" of Musa Qaleh, first in December 2007 and then once more in June 2008, illustrate this point.[70] Given this outcome, the sought-after "effect" of increasing stability or providing a platform for improved economic development and good governance remained elusive.

Another indication of the flaws in the new approach was the British experience with Operation Panther's Claw. As US Marines started reinforcing Task Force Helmand in the summer of 2009, the coalition launched two of the biggest operations since the invasion in 2001: Operation Strike of the Sword, led by the US Marines, and Operation Panther's Claw, led by UK forces. The aim of the British operation was to clear and hold the area between Lashkar Gah and Gereshk in the green zone of Helmand—an area that had been under Taliban control for years and served as a key corridor for insurgent activity and supply.[71] The intent of the operations was to expand security in advance of the August 2009 presidential election. However, the British forces struggled in both the clearing and the holding phases: the Taliban refused direct confrontation, and the British military had neither sufficient troops to control the area nor indigenous forces with whom it could work. This last point deserves some emphasis because partnering with local proxies represents a vital and historically consistent counterinsurgency practice, crucial in any attempt by a foreign power, particularly one so critically undermanned, to exercise control and legitimacy.

Panther's Claw expanded the area under coalition control but still fell short of its intended objectives. The green zone—the fertile, populated areas along the Helmand River valley—was never comprehensively and methodically cleared. The enemy presence even in the cleared area remained quite strong, and the British holding force was able to control only the Babaji district center, leaving the remainder of the green zone relatively free for insurgent reinfiltration. Indeed, because the insurgents could return during the nights, the transition to the holding phase in the cleared areas proved premature.[72] Launched with only weeks left until the election, this operation was unable to achieve the security required for voting: less than 10 percent of the population turned out to vote, and complaints of election fraud were widespread.[73]

It is interesting to note that the increased theoretical emphasis on counterinsurgency in Afghanistan took place during the American "surge" in Iraq, which included an increase in US ground troops, their partnering with local forces against common adversaries, and their combined conduct of sustained and successful clearing and holding operations, particularly in and around Baghdad and Anbar Province. In Iraq, this shift managed to halt the vicious cycle of violence gripping the country and dramatically increase security for the following months and years. Why did the increased emphasis on counterinsurgency principles in Helmand not yield the same strategic successes? More fundamentally, what does this patchy track record say about counterinsurgency's credibility as a concept?

The answer lies in what counterinsurgency as a concept can and cannot do. Counterinsurgency offers a collection of insights and guidelines collected from past operations, which, if used and adapted in a manner sensitive to local context, can help in the design and execution of a specific campaign plan. Yet counterinsurgency is *not* a strategy. Instead, it should be seen as an approach to operations, involving a collection of principles and practices detached from any one campaign and operating below the realm of strategy. To the degree that the principles and practices of counterinsurgency worked in Iraq, it was because they were tied to a campaign plan informed by the specific enabling factors relevant to that operation. This is also precisely where the British campaign in Helmand failed; instead of using counterinsurgency as an operational approach in support of what should have been a substantially overhauled strategy with clearer aims supported by appropriately resourced military and civilian units, the British used the language and slogans of counterinsurgency as an ersatz strategy and without the resources required to make it work.[74] In the absence of a clear strategy, the catchwords of counterinsurgency (*population security, governance, legitimacy*) were confused with strategic ends and pursued all at the same time, with no prioritization or clear end in mind. Missed in this hurried embrace of newly rediscovered theory was the need to adapt its premises and principles to meet specific political goals.

Alternative approaches, given the restricted means, could have included limiting the geographical reach of the force to those areas that could truly be controlled and where a difference could be made—either by not deploying to northern Helmand or, if these districts and the relationship with the provincial governor were considered key to success, by abandoning central Helmand to enable a northward redeployment. As highlighted earlier, being thinly spread throughout the province meant that the few military tactical successes that were achieved in various clearing operations could not be capitalized upon to provide lasting results. A second option could have been to invest more heavily on local security structures and use them to extend the footprint of the limited British force. A third option could have been to approach operations in a more conventional way as the severity of the security situation became clear—maximizing the availability of combat troops and heavy firepower to tackle the Taliban's onslaught. Such an approach should not be confused with the initial deployment of 16 Brigade that was planned as a counterinsurgency/peace operation and not as conventional combat operations. A conventional charge on Helmand by the British paratroopers of 16 Brigade or by the Royal Marines of 3 Commando Brigade with the purpose of securing terrain would surely have looked very different and would probably not have been attempted with the limited resources at hand.

There is no way to prove counterfactually that any of these approaches would have been more successful—the point is to highlight that the British forces had several ways in which it might have implemented their political mandate. Instead, they seem to have "locked in" on a comprehensive counterinsurgency approach no matter the size of the operational area and the resources available. Key lessons from this British experience, therefore, are that talking a good fight is not enough and that counterinsurgency requires either great investment by the states involved or demonstrable creativity and acumen so as to make the most of limited resources.

SALVATION: US REINFORCEMENTS AND THE TRANSITION PROCESS

The operations launched in 2007–2010 can be described as a number of misguided attempts to overcome a poor start at the time of deployment, followed by the ill-conceived attempt to make up for such errors through a counterinsurgency approach entirely unsuited to the resources provided. In contrast to this narrative of false starts and setbacks, Operation Moshtarak II, launched in the spring of 2010, marked a break in fortunes, at least on the tactical level. Moshtarak II was the opening gambit of NATO's "surge" in 2010 and the first test of the strategy put in place by the newly appointed ISAF commander, Gen. Stanley McChrystal. The surge provided 30,000 new troops to Afghanistan, and the strategy involved a strong emphasis on politically led operations, geared toward gaining the support of the local population and conducted in partnership with Afghan National Security Forces (ANSF).[75]

Moshtarak II involved two simultaneous offensives launched on February 13, 2010. One was the amply discussed US Marine Corps offensive in the Taliban stronghold of Marjah; the other was a supporting offensive conducted by the British-led Task Force Helmand in northern Nad-e-Ali.[76] Although progress in Marjah was initially slow, Theo Farrell, author of a major assessment of Moshtarak II, notes encouraging progress in Nad-e-Ali that resulted in increased freedom of movement for civilians and security forces, the appointment of an effective governor, improved public services and police forces, as well as the election of a more representative district community council. According to Farrell, the operation demonstrated that in southern Afghanistan ISAF was indeed implementing a more population-oriented approach to counterinsurgency in line with Gen. McChrystal's strategy for the country.[77]

McChrystal's strategy represented, in essence, precisely what the British had attempted since it had first deployed to Helmand in 2006. It spoke of protecting the population rather than hunting down insurgents and put the counterinsurgency principles at the heart of the effort. More specifically, the idea was to push troops into more densely populated areas, such as the Helmand River valley and Kandahar city, to establish "ink spots" of control—directly comparable to the British Afghan Development Zones—in the midst of enemy territory. Although the approach rings familiar, at this stage the international coalition, increasingly working with their Afghan partners, displayed an improved ability to clear key locations of insurgents in both Helmand and Kandahar and finally also to hold such territory, if on a more limited basis.[78]

Several factors help explain why the British and their coalition partners managed at least to halt the momentum of the insurgency in Helmand and

Kandahar in late 2010 and early 2011. As the Americans had gotten more heavily involved, the first crucial difference was an increase in the level of resources available to complete this effort, specifically the addition of about 20,000 US Marines in Helmand alone. The increased general focus on Helmand and neighboring Kandahar by NATO as a whole and by the United States in particular also contributed to a superior understanding of the province and its politics, which in turn informed the conduct of operations.

The conduct of Moshtarak II also reflected ISAF's increased emphasis on provincial and local governance. This change was not just a shift in rhetorical emphasis; during the surge, the United States tripled the number of engineers, civilian-assistance workers, and diplomats in Afghanistan, so that they now numbered more than 1,100, and substantially increased the budget for civilian affairs.[79] In practice, this new approach entailed closer collaboration with Afghan political leaders and development officials: to set up governance structures in cleared towns, to enable local leaders and officials to make positive first impressions on the local population, and thereby to gain at least a minimum level of local legitimacy and support. The stress on governance was evident in the rapid establishment of district governance in north Nad-e-Ali, in the similar attempt in Marjah, and in ISAF's efforts to engage Afghan authorities at the national, provincial, and district levels in both the planning and the execution of the operation. The provincial and district governors, for example, played an important role in briefing Kabul, in identifying key villages and routes, and in helping the British define and recognize "normality" of life in certain areas.

The added resources critically allowed the British forces to focus more on the training and mentoring of Afghan forces as well as on leading and commanding the operations of others, often to good effect. This work proved essential because it enabled more effective employment of local forces within the Afghan security apparatus—something that contributed greatly to the relative stabilization of Helmand in 2011 and 2012. By this time, ISAF forces were generally well integrated with ANSF through the OMLTs, although the effectiveness of such partnerships remained highly uneven.[80] Even so, the OMLTs proved important in compensating for the inadequacies of the Afghan forces in terms of leadership and command competences as well as training and equipment. Regarding the latter, it is worth noting the provision of indirect fire and aerial support to Afghan units by embedded coalition officers working within the units' ranks.

The supporting role has clearly proven more fruitful for the numerically limited British forces. It also resonates more with the successes of the imperial past, when British forces managed the security of vast territories through local police and military forces trained, equipped, and often supported by the British Army. Required for this approach to be successful, of course, is the existence of indigenous forces with whom to work. This factor had been notably absent during the early years of the campaign in Helmand, in part because the development of the Afghan army and police had been neglected since the invasion in 2001 and in part because the British forces chose not to work with the militias that did exist in the province. A partnership of this type would have required a deep understanding of the local structures and environment, not least to gauge the local legitimacy (and accountability) of those actors willing and able to support stated mission objectives. Yet, as discussed, such knowledge and initiative were wholly lacking in Britain's efforts in Helmand, at least until 2011. When the shift was made, the results became apparent. Although some of the districts under British responsibility are still (as of 2013) among the most violent in Afghanistan, two of them, Lashkar Gah and Nad-e-Ali, began a transition process in 2011 whereby responsibility for security was over time and in several steps handed to Afghan forces. The final British area of control, Nahr-e Saraj, entered the transition process in May 2012.

The British also displayed great command and leadership capabilities as the British Headquarters 6th Division was put in charge of planning and executing the operations from November 2009 to November 2010. This included Operation Moshtarak II during the offensives on Marjah and Nad-e-Ali as well as Operation Hamkari in and around Kandahar city. Headquarters 6th Division was an old infantry division specifically reformed in 2008 as a deployable two-star headquarters with the purpose of taking charge of Regional Command South in Afghanistan.

The planning and leadership displayed by 6th Division during its time in command were truly an accomplishment because these operations were the most significant since the invasion of Afghanistan and involved a great variety of actors and activities that were coordinated to good effect. Interestingly, 6th Division was built around staff with recent operational experience in southern Afghanistan. Members of this staff strove to understand the local political situation, conducted in-depth analysis together with local partners, and thereby developed more solid intelligence for subsequent planning.

Gen. Nick Carter, commander of Regional Command South, created an operational plan that in many ways reflected the old tradition of military duties in aid of political power. Operation Hamkari was defined primarily as a political operation to extend the Afghan government's hold over Kandahar or, in Gen. Carter's words, "to connect credible Afghan governance to the population."[81] In practice, this meant an attempt to increase the credibility and legitimacy of the provincial governor, Tooryalai Wesa, and to bring local power brokers into the process of stabilization. The intent obviously echoes the rhetoric of previous plans, but this time the approach was at once more pragmatic and realistic about what British forces could themselves achieve. For example, in the combat phase of the Hamkari project (Operation Moshtarak III), the British military, rather than seek to achieve stability by itself, made great use of notorious local power brokers Ahmed Wali Karzai and Colonel Abdul Raziq, who would authorize and execute essential clearing operations.[82]

The effect of this transfer of responsibility to indigenous forces was substantial because they had greater situational awareness, political clout, and, in many cases, legitimacy than their British or American counterparts. By using local political networks to secure the area, Colonel Raziq and his Afghan border police successfully and quickly completed the clearing operations with minimal resources and collateral damage.[83] Like the added resources provided by the surge, the transfer of responsibility to indigenous forces allowed the British military to focus its limited resources on other important tasks—such as the training and mentoring of Afghan forces, supporting newly instated political leaders, and providing strategies and leadership for operations.

The involvement of Colonel Raziq and Ahmed Wali Karzai in the Hamkari project stands in stark contrast with the removal of the local big man, provincial governor Sher Mohammed Akhundzada, before the initial deployment in 2006. By 2010 standards, he and his militia would have been ideal partners in the counterinsurgency campaign, yet at the time the context of state building and democratization made such partnerships politically impossible. As the transition process to Afghan control got under way in 2011, these lofty ideals were replaced by a far more pragmatic concept informally called "Afghanistan good enough." The meaning of this phrase is contested, but the goal is generally seen as an Afghanistan with strong-enough security forces to conduct the counterinsurgency campaign on its own and a central government stable and capable enough to control and maintain the campaign with Western support. Although the downgrading of aims has much to do with the international coalition's efforts to withdraw the bulk of its force by the end of 2014, it also points to a more realistic appraisal of what is possible in Afghanistan. As part of this new effort to use real means to meet achievable ends, the US-led NATO Training Mission Afghanistan was propped up with a budget of around US$10 billion annually to form and train Afghan security forces.

The downgrading of ambitions has been essential to whatever success has been seen in Afghanistan, but it also threatens to undermine these very same achievements. This period finally saw the successful implementation of a tactical-level counterinsurgency approach developed in accordance with the specific context of operations in Afghanistan. By increasing the resources for the operations, employing indigenous forces to good effect, and striking a more useful balance in the application of force, the campaign seemingly narrowed the gap between ends and means. Moshtarak II and Hamkari also achieved substantial tactical successes, both in clearing and holding ground, but also, to a more limited extent, in initiating political transition and reconstruction. There are plenty of positive reports of areas cleared, district governors instigated, trade routes and local markets reopened, roads and bridges constructed, as well as schools and universities built or reopened.[84]

The problem is that these tactical achievements have not translated into strategic gains—and are unlikely to do so. In Iraq, the purpose of the surge initiated by President George W. Bush and Gen. David Petraeus was to halt the ongoing civil war, limit the level of violence, and thereby provide the "breathing space" needed for political negotiations and settlements. Through the implementation of a carefully calibrated campaign plan and effective exploitation of the contextual opportunities provided at the time, the US military contributed to a sharp drop in violence. It partnered with former adversaries, put pressure on the obstructionist elements of the Iraqi government, and set the conditions that would, it was hoped, enable longer-term reconciliation. In Afghanistan, by contrast, the surge first of all failed to achieve a substantial drop in the number of insurgent attacks or the general level of violence beyond the geographically limited ink spots. As Gen. John Allen, commander of ISAF, noted in August 2012, ten districts in Afghanistan now account for a full half of the insurgent violence in the country: three in Kandahar, six in Helmand, and all three districts under British control—Lashkar Gah, Nad-e-Ali, and Nahr-e Saraj.[85] NATO's effort in Afghanistan has also failed to achieve a political settlement with former adversaries—a vital force multiplier in Iraq—much as it failed to address the deep problems of accountability and legitimacy within the central government in Kabul. At the time of writing (late 2012), many of the possible indicators of success—such as the numbers of insurgent attacks and of civilian, ISAF, and ANSF casualties; popular approval rates of government performance; and the total proportion of Afghan territory controlled by the Taliban—still refuse to point in a conclusively positive direction.[86]

Part of the problem in Afghanistan was timing. Had the surge been conducted earlier, in 2006 or before patience with operations had run thin among Western politicians and constituents, proper follow-up might have enabled the tactical successes to be turned into strategic gains. On the basis of a change in momentum, action would then have been needed to build on these successes; pursue serious political negotiations and possibly a settlement; increase government capability, accountability, and legitimacy; as well as boost the local economies within the newly established pockets of stability. However, by 2012 there was no longer any patience or interest in any such follow-up: the focus had shifted to transition and withdrawal, for eminently understandable reasons, yet in ways that will imperil the tactical gains made. Given this strategic context, the efforts expended at the tactical level in 2012 can be seen as the correct approach implemented at the wrong time, or—more damningly—as too little, too late. At this stage, the resolve to achieve anything beyond "Afghanistan good enough" has been lost, and, with the surge troops already returning home, it is uncertain who or what will consolidate and build on the tentative tactical progress achieved to date.[87]

As we turn again to the time wasted and opportunities squandered in Afghanistan, it is necessary to raise once more—as a fundamental problem in the campaign—the ambiguity in aims sought and strategies employed. Despite great variation in approach and meaning since 2001—the usual evolution of strategy and operational art—the underlying purpose of this mission has never been adequately settled. As the West is increasingly focusing on withdrawal, these ambiguities are resurfacing and complicating the attempts to gloss over the cracks left behind by a decade of war. Whatever the metric, assessments of post-2014 Afghanistan are in 2012 generally bleak.[88] Not only have the democratic ideals that once justified the operation been more or less abandoned, but there are also signs that the Western military withdrawal will lead to an escalated civil war in the country, compromising NATO's achievements, however they are defined.[89] What the Afghan campaign reveals about NATO and about its main troop contributors in particular is a failure to operate and think strategically or at least coherently.

What do the relative tactical achievements between 2010 and 2012 as well as the failure to achieve lasting strategic effects say about the British ability to make substantial contributions to complex expeditionary operations? The British campaign as a whole can hardly be described as a success—far from it—and the operations in Afghanistan have bluntly displayed that Great Britain lacks the civilian and military resources to conduct large-scale counterinsurgency operations on its own. Just as worrying, Britain's inability to compensate for its own resource limitations by identifying and partnering with acceptable local forces represents a capability gap that will need to be urgently addressed before British troops are deployed on any similar type of mission. Against this assessment, the late British achievements—the effective command of operations in Helmand and Kandahar in 2010–2011, the training and mentoring of Afghan forces, and the initiated transition process—provide signs of less ambitious but perhaps more successful approaches to future British contributions to expeditionary campaigns. Given the right leadership, there is clearly potential within the British military to conduct these operations in coalitions or with the use of indigenous forces, but even then, as noted, the paramount and most fundamental challenge will be to support these activities with a viable strategy backed by commensurate resources.

* * *

When the British military deployed to Helmand province in 2006, it was again—as in Basra—badly prepared, lacking in plans, and unfamiliar with the nature of the campaign. Back in London, the British government spoke of a comprehensive approach being applied in Helmand that was to bring development, democracy, and security to the province. Yet starved of resources, partners, and troops and facing a fierce adversary, the British military was unable to put such lofty ideals into practice. Instead, successive units applied largely improvised solutions to the problem as they perceived it, never quite succeeding in bridging the disconnect between ends and means or substantially improving the situation on the ground. Seeking to apply the lessons from Iraq and correct past errors, 52 Brigade deployed in October 2007, looking to counterinsurgency as a way of stabilizing the province. Here, too, operational adaptation occurred in the absence of a concomitant shift at the strategic level, resulting in further disappointment and frustration. When the US military was sent to assist the British forces, it finally became possible to speak of a counterinsurgency campaign in Helmand, yet by this point the strategic intent was shifting from state building to damage limitation, thus undermining the effects of the tactical progress under way.

As noted earlier, it is clear from operations in Helmand as well as in Basra that neither the British armed forces nor their civilian counterparts in the Foreign Office and DfID have the capacity to conduct and sustain large-scale counterinsurgency operations—despite increasing numbers and late tactical adaptation. Without substantial support from US troops (amounting to twice the number of British troops), Task Force Helmand did not come close to tackling the insurgency or establishing the stability needed for the necessary civilian aspects of operations. This issue is in large part one of numbers. As Anatol Lieven argues, regardless of the courage, endurance, and fighting power of the British military, its real resources as well as the limited collective national will are simply not tailored to mounting demanding operations in the manner attempted in Iraq and Afghanistan.[90]

There is no doubt that the troops deploying to Helmand were short-changed by the political and military leadership. However, the military also failed to make the most of the limited resources provided. The decision to disperse the small number of troops available throughout the province, for example, and the perceived need to accommodate the American commanders in charge of Operation Mountain Thrust were operational-level decisions or interpretations of political intent. Moreover, not until late 2007 did British units move beyond the strictures of regimental culture to form plans and approaches based on the challenge as it presented itself. Underlying these difficulties, in part, are the problems encountered in identifying, training, and partnering with local indigenous forces—a critical enabler for successful counterinsurgency. The failure to make use of indigenous forces, in combination with the gaps in the civilian aspects of operations, meant that the British forces were made to stand alone in what should have been an effort involving many more actors. The solitude of the British Army in Helmand stands in stark contrast with historical operations in the colonies. Finally, even with the necessary resources, Britain lacks the administrative structure and competence at the strategic and operational levels of command needed to coordinate different actors and activities. Relying on host governments to provide these structures and planning resources in countries such as Afghanistan and post-Baathist Iraq is obviously highly problematic but often unavoidable.

The case of Afghanistan thereby points to the significant problems in the British way of preparing for and prosecuting modern wars: the failure to properly formulate and resource strategy; the failure of civil–military coordination at both the strategic and operational levels; the limitations of military improvisation and of "muddling through" in the absence of a plan; and the dangers of letting strategic intent and operational approach develop independently.

If the British military and its political masters will want to conduct expeditionary operations in the future, it will be critical that the capability gaps exposed in Afghanistan (and in southern Iraq) are urgently addressed.

4

"A HORSE AND TANK MOMENT"

THE BRITISH MILITARY'S engagements in Iraq and Afghanistan severely dented its standing as a force uniquely capable, by dint of its history and culture, to conduct counterinsurgency. The setbacks experienced in these campaigns cannot be placed solely or even mainly at the armed forces' door: the troops were too few in numbers, too lacking in partners (both civilian and host nation), and, perhaps most fundamentally, without clear strategic direction or political support from the homeland. Yet alongside these factors the setbacks also related intimately to the British military's own lack of preparation and familiarity with the tasks and type of knowledge needed: to understand the local political context and engage with its actors; to establish local partnerships (so as to offset the limited number of its own troops); to address the developmental, reconstruction, and governance-related aspects of military occupation; and—on a more senior level in particular—to understand the character of the conflict in which they were now engaged.

The armed forces' lack of preparedness is relatively easy to explain: as described in chapter 1, throughout the 1990s the British military had followed the dictum that a soldier well prepared for high-intensity combat can adapt to the challenges of counterinsurgency, but not vice versa. This approach had encouraged a predominantly "conventional," state-on-state conception of war. Nor did the MoD and senior command's fascination with the US-driven concepts of "force transformation" help prepare British soldiers for the field; instead, constant repetition of a new generation of buzzwords— *network-enabled operations, information superiority,* and *effects-based operations*—encouraged a reductive understanding of war as a sophisticated targeting drill to be controlled and won through advanced technology. At best, the discussion in the decade leading up to the Iraq War had focused on various forms of peace-support operations, which although marginally related to counterinsurgency still operate by a different set of principles and logic.[1]

The lack of institutional interest in counterinsurgency has deep historical roots. Even at the height of British military involvement in such missions during the mid–twentieth century, efforts to institutionalize lessons from the field rarely produced more than the occasional update to doctrine or revised training pamphlet. The lack of a more concerted institutional focus on counterinsurgency has forced the British military to reinvent the wheel with each nominally similar campaign. In the past, such campaigns were sufficiently frequent to allow for individual vice institutional recollection of what worked, which greatly facilitated operational adaptation. Yet by the time of the Iraq and Afghanistan wars, far fewer leaders and troops had the relevant experience and no refresher courses were provided to help sustain the awareness of earlier times.

Since Britain's reencounter with insurgency following the invasion of Iraq in 2003, efforts have been made to amend this failing. Counterinsurgency and counterinsurgency-related operations and challenges have gradually received greater institutional attention, as reflected in doctrine, training, curricula, and the establishment of new organizations and structures. Three overlapping factors have driven this process. First, both Basra and Helmand came to be understood as threatened by "insurgency," and the troops deployed to these zones therefore required counterinsurgency instruction. Thenceforth, predeployment training, curricula, and resource allocation changed over time. Second, the MoD gradually came to espouse an understanding of the future character of conflict as encompassing many of the challenges encountered in Iraq and Afghanistan: operations conducted in populated areas, in foreign cultures and languages, and against elusive adversaries capable of offsetting their military inferiority.[2] The turn toward counterinsurgency was thus also intended to produce a more general familiarity with the complexities of *modern warfare*—that is, beyond Iraq or Afghanistan. Third, the MoD saw a continued need, even with the costs of the Iraq and Afghanistan campaigns, to maintain the capability and capacity to conduct "an enduring stabilisation operation at around brigade level."[3] This requirement stemmed from a view of "weak and failing states" as posing national-security threats to the United Kingdom and the corresponding need to be able to conduct "post-conflict stabilisation."[4] Given these planning assumptions, many of the lessons of Iraq and Afghanistan had to be retained.

To reformers, these three drivers provided the impetus for much-needed change: rather than presume expertise and be caught out when tested, the British armed forces would ensure that the knowledge and capabilities relevant for the most complex of operations be fully institutionalized. Yet if this was the basis of a possible reorientation, actual reform faced concerted resistance. This resistance was (and remains) primarily institutional and largely reactionary, resulting in the blockage or delay of many innovative types of reforms. The resistance to change relates also to Britain's weakening financial position, which has complicated the simultaneous pursuit of disparate priorities. Finally, given the cuts to defense budgets and the bruising experiences in Afghanistan and Iraq, there is little appetite to prepare for similar operations elsewhere.

Change and continuity will always coexist in assessments of institutional adaptation, and for this reason the purpose of this chapter is not to determine whether the British military had, by any given time, "learned counterinsurgency." Instead, this chapter assesses the common assertion of British military adaptability by examining the manner in which Britain reacted to its less than optimal operational experience with counterinsurgency and prepared for operations of similar (or greater) complexity elsewhere. The assessment reveals a learning process that was slow to start, but that since 2009 has showed genuine potential for change. Even then, the most promising of initiatives have occurred against a broader backdrop of continuity, particularly in the key foundational areas of resource allocation and force structure. With the withdrawal from Iraq and the impending exit from Afghanistan, it is doubtful whether the innovation seen to date will be sustained or give way to more "traditional" priorities.

A SLOW RESPONSE

It took some years following the occupation of southern Iraq for the British armed forces to react institutionally. Buoyed by the swift overthrow of Saddam Hussein and the relative stability in southern Iraq (compared to the rest of the country), the British armed forces saw no immediate need for reform. At this point, problems experienced in the field were commonly ascribed to the weaknesses of the military's civilian partners; more than anything, their meager presence and resources in the field were perceived as the campaign's missing link.[5] The military was therefore a great supporter of the Post-Conflict Reconstruction Unit (PCRU), a body set up in 2004 to improve interdepartmental coordination for the stabilization of postwar countries.[6] The hope was that the PCRU would help involve the Foreign Office and DfID, so that the military could concentrate on its "core" tasks: patrols, raids, and security.

This focus on the civilian agencies was justified, but also problematic. First, concern with civilian weaknesses belied the need for serious reform also within the military, which did not make much headway during these initial years.[7] Some steps were taken, such as the quick adaptation of the Operational Training and Advisory Group (OPTAG) and of predeployment training to put more emphasis on local culture, language, and conditions.[8] In 2003, Land Forces Standing Order 1118 was issued, which assigned responsibility within the army for a lessons-learned mechanism based on its experiences in Iraq.[9] Nonetheless, there was little evidence in 2003–2005 of a more concerted reconsideration of counterinsurgency or of an institutional reorientation toward these types of campaigns.

Second, the military and others were far too hopeful about the government's ability to "fix" the civil–military imbalance, which skewed expectations of how labor might be divided in future campaigns. On paper, the PCRU promised a great deal: owned jointly by DfID, the Foreign Office, and the MoD, it was mandated to "develop strategy for post conflict stabilisation" and to "plan, implement and manage the UK contribution to post conflict stabilisation."[10] With three masters but none of its own, however, PCRU was burdened by an unclear chain of command and struggled to establish itself. The unit was not declared operational until July 2006, at which point it accounted for twenty-eight personnel, drawn from five government departments, and a yearly budget of £10 million.[11] Its civilian parent agencies, DfID and the Foreign Office, lacked "both flexibility in funding arrangements . . . and career incentives for staff to deploy" and operate in conflict environments.[12] At this point, neither these weaknesses nor their long-term implications for the military's own remit in postconflict settings were grasped. Instead, frustration at the civilian agencies' current weaknesses and misplaced hope in their swift remediation absolved the military from closer self-scrutiny.

It was not until 2006 that the military took more significant steps to reorient its forces. Three factors brought on this change. First, as security in Basra deteriorated, questions surfaced regarding the British approach to operations there and the need to adapt.[13] Second, in its reassessment of the campaign, the British military was swayed by the rediscovery of counterinsurgency in the United States, where the Army and Marine Corps were working on a new counterinsurgency manual. Given the close involvement of select British officers and analysts in the drafting of the new doctrine, this rediscovery of counterinsurgency bled back into the discussion ongoing within the United Kingdom at this time. Finally, the Blair government's January 2006 announcement of troop deployments to Helmand gave added salience to the study of counterinsurgency; at least it provided reasons to focus, in both predeployment training and education, on the challenges of operating among civilians and against insurgent groups.

The convergence of these factors led to reforms in the way soldiers were prepared and instructed for duty. Urban training, hitherto limited to a fairly rudimentary "mock Arab" village at Copehill Down Village, was expanded with the revamping of the Battle Group Training Unit at Salisbury Plain and the Training Unit in Suffield, Canada.[14] The writing of an updated counterinsurgency doctrine, last published in 2001, also began, which led to the release in March 2007 of *Counter Insurgency Operations (Strategic and Operational Guidelines)*. The update reflected a growing consensus within the army leadership that the situation in Basra resembled an insurgency rather than an unusually violent peace-support operation and that new doctrine was needed. Because doctrine must be taught to truly matter, it was noteworthy that the new publication coincided with an increased focus on counterinsurgency-relevant instruction at the Joint Services Command and Staff College. Students taking the Higher Command and Staff Course benefited from having instructors with multiple tours under their belt—officers returning from theater as full colonels or equivalent and who could share their operational insights. At the advanced and intermediate command staff courses, counterinsurgency had since 1997 been taught in small bursts and through optional courses. Now external speakers were brought in as part of a new focus on this topic.[15] Notably, many of the expert speakers involved in the course hailed from the United States; no longer were British officers advising their American counterparts on counterinsurgency, but rather the reverse.

It was also in 2006 that the MoD and the British Army began taking more concerted steps to equip the force in theater for counterinsurgency. As violence spread across the Iraqi South and in Helmand Province in Afghanistan, it became clear that British troops were ill equipped for the typical military tasks of counterinsurgency: to maintain presence, conduct strike operations, withstand unpredictable threats and dangers. In the media, stories detailed shortages in protective vests, up-armored vehicles, and other force-protection gear. Helicopters—needed for tactical mobility, particularly in contested environments—were also lacking.[16] Most controversial at the time was the continued use of Snatch land rovers in Iraq; these vehicles had been employed in Northern Ireland but offered inadequate protection against the threats of roadside bombs and grenades. In response to mounting pressure, both Tony Blair and Armed Forces Minister Adam Ingram in 2006 made public pledges to provide the deployed troops with any equipment they might need. This effort led to various Urgent Operational Requirements (UOR) orders, by which armored Mastiff vehicles and other surveillance and force-protection capabilities were sent to the field. Although many criticized this corrective action as "too little, too late," it nevertheless reflected a growing awareness of and willingness to meet the specific material requirements of counterinsurgency.

It had thus taken three years of engagement in Iraq for the military to begin to reform its doctrine, education, training, and resource allocation in line with ongoing operations. On the ground, tactical-level adaptation had been occurring throughout this period, sometimes with impressive speed, but it was only in 2006 that higher-level institutional reforms became apparent. Even then, the response was at this point modest. The revised *Counter Insurgency Operations* manual did not have the same effect as the US counterinsurgency manual released three months earlier, either in terms of prompting a conversation or changing the military's mindset. Nor can it be said that it necessarily filled a gap: the 2001 field manual on counterinsurgency was fundamentally sound and had informed the drafting of US doctrine in 2006. So the problem was not that no such manual existed, but instead that it was not being read and not being taught in the staff colleges; indeed, not consulting the manual was too often held up as a source of pride. On that front, the renewed focus on counterinsurgency at the Joint Services Command and Staff College was welcome to those who sought greater institutional focus on these types of operations, but even then the advanced and intermediate courses still devoted only a handful of days specifically to this important topic. The reforms to training were similarly slow in coming, in part because of the difficulty of changing the army's focus from "major combat operations" to counterinsurgency. Even in late 2006, the commander of the Land Warfare Collective Training Group at Warminster noted that "what we do today is still a bit sterile and Cold War" and that "this paradigm shift . . . has not really borne down on our training, so we have now got to make bold corrections."[17]

THE COST OF CHANGE

To a degree, these "bold corrections" were just a matter of time given the trickle-down effects of the ongoing counterinsurgency campaigns. Yet while these deployments continued to push new priorities onto the British military, they also brought unanticipated tensions to the fore, between longer-term institutional reforms and short-term operational requirements. Added to these tensions was the gradual onset of a financial crisis that fueled a fiercer competition—between governmental departments for scarce funds and between military services for declining defense spending. At times, the attempts to reconcile the need for adaptation on the one hand and austerity on the other produced somewhat contradictory results. Doctrine for counterinsurgency would be published all while funding was cut for those centers seeking to teach it. Training exercises were adapted in line with ongoing operations, but only within a broader structure still predicated on conventional combat. The mixed messages belie a lack of institutional consensus that has limited the scope for possible change.

Reform was easiest and most evident where new initiatives did not have to compete with or displace older ones. Doctrine was one of these areas. Following *Counter Insurgency Operations* in 2007, work got under way on an entirely new field manual. Mirroring the approach of the team behind the influential American counterinsurgency manual, the British Army engaged with various civilian and academic institutions to vet its forthcoming product. Finally, in October 2009, *Army Field Manual*, volume 1, part 10: *Counter Insurgency Operations*, was released. The manual was more concise than its predecessor, cut down on jargon and theoretical abstractions, and offered a more readable guide to the problem of insurgency. Inspired again by their American counterparts, the British writing team ensured a greater impact than with previous field manuals (all of which had been internal products): twenty-five thousand copies were printed, electronic versions were made available, and the manual was presented at conferences worldwide. It was taught in every internal course on counterinsurgency, both at Sandhurst and the Staff College.

The counterinsurgency manual was published jointly with MoD Joint Doctrine Publication 3-40, *Security and Stabilisation: The Military Contribution*. This significantly longer publication, intended for the joint services and other government departments, provided a broader take on the problem of political instability and state failure. For the military, it was noteworthy for its recognition that civilian governmental partners often struggle to deploy to insecure environments and that the military then has an important, if hopefully temporary, role in supporting governance and building institutional capacity as well as in enabling economic and infrastructural development.[18] This stance—that where civilians can't, the military sometimes must—was a departure from previous counterinsurgency doctrine and mirrored the line taken in emerging US doctrine.[19]

One may fault the British Army for the delay in getting new doctrine out: by the time these two manuals appeared, the six-year campaign in Iraq was already over. Also, despite close cooperation between the two writing teams, it was not entirely clear how the two manuals meshed. The attempt in the *Stabilisation* manual to differentiate its remit from that of the *Counterinsurgency* manual was particularly questionable, given the close overlap between the two terms.[20] These issues aside, the publication of doctrine remains a relative success story in terms of army innovation. One reason for this progress is the low opportunity cost of issuing new field manuals: whereas there is a finite number of classes in a curriculum or days in a training cycle, there is no similarly immediate limit to the production of doctrine. It is therefore far easier to write new doctrine than to ensure it is taught, understood, and embraced by the institution because it is at these critical stages that preexisting priorities are upset. Indeed, where new priorities have had to be advanced at the expense of old ones, change has been significantly more difficult.

This is obvious within military training. On the one hand, operational needs resulted in some significant reform. The army adapted its 2,690-square-kilometer training site in Suffield, Canada, and began launching five scalable predeployment exercises per year. Named "Medicine Man," these exercises involved live-fire scenarios that mirrored the challenges faced in the field, from elusive adversaries mingling with civilians to the constant media presence.[21] In December 2008, work began on a 51,000-square-meter village at the Stanford Training Area (Stanta) in Thetford, to be used for predeployment training.[22] Every nine months, the grounds put up to 9,500 personnel through Afghan-specific scenarios, overseen by subject-matter experts and OPTAG to ensure verisimilitude with the field. OPTAG played a similar role at Camp Bastion Training Centre in Afghanistan, which opened in October 2009 and provided incoming units a "last-minute" weeklong training course. OPTAG also provided direct training to unit leaders, following an established British counterinsurgency tradition of "training the trainer"; commanders were put through an intense one-month program and then passed this knowledge on to their respective units.[23]

These and other initiatives were significant, yet listing them in this manner belies the challenges the British military faced in undergoing reform. These challenges speak to the difficulty of adding priorities to an institution already stretched by ongoing commitments and expected to maintain proficiency in all types of military operations. First, there was the problem of scale; even in 2009 the army "lacked sufficient training facilities to replicate an Iraqi/Afghan environment," and those that were sufficiently realistic were in such high demand as to compromise the quality of the training.[24] The construction of the Stanta village would later mitigate though not entirely address this shortfall. Second, it proved difficult to fit the new exercises into the training cycles without sacrificing preexisting material.

Until 2009, training within the British Army was based on the so-called Adaptive Foundation, an eighteen-month training cycle that emphasized skills thought essential to all military operations. This training typically focused on conventional combat, which is seen as foundational, and troops were then given a further six months of predeployment training on more specific, mission-relevant tasks.[25] There is merit to this system, but it raises two problems. First, both the Iraq and Afghanistan campaigns demonstrated the limits of predeployment training in quickly reorienting a force to the challenges of counterinsurgency. Six months, it turns out, is a fairly short time.[26] Second, the division between foundational and specialized training did not change significantly despite years of applying the latter more than the former in theater. Much of what is learned in the foundational training was truly generic: how to drive a tank, fire a gun, build a bridge, or carry out resupply. Nonetheless, the broader context and assumptions underlying this basic training remained broadly conventional, producing a gap between training and practice and leaving very little time for the required reorientation.[27]

At what point must what is deemed "foundational" be adapted in line with ongoing and anticipated challenges?[28] The British Army has made some efforts to bridge the gap, but the question remains whether the measures go far enough or too far or are simply the wrong approach to solving this particular dilemma. First, between 2008 and 2010, the army modified its foundational training program by temporarily closing its jungle-warfare training ground in Belize and increasing to six (from three) the number of six-week battle-group exercises held at Training Unit Kenya. This shift was intended to narrow the gap between foundation and predeployment training as the terrain in Kenya is more alike that in Afghanistan.[29] More generally, the army has also cancelled the less essential exercises of the foundational training so as to save money and make time for more pressing priorities.[30] By 2007, a total of 357 training exercises had been cancelled in this manner.[31] Finally, in 2009, the army renamed the Adaptive Foundation in favor of "Hybrid Foundation Training," which was intended to provide a more versatile preparation for wars of any type. Since then, more mission-specific challenges have bled into the foundational training: the focus on nuclear, biological, and chemical weapons has, for example, lost out to countering improvised bombs—an arguably more urgent requirement. Despite such changes, the focus of foundational training remains, perhaps inevitably, on traditional military tasks—"fire and maneuver, all arms integration, leadership and team building"—which, although critical to any force, still provide scant preparation for the equally challenging requirements of ongoing operations.[32]

These tensions speak to the longer-term dilemma of how to prioritize between two disparate conceptions of war. On the one hand, there are already concerns, despite the limited changes made to date, that the Hybrid Foundation Training is becoming too focused on "the last war"—Afghanistan—and is therefore failing to prepare soldiers for the "major combat operations" of the future.[33] On the other, foundational training is still not providing the type of training that appears necessary for counterinsurgency, or any operation in which the army must fight among and alongside civilian populations. For example, given the emphasis in military thinking on the need for "situational awareness" and "in-depth knowledge of . . . culture," it may be necessary, as the MoD's Development, Concepts, and Doctrine Centre once recommended, to insert "general themes of culture and the significance of cultural capability" into the foundational training and to complement this element with "culture-specific" instruction during predeployment training.[34] Reforms of this scale and ambition have not taken place and would be hotly contested the moment they challenge more traditional training priorities.

One attempted way out of this dilemma has been to rely on ad hoc measures to fill gaps in troop preparedness. For example, postoperational reports from Helmand revealed an acute need to enhance deploying units' cultural knowledge and awareness. Even as late as 2010, "most Service personnel got just half-a-day's cultural awareness briefing before deploying to Afghanistan, and the training need was poorly defined."[35] To Gen. (ret) Sir

John Kiszely, former head of Britain's Defence Academy, army complacency regarding its "inherent strengths" with respect to other cultures was part of the problem in that it had limited cultural training to "what basic errors to avoid [and] a smattering of a few handy phrases."[36] To remedy this deficiency, the MoD created the Defence Cultural Specialist Unit (DCSU)—a pool of deployable military cultural advisers, or CULADs, who train and assist the deployed forces.

Since the initial deployment of these CULADs in 2010, the feedback for the DCSU has been mostly positive. At the same time, the new unit is suffering from the almost inevitable teething problems of any new structure, established midstream to make up for urgent capability gaps.[37] First, in terms of scale, the DCSU has to date deployed only six CULADs at any one time. Where present, CULADs are seemingly appreciated, but one wonders about the impact of such a small unit on the force as a whole. Second, in terms of mandate, uncertainty as to their exact role meant CULADs were at times misapplied. On their first deployment, in 2010, their language skills—another rarity in theater—meant that they were used as "Afghan liaison officers" rather than as cultural advisers; important as this is, it was not what had been intended. Third, in terms of training and competence, on top of their language instruction, CULADs received just three weeks of additional training, which necessarily limited what they could bring to the field. Finally, in terms of permanence, there has been scant progress toward institutionalizing the DCSU within the army. Since October 2010, it has helped oversee a one-week cultural training course run by Cranfield University and provided to some deploying units. Yet the DCSU more broadly relies on the perception of its utility for its survival, which makes it doubtful whether it will thrive or even survive post-Afghanistan, at which point the force will revert to the same minimal cultural capability as it had previously.[38] The question, then, is whether an ad hoc and belated fix such as the DCSU, however positive its contribution, is the best way of addressing more deep-running capability gaps or whether it might not be more prudent to address this and other similar shortcomings through concerted institutional reform.

Beyond the tension between "foundational" and "specialized" skills, army training also confronted the financial strains of balancing "force preparation" and "force generation"—or, put more plainly, between training the force and having it available for combat. Although UORs have helped bring much-needed equipment to the field, simultaneously equipping the troops who are *preparing* to deploy has been difficult. As a result, many troops arrive in theater untrained on the kit they are expected to use. In December 2007, the army sought to remedy this problem by establishing the Operational Training Equipment Pool, which has availed new vehicles and weapons to troops in training. Yet as the National Audit Office makes clear, even then the numbers are "insufficient to support the scale of pre-deployment training."[39] To some degree, the use of simulations and software has offset shortages such as these and in realistic training sites. Since 2007, drivers from the Royal Logistics Corps, along with more than 6,000 deploying troops, have been trained on the Joint Combat Operation Virtual Environment program, which creates an entire virtual town, complete with insurgents, roadside bombs, and civilians.[40] The army is also using the Combined Arms Tactical Trainer to simulate various platforms used in theater. Yet whereas computer simulations have the benefit of scalability, lend themselves to "play-by-play" review, and are more financially viable, there are limits to how effectively they can prepare troops for the full experience of actual combat.[41]

Despite slow but notable improvement in the area of training, significant dilemmas clearly remain. The broader dilemma, one that cannot easily be met by tinkering on the margins, is how to incorporate two different conceptions of war—one "conventional" and one "irregular"—so as to prepare for both or, even better, how to arrive at one *integrated* vision of likely future threats and to prepare accordingly. In theory, the MoD already has the vision: the *Strategic Trends Programme: Future Character of Conflict* report, commissioned by the vice chief of defense staff and published in February 2010, provided a ministerial statement on the future operating environment, which it predicted would be crowded, replete with "irregular" actors and adversaries, and plagued by weak institutions.[42] It added that conflict in these types of settings "will challenge military forces structured and prepared for industrial-age war between global superpowers."[43] In a similar vein, the introductory paragraph of the MoD's report *Future Land Operational Concept* of 2008 stated that "the requirement to conduct complex operations, where political stability is the goal, is most pressing and directly challenges previous assumptions regarding existing structures, training and the demands on our people."[44]

It can be hoped that the resources and time freed up by an eventual withdrawal from Afghanistan will provide a golden opportunity to prepare for these types of challenges, both in training and in education. At the same time, in a fiscally constrained environment where Afghanistan and Iraq no longer provide clarion calls for adaptation, it is also possible that the military's priorities will revert to status quo ante. New exercises and capabilities have so far been grafted onto the core through steps that can easily be reversed, and the foundation remains more or less the same. Moreover, notwithstanding the MoD's various concept papers, the operations in Iraq and Afghanistan have been damaging in so many ways that preparing for similar or even more complex contingencies elsewhere is likely to strike both governments and militaries as a singularly unattractive proposition. Finally, training for conventional warfare has had to be sacrificed in the past half-decade, and there will be an understandable desire to compensate for these cuts once the operational demands of counterinsurgency subside. For these reasons, following through on the MoD's futuristic visions is likely to be highly problematic or at least require very persistent senior-level lobbying.

UNDERSTANDING THE WORLD ON A BUDGET

A similar difficulty in financing new initiatives without sacrificing older priorities expressed itself in the battle to overhaul the military's analytical and intellectual capabilities—in other words, its capacity to understand emerging threats, foreign cultures, regional politics, and operational effects. Improvement in this area is central to the reorientation toward counterinsurgency—missions that typically demand a "learning organization" that is culturally savvy, comfortable in foreign environments, and able to understand and work with local actors. It is also seen as critical to preparing the military for future "complex operations"; the argument here is that whereas technology can be produced surprisingly quickly in wartime, competent leaders with the required knowledge and cognitive capacities can only be matured over time. Yet despite the emphasis on such capacities in doctrine and concept papers, investment in the relevant enablers has typically lagged, with resources devoted instead to more traditional areas. There are signs of change here, particularly since around 2009, but as with innovation in training, it is uncertain whether investments in knowledge, education, and understanding will be allowed to flourish in a cost-saving environment where the urgency of operations in Iraq and Afghanistan has diminished.

One of the first promising initiatives to boost army learning was the creation in 2009 of the Lesson Exploitation Centre (LXC). Located within the Land Warfare Centre (LWC) and the brainchild of Maj. Gen. Andrew Kennett, then the director-general of land warfare, the new center was to enhance the lessons-learned process within the British Army: to identify, analyze, disseminate, and track lessons from the field. It would go on to assess the utility of predeployment training (through a review process occurring "immediately after training and six weeks into deployment") and act as a repository for postoperation reports and interviews with commanders across the ranks. Since its inception, the LXC has come to involve international partners in its search for salient lessons. In 2010, it began disseminating four-page briefs to deployed troops to communicate the "tactical lessons which require implementation"—in other words, fusing the field and the institution in a continuous cycle of learning.[45]

Some months after its establishment, the LXC was conferred added hierarchical weight through the establishment of the Force Development and Training (FDT) Command. Modeled on the US Training and Doctrine Command, the FDT was established as a three-star command responsible for overseeing the capture of lessons from ongoing operations, the development of new concepts and doctrine, and the provision of training and new equipment to deploying units. In its responsibilities, the FDT is central to the army's modernization, providing one focal point for all aspects inherent to change. As such, the command comprises four components: Royal Military Academy Sandhurst; the LWC (including the LXC); Army Recruiting and Training; and Logistics, Support, and Equipment.[46]

Though it is too early to assess its full impact, the FDT Command represents a radical top-down effort at turning the British Army into more of a "learning organization." Already within its first years, Gen. Paul Newton, the first FDT commander, had institutionalized various measures to increase military learning and spur debate. Starting in 2010, the FDT introduced "mission exploitation," referred to by Gen. Newton as "the mother of all debriefs." As described by the general, mission exploitation meant that "every time a British brigade now comes back from Afghanistan, we debrief it in detail to squeeze every bit of insight out of it. . . . We put them together with the people who write the doctrine, who write the training and education courses, who do the recruiting, and with those in industry who design and build the equipment to try and shorten our decision cycle."[47] The FDT was also actively involved in a major annual planning exercise, Agile Warrior, designed to provide an "authoritative evidence-based analysis of future land-force requirements."[48] Part of Agile Warrior was the Urban Warrior exercises, used to identify the army capabilities required for complex, urban operations—the type of environment forecast in the *Future Character of Conflict* and one not too dissimilar to the environment encountered in Iraq.[49]

A third notable innovation was the Afghan COIN Centre (ACC), also established in 2009 as part of the LWC to "develop new doctrine and tactics and to educate soldiers and their civilian counterparts in current thinking" on counterinsurgency and stability operations.[50] The initiative restored an old British "counterinsurgency tradition," as similar centers had been established during Britain's previous campaigns in Malaya, Kenya, and Northern Ireland. It also mimicked the approach taken by the US military, which had created a Counterinsurgency Center at Fort Leavenworth in 2006. Much like its American counterpart, the ACC produced publications, hosted and attended conferences, and engaged in outreach. It was also mandated to gather best practices from a range of studies and actors; to develop tactical doctrine and advise on operational doctrine based on said practices; and to promote and inform military education on the topic of counterinsurgency.[51] To its proponents, the center had "focused our thinking about [counterinsurgency]" in Afghanistan and beyond.[52]

Another of the ACC's functions was to help populate Army Knowledge Exchange (AKX), an online classified site set up by the LWC's Land Warfare Development Group in early 2010 to provide troops with the latest material on and a forum where to discuss ongoing land operations. AKX provided an easy way of collecting and disseminating the publications produced by the emerging lessons-learned organizations, including the main findings of the FDT's mission-exploitation exercises. By February 2011, AKX was receiving "more than 2,000 hits each day and usage [was] growing rapidly."[53] Later that year, an unclassified version of the site was launched, bringing together a broader community of soldiers and civil servants.

These and other steps denote army innovation in research and operational assessment. Indeed, the construction of a lessons-learned structure within the army is arguably the most high-profile success story of British institutional learning since its rediscovery of counterinsurgency. Of course, not all of these structures were created with counterinsurgency in mind, but they seek to prepare soldiers for the complexities of the future battlefield, many of which (but by no account all) were also present in Basra and Helmand and typify what Gen. Rupert Smith has famously referred to as "wars among the people."[54]

Yet although these instances of innovation are important, it is uncertain whether they will be sufficient or sufficiently sustained to prepare the organization for the "future character of conflict," as defined by the MoD. Some argue that the focus in these new structures is too tactical, too "enemy centered," and that the analysis therefore does not break substantively enough from the army's own comfort zone.[55] Whatever the merits of this charge, the relevant organizations cannot but constitute a first important, although in itself insufficient, step along the way. As Anthony King has noted, "Major innovations need more than lessons learnt changes; it requires fundamental reorientation. It needs a reforming concept which unites and impels changes at every level and it needs a leading group to have this idea and to drive it through."[56] King goes on to identify a group of reform-minded senior officers who have had an effect on the institution that is wholly disproportionate to their number. Despite their best efforts, however, it is disconcerting to see how badly such innovation sits with other and notably broader trends within the armed services.

First, the measures highlighted earlier were established only after a combined nine years of engagement with a new, unfamiliar, and highly challenging operating environment. By the time the FDT really got off the ground,

British soldiers had long left southern Iraq, and British politicians were already preparing for a withdrawal from Afghanistan. Second, efforts geared at learning, both institutional and individual, also tended to be understaffed and struggled to affect the main muscle of the organization. Despite the many challenges faced in Afghanistan, the ACC, for example, was given only a staff of nine and faced a constant struggle to retain its modest funding and fill its posts.[57] One wonders what will happen to the ACC as the Afghanistan campaign comes to a close. The FDT is undoubtedly on firmer ground, yet it was a matter of some internal debate whether the organization's many initiatives would survive Gen. Newton's retirement from the army in 2012—that so many did was certainly not taken for granted, but rather celebrated, given the context.

The context of course has much to do with funding constraints—the stock answer for why these types of initiatives only rarely got off the ground. A lack of funds was the reason given for the early termination of the Defence Academy's Advanced Research and Assessment Group (ARAG), founded in 2005. ARAG conducted research and analysis on a range of geostrategic and operational issues so as to influence the development of defense and security capability. It also contributed to doctrine, instructed deploying units, taught statecraft and governance, and comprised a roster of experts with specific and rare linguistic skills and academic knowledge. Finally, the group managed the Defence Academy Reserve Cadre, a thirty-five-strong unit of Reserve Force personnel with civilian and linguistic skills relevant to emerging threats and opportunities. Plans were also in the making for a Cultural Institute, led by ARAG, to provide open-source analysis of culture-relevant issues, develop curricula on these topics, and provide a focal point for cultural experts from various backgrounds.[58] To its proponents, ARAG offered the MoD invaluable intellectual capital, yet despite its modest annual budget of £1.5 million the unit did not survive. Some have pointed to a possible back story involving poor leadership, a muddled mandate, or simply "internal politics"; regardless, no attempt was made to reform ARAG or to establish an equivalent deemed more functional. The net result, therefore, was a continued shortage of staff and centers to conduct the type of analysis so often needed in expeditionary operational environments.

Other similarly oriented programs shared the same fate, resulting in the further weakening of the MoD's intellectual backbone. The army's Defence Fellowships program, which had enabled promising soldiers to spend a year conducting research at the United Kingdom's leading civilian universities, has "largely fallen into abeyance" and relies now on "the charity of individual commanders to find funding 'at risk' to their own budget."[59] Some of the few officers awarded these fellowships—notably Col. Alexander Alderson in 2008 and Col. Richard Iron in 2010—have tended to go on to play major roles in the transformation of the army, but they are also exceptions to the rule. Indeed, because postgraduate education increasingly has to occur at an officer's own time and without any clear institutional reward, the British Army boasts a far smaller proportion of officers with advanced postgraduate degrees than does the American army.[60] In terms of institutional innovation, this distinction is notable since the US Army's "soldier scholars" have played a disproportionate role in transforming this institution and its conduct of operations.[61] In contrast, in 2009 the Defence Academy's research capability was halved. Further contributing to an absence of deep specialist expertise within the armed services was the reduction in the Defence Intelligence Staff and the removal of many Defence Attaché posts.[62] By 2011, the Modular Master's Programme was terminated; the army had previously used this program to help pay for several soldiers' master's degrees, and it had resulted in closer ties between the military and academia. The program's cancellation shocked many of those concerned with military education, given its comparatively low cost and high impact, along with the MoD's own long-standing rhetoric about the need for an "educated soldiery" able to grapple with the complex and uncertain challenges of tomorrow.[63]

It is undeniable that the MoD was facing a challenging financial situation. In 2009, the National Audit Office reported on an estimated gap of between £6 billion and £36 billion in the defense budget over the next decade, depending on Britain's overall financial health.[64] Even then, the targeting of educational initiatives and structures belied the MoD's particular prioritization—to wit, that the benefits of the related institutions did not justify the comparatively small monetary outlay they required. By and large, such funding was allowed to subsist only so long as there were spare funds. In contrast, the MoD was in no shortage of other, more expensive programs that were underperforming, experiencing delays, or outright failing, yet that were far less likely to be cut.[65] Within this type of environment, and given the ever-shrinking horizons of what is financially possible, it is uncertain whether even the FDT Command, the most promising manifestation of institutional learning, will be able to fulfill its ambitious programs and potential.

RADICAL CHANGE FOR A CONSERVATIVE ORGANIZATION

To understand the conflicted nature of institutional reform, it is necessary to go beyond monetary factors. Monetary prioritization reflects institutional prioritization, so there being insufficient funds often stems from choices taken backstage or by default. In the case of the British military, resource allocation reflected the political and cultural/bureaucratic environment of the institution at this time, both of which militated against change and require closer scrutiny.

From the outset, it became more important politically for the British government to project success in its military operations than to identify errors and correct what had gone wrong. The Iraq War was always divisive for the Labour government, and when the situation in Basra deteriorated, a major priority was not to allow the perception of failure to inflame an already fractious debate. The specter of embarrassing headlines or of providing fodder to the political opposition ensured that admissions of fault were rare, which in turn stifled the debate and blocked attempts at reform. Curiously, in this regard, the success of Operation Charge of the Knights had a perverse side effect in that it allowed some leaders to use its propitious outcome to validate the campaign as a whole. Glossed over in this narrative were the relatively minor role played by the British armed forces in turning things around and the major problems affecting the British campaign in the previous five years.

The need to present an image of success extended to the military, where it contributed to self-censorship. Here, senior-level fear of undermining the political leadership at Whitehall combined with lower-level fear of harming one's career or deviating from a deeply hierarchical order. Opportunities for frank communication were rare: former brigade commanders were discouraged from speaking publicly of their experiences in the field, and there were few outlets where reform could be discussed. High-level conferences organized to discuss lessons learned in the field were characterized by some reform-minded officers as "exercises in complacency," focusing on technical nuts-and-bolts issues (e.g., air–ground integration, resupply) rather than on more significant capability gaps.[66] At most, the debate on ongoing operations and the acknowledgment of errors occurred behind closed doors and was otherwise kept at a minimum.

It has been suggested that the fifth column setting this particular mood of conservatism and censure is the middle tier of bureaucrats within the army and the MoD. In the words of one two-star general with responsibilities that include reforming the army for future challenges, there is an "unpleasant amount of institutional inertia" and a "stifling process of scrutiny and approval which engenders the most appalling delays."[67] To David Betz, the problem is "the thick band of bureaucratic cellulite composed largely of colonels and brigadiers which basically defies change, protects privilege, and is essentially about process and not result."[68] Added to this force for continuity is the "time-serving civil servants," who to some reform-minded senior officers "have little understanding or sympathy for what the army has to do on the ground, and whose main objective is to spare embarrassment (supposedly to ministers, but also to themselves) and extra work."[69] Thus, reform-minded officers coming back from the field who seek to bring about change have found themselves mired in process, and the handful of senior generals seeking to push the organization in the right direction face unexpected resistance.

As one example of this trend, it took determined internal lobbying to get the *British Army Review* to devote merely a part of one issue to the Basra campaign. The issue was to feature five articles assessing the conduct of operations in Basra, yet for this very reason its release encountered institutional resistance from within. Despite the fact that access to the journal is already restricted to the army, just two articles ended up being published, and both were subjected to close scrutiny—even censorship—by the MoD; three other articles, deemed too critical, were dismissed. This episode contrasts with the liberty afforded US officers to discuss the US military's conduct of operations in professional journals and with the openness of the US discussion on counterinsurgency as a whole, be it on blogs or community websites.[70] Indeed, it is curious that the MoD insists on restricting access to *British Army Review* to the armed forces at all. According to a statement in 2009 by the MoD director of media and communication at the time, the restriction is in place to prevent the British media from misusing or mischaracterizing the internal debate—to "avoid giving such propaganda gifts to the enemy."[71] Even if one acknowledges the peculiar bloodthirstiness of some of the British press, it must still be asked why US equivalents such as the army's *Military Review* and *Parameters* are able to remain open source and readily accessible on the Internet. The MoD's insistence in restricting access to these types of publications gives the impression of a closed intellectual environment or one where fear of criticism and public "outings" has overridden the need for open debate.

In combination, the political climate and institutional obstacles help explain the generally slow pace of reform. Astonishingly, this slowness has persisted despite vocal, senior-level appeals for change. In January 2009, Chief of the General Staff Richard Dannatt noted that "we must address the way in which our Army is structured, equipped, trained and motivated if we are to ensure that we remain relevant."[72] His successor, Sir David Richards, argued that "we must be capable of being among the people" and that the army needed more "interpreters, cultural experts, intelligence officers, CIMIC [civil–military cooperation]."[73] The problem was in giving substance to these words—or, more accurately, in gaining institutional acceptance for them even when they threatened traditional priorities. Hence, the need for such efforts as Gen. David Richards' Operation Entirety: an attempt in mid-2009 to get the army as a whole actually to focus on the ongoing war in Afghanistan. Although in many ways successful, even this effort (instigated by the chief of the general staff) ultimately struggled to overcome the systemic resistance to change: it remained largely unfunded, and its proposed changes were in any case designed to be reversible.[74] Absent was a more fundamental reworking of priorities that would mirror in scale what Gen. Richards characterized as his generation's "horse and tank moment."[75]

TWEAKS VERSUS CHANGE

Given this environment and the difficulty of sustaining deep-rooted change even in training and education, it should not be a surprise that more ambitious reforms struggled to get off the ground. Both in the MoD's budget allocation and the army's force structure, policy appeared to assume that the challenges experienced in Iraq and Afghanistan were aberrational and avoidable and should therefore not inform policy. This disconnect is a key indicator of organizational innovation since the structure and budget of an armed force indicate the types of missions for which it is primarily intended.

In terms of force structure, the innovative proposals of various reform-minded leaders tended not to have much effect. As chief of the general staff, Gen. Dannatt directed the army to explore the creation of specialized units dedicated to training and advisory missions, a central yet challenging facet of counterinsurgency operations.[76] To Dannatt, these "stabilization units" were to "be capable of both fighting alongside local forces, and delivering reconstruction and development tasks in areas where the civil agencies cannot operate" and to "form the spine of our enduring cultural education and understanding." Dannatt also spearheaded the Transforming to Contact initiative, which was to "*optimise* the One Star Brigade level for Stabilisation Operations" yet retain the ability to task organize for conventional combat within a divisional framework.[77]

Despite Dannatt's personal support as chief of the general staff, these efforts were only partially implemented and did not in the end enhance the army's suitability for counterinsurgency or other complex campaigns. Specialized units for training and advisory missions have not emerged; the army's approach to selecting trainers and advisers has instead remained "mostly ad hoc or based on availability," with no concerted effort being made "to pinpoint individuals with advisory experience or time in country."[78] More broadly, despite an ongoing process of force-structural reform, the requirements of ongoing operations did not inform the changes under way. Instead, reforms aimed narrowly at making the army more deployable or, later, at increasing dwell-time between tours for individual soldiers—important undertakings, but that do little to enhance the force's structural suitability for the operations it was asked to conduct.

In terms of force sizing, troop numbers had been a constant concern both in Iraq and Afghanistan. It is easy to see how this issue would confront the army in future campaigns, particularly if these campaigns were to include "enduring stabilisation operation[s] at around brigade level" (as forecast in the 2010 *Strategic Defence and Security Review*, or *SDSR*).[79] Size in these types of campaigns is not in itself strategically decisive, but as the British forces found in Basra and Helmand, the effects of *undermanning* a stabilization effort are often severe. It is therefore strange that despite the ongoing campaigns in Iraq and Afghanistan *and* the need to prepare for brigade-level engagements elsewhere, the army reforms during this period consistently advocated incremental *decreases* to the force's end strength. The first cut came in 2003 with the Future Army Structure program, by which the army's forty single-battalion regiments were to be reorganized into twelve large infantry regiments. This shift's net effect on the army's size was a cut of 1,500 personnel (to 102,000), most of which came from the infantry, which lost four of its forty battalions.

If a cut in infantry and in end strength in 2003 appears out of touch with the challenges then confronted in Iraq or with the army's ability to conduct complex campaigns in the future, it is because such concerns were not the main focus of the reform. Instead, the idea was to create a smaller yet more deployable military for "better targeted action and *swifter* outcomes."[80] In its language and assumptions, the initiative borrowed from the US military's program of "force transformation," which posited modern technology and emerging information capabilities as future war winners and by whose logic large land armies for protracted engagement were no longer needed.[81] For Britain, this approach meant fewer infantry and greater investment in over-the-horizon defense capabilities.

The damage was in a sense doubled because the modern technological capabilities that were to compensate for the reduced manpower were too ambitious to be delivered on time. The 2003 White Paper envisaged self-sustaining networked brigades structured around the emerging Future Rapid Effects System (FRES). As originally intended, FRES would mirror the US Army's Future Combat System: both were predicated on "network-enabled" technology; both involved a series of vehicles joined through such a network; and both emphasized lethality, lightness, and deployability above survivability, mass, and protection. Both fatefully also stumbled due to their infatuation with emerging technology, which resulted in skyrocketing costs and serious delays. As a result, the British Army lost strength while missing out on the capabilities that, in theory, were to compensate for this shrinkage. Seven Challenger tank squadrons (around one hundred tanks) were phased out, even though there was no FRES-based equivalent to take their place. Four infantry battalions were cut, but there was never a technological equivalent to make up for this loss.

The disconnect between reforms and ongoing operations is also evident in the explicit assumption of Future Army Structures that expeditionary activity would decline, beginning with the drawdown from Northern Ireland. This prediction did not square with the several overseas engagements, excluding Iraq, that the army was then involved in and also ran counter to the prediction in the 2003 White Paper that the British Army would be "frequently employed on peace support and counter-terrorist operations where the focus will be on conflict prevention and stabilization."[82] Rather than inform force sizing, such contingencies and the ongoing Iraq campaign were treated as aberrational.

Nor were these cuts reversed as the complexity of ongoing operations manifested itself. In the United States in 2004, the Pentagon was authorized to increase total end strength by 36,000 troops—a temporary measure to alleviate the strains of a heightened operational tempo. In 2007, US Secretary of Defense Robert Gates instated a more permanent increase to address the shortfall in ground troops for the Iraq and Afghanistan campaigns. No similar action was taken in the United Kingdom. Instead, despite the *SDSR*'s language about brigade-size stabilization campaigns, it also cut the army—this time by a further 7,000 troops. It was initially pledged that the combat units in Afghanistan would not be affected by these cuts, yet this guarantee was merely a temporary and politically motivated reprieve that simply postponed further reductions. Indeed, leaks to the press in February 2011 suggested that given the financial crisis, the army was to be cut to 82,000 following the withdrawal from Afghanistan. In the end, the respite lasted only until July 2010.[83]

These cuts were given intellectual foundation in various policy papers that suggested an imbalance in the British armed services in favor of the army. According to Malcolm Chalmers, "By 2015, land forces will account for around 65% of total service personnel, compared with current levels of around 55% in the US and France, 53% in Canada, and 50% in Australia."[84] The analysis was influential but problematic. First, as highlighted on the blog *Think Defence*, these types of calculations vary greatly depending on which units are included.[85] Second, talk of balance suggests the need for equality between the services, but these decisions should not be "about equal pain . . . or some vague notion of equity and fairness"; "they should be about strategic effect."[86] In that sense, one wonders why force ratios derived from other countries should be relevant to UK defense planning assumptions. Also, the notion of returning to a "normal" proportion, one established prior to the most recent campaigns, appears somewhat suspect because it suggests that none of the lessons from these campaigns—of how to achieve strategic effect or of the troop numbers required to do so—had been noted.

Indeed, it is difficult to see how a force of 82,000 might deploy and sustain a brigade-size campaign when the larger, pre-*SDSR* army struggled to meet this very requirement. According to a study published by the RAND Corporation, the British Army of January 2008 comprised 98,510 full-time personnel, 3,290 less than its total required strength.[87] A typical battalion would at this point be 10–20 percent short of its intended strength.[88] At this strength, and given the operational tempo of the Afghan campaign, the MoD's Harmony Guidelines were being systematically breached: by these guidelines, no more than 20 percent of army personnel are to be deployed with less than twenty-four months of dwell time.[89] Such breaches and the strains on the force that they impose would only be more severe in a 20 percent smaller force. Whether the Harmony Guidelines remain a suitable benchmark for a wartime military is in itself a worthwhile question and arguably another indication of peacetime orthodoxy lagging behind the demands of ongoing operations.[90] Regardless, at a force of 82,000, recent issues with troop numbers will only be accentuated.

With Army 2020, the army's modernization plan of 2012, the figure of 80,000 was confirmed, making the British Army the smallest it has been in more than a century. In this latest iteration of the army's plans for the future, it was hoped the small size of the active force would, when needed, be complemented by the Army Reserve, which was to be boosted to a strength of 30,000. This effort to counteract the effect of some of the cuts to the active force is laudable but raises new questions of how this new reservist force is to be recruited, equipped, trained, and prepared. As argued on the blog *Think Defence*, this process will require substantial funds, probably more than the £180 million per year allocated to it per Army 2020—all of which raises the additional question of whether this solution is viable and will stick.[91] If not, and if the assumptions do not hold, the army will, due to its new size, be seriously circumscribed in what it can do.

Besides growing the force, another means of increasing the availability of troops is to extend the length of tours, either for headquarters staff or for combat troops or for both. Throughout the Iraq operation and for most of the Afghanistan campaign, every member of the armed forces—regardless of rank or function—served on a six-month tour. The frequent rotations led to a lack of command continuity and theater familiarity, which produced an approach often fractured in style and substance. Frank Ledwidge describes how in both Iraq and Afghanistan tasks whose completion required more than six months were downgraded in favor of "quick wins."[92] In recent years, the MoD has begun to recognize this problem and extended the tour length for some senior commanders and headquarters staff in Afghanistan to as much as a year.[93] If Britain truly wants to be an expeditionary power, there may also be a need to revisit the tour lengths of deployed soldiers and civilians. These types of decisions are clearly never easy because longer tours strain the force—those deployed and their families—yet they can also be necessary. In the United States, Robert Gates's first decision as secretary of defense was to extend US Army tours from twelve to fifteen months so as to increase the availability of deployable forces. Gates would later look back at this measure as "perhaps my most difficult decision over the past four years."[94] In Britain, by contrast, the ring-fenced six-month tour has undermined the army's effectiveness as an expeditionary actor, at least in protracted campaigns. It certainly makes it difficult to draw parallels between today's force and that which established the British Army's counterinsurgency credentials in Malaya, where tours would commonly be twenty-four months long.[95] Of course, there is no going back to the army of the 1950s, but nor has an alternative solution been found to the problem of sustaining a presence abroad. So far, a peacetime rotational policy has prevailed.

Nor has the British Army adapted much in terms of its force structure. Some rebalancing was seen in 2004–2005, when 500 of the 2,000 infantry cut were reinvested in support roles—such as engineers, logisticians, and intelligence personnel—found to be valuable in a counterinsurgency environment.[96] At the same time, the fact that these additions were drawn from the infantry, another prized counterinsurgency asset, puts the net utility of this reform into doubt. Indeed, the infantry trade is one of the army's so-called pinch points, an area where demand significantly exceeds supply, and between July 2008 and August 2009 the deficit in manning this role grew from 8.5 percent to 10.6 percent. In effect, one hole was dug to fill another.[97]

Beyond this rebalancing, most changes have focused on enabling smoother army rotations rather than creating new capabilities. The focus on rotational policy was essential, given the demands placed on a relatively small force operating on six-month tours. For the conduct of operations once in the field, however, it would have been equally, if not more important to focus on strengthening those capabilities needed in theater: military police, trainers and advisers, linguists, medical units, engineers, and those specializing in civil and public affairs, law enforcement, human intelligence, and countering improvised explosive devices.[98] An insufficient number of personnel in these trades has not only undercut the British Army's expeditionary effectiveness but put tremendous strain on those soldiers who do have the needed skills—a strain that various reforms to force structure have failed to address. As the National Audit Office and the Foreign Affairs Select Committee have noted, the number of trades considered "pinch points" increased by 15.4 percent between 2004 and 2008 and included ammunition technicians, information system engineers, recovery mechanics, explosive ordnance disposal (EOD) technicians, and medical staff.[99] Troubled by these "pinch points," the MoD classified the relevant figures in 2010, but data obtained in 2009 by the *Independent* show shortfalls in medical staff, helicopter pilots, and EOD ranging anywhere from 17 to 72 percent.[100] The shortfall in EOD is particularly disconcerting given that homemade bombs at the time accounted for almost 80 percent of British casualties in Helmand.[101]

Addressing these shortfalls would help reform the army's force structure in line with the ongoing operations, but it would be only a first step, given the unexpectedly broad range of tasks foisted on the armed forces in today's operations and likely in future land campaigns. In an article for *British Army Review*, Maj. A. R. Pitt points to one example—namely, "the inability of Defence to establish a properly resourced and credible media operations capability despite repeatedly identifying it as a critical operational gap, including in Afghanistan, Iraq and Kosovo."[102] There are other examples: Does the army have sufficient expertise with human intelligence, civil affairs, influence operations, culture, language, and civil–military cooperation at the battle-group level and below?

Similarly, has the army fully thought through the force-structure implications of an enduring shortfall in civilian capacity in the field? The Stabilisation Unit is certainly an improvement on its predecessor, the PCRU, but the problem of capacity remains. Furthermore, even with the right capacity, civil–military coordination is still likely to be found lacking. In part, it is a matter of timelines: in Afghanistan, civilians spend one to three years on a PRT, with two weeks off every six weeks, which effectively means they are in theater for only 75 percent of a six-month army tour. Because of their different timelines, the civilian and the soldier will also have different horizons for when progress must be achieved.[103] This may be one reason why Keith Mackiggan, the head of the Basra PRT in 2008–2009, noted in his testimony to the Iraq Inquiry that despite great progress in building up a civilian stabilization capacity, "the organisational cultural differences between different departments make me wonder whether there isn't still a need for some kind of hybrid civil/military capacity in Whitehall, which we don't yet have."[104]

The latter conundrum—the lack of a workable and deployable civil–military force—is compounded by the military's institutional reluctance to engage in "civilian activities." For many years in Iraq, the British military resisted engaging with various civilian aspects of the mission—surveying electricity substations, rubbish collection, the provision of water—probably because it was felt that these tasks should be conducted by civilians.[105] Similarly in the

SDSR, military responsibilities are clearly limited to *"providing security* for stabilization,"[106] whereas in Helmand it was the PRT, not the military, that "owned" the governance and development "lines of operation." In theory, this division of labor appears to conform to the view of the soldier as a war fighter and the civilian as concerned with everything else. In practice, soldiering has often meant much more than war fighting, and there is typically a need for far greater flexibility. This is particularly the case where insecurity is prevalent, the number of civilians limited, and the military operates across a significantly larger area of operations.[107] Given the difficulties faced in rectifying this problem, the army may very well find itself without civilian support in future campaigns, and where this is the case, it would only jeopardize mission objectives for the military to stay intransigently within its own narrow lane. Rather than refuse on principle to adapt to this reality, the military might want to consider reforming its force structure in line with likely tasks and responsibilities so as not to fall into the capability gap with the next deployment. So far there have been few signs of such change.

ALL THINGS TO ALL PEOPLE

The coexistence of superficial change against a backdrop of deep-rooted continuity has one underlying reason: the British military has not allowed a decade of engagement in counterinsurgency or its expectations for operations of similar complexity to affect its institutional self-perception and understanding. Instead, the British military has remained committed to and hamstrung by a deep-rooted contradiction—namely, that of building a technologically advanced and globally deployable force without the means necessary to do so and while allocating substantial resources toward ongoing operations. It is a contradiction built on three flawed premises: first, that the operations in Iraq and Afghanistan were aberrational and should not inform policy; second, that the British government has the financial foundation to build a first-rate military with global reach; and, finally, that its institutional concentration on major combat operations will not compromise its ability to conduct stabilization and counterinsurgency in the future. The effects of these premises converging should now be clear. The British military's finite means have been spent on building an advanced force that not only is unsustainable from a financial perspective and has had to be cut, but that is also incapable of following through effectively on whatever battlefield victories it can claim. Meanwhile, the deployed military does not receive the institutional support that it feels it deserves.

What is curious about British military modernization is that the grand plan underpinning it remained virtually unchanged despite a sea change in the political, strategic, and fiscal environment in which it was pursued. Absent during this time was a truly strategic process of identifying what type of armed forces Britain wants, can have, and is willing to pay for. Many policy stances were instead unquestioningly perpetuated while claiming vast sums of money at a substantial opportunity cost in terms of reform. The corrective steps taken to address the gap between extant and needed capabilities typically took the form of improvisational fixes, and their long-term effects were rarely fully thought through.

How is one to understand the origins of this dilemma? Much can be explained by two parallel developments in the 1990s. First, the increased frequency of British experiences with "peace enforcement" during the 1990s fostered overoptimistic expectations for expeditionary interventions to come. With the end of the Cold War, Britain was reinventing itself and its role internationally. Operations in the Balkans and Sierra Leone appeared to provide reassuring evidence of Britain's untarnished status as a great power with global reach. Second, influential sections of the British military concluded from the Iraq War in 1991 and the Balkan bombing campaigns that precision-guided munitions and other emerging capabilities would be decisive in future interventions. The MoD therefore sought to follow the United States through the vaunted revolution in military affairs, which by the turn of the century had resulted in wholesale institutional acceptance of concepts such as "effects-based operations" and "network-enabled capabilities" as well as ambitious plans for defense modernization.

Optimism about the British capability to intervene effectively and about the potential of emerging technology resulted in grandiose statements about Britain's role in the world. Politically, it fueled an ambitious "doctrine of international community": a vision of Britain as actively involved in underwriting global order, also through military means. On this very point, in 2002 Defense Secretary Geoff Hoon spoke confidently of "proactive military intervention," whereby Britain would engage its "enemies in their backyard" and "at a time and place of our choosing."[108] Little thought went into the full requirements of these interventions because, based on a partial reading of past "peace operations," they appeared minor or at least manageable. Also overlooked was the costliness of the required modernization, the strictly limited application of its main assets to strike operations, and the need to invest in a different range of capabilities for protracted land-based campaigns. Instead, excessive confidence about the British role in the world allowed ambitions to soar—without a concomitant increase in the defense budget. Yes, the British defense budget increased in 1998–2008 for the longest sustained period since the 1980s, but as a proportion of gross domestic product (GDP) it actually declined from 2.57 percent to 2.47 percent, as compared with 4.05 percent at the end of the Cold War.[109] As Anthony Forster points out, "The cost of adapting the force structure toward expeditionary warfare—but keeping previously approved procurement programmes that did not meet current operational requirements—has been consistently underestimated."[110]

Rather than increase the defense budget or, better still, revisit the assumptions behind this type of modernization, the tendency has been to find "solutions" that avoid the substance of the problem. One "solution" has been to delay overly ambitious orders or to make cuts in the number of platforms ordered. In several cases, such delays have resulted in temporary savings but later costs. As detailed in the *Review of Acquisition* authored by Bernard Gray in October 2009, on average programs end up costing 40 percent more and are delivered 80 percent later than originally expected.[111] A more dramatic example is the armored vehicle for FRES: by 2010, more than ten years of investment and a total of £255 million had been dedicated to this vehicle, a critical component in the army's modernization into a networked, deployable, and more lethal force, yet the vehicle had not even left the drawing board.[112]

FRES is an interesting case because it represents the military's willingness to pour increasingly sparse funds into a capability for predominantly "conventional" settings,[113] all while its army, the principal user of the armored vehicle, was fighting and instructed to prepare for future complex operations against "asymmetric" or "irregular" adversaries. In his written evidence to the Iraq Inquiry, Lord Paul Drayson, who between 2007 and 2009 was the minister of state for defense equipment and support, made the mismatch explicit: "The impression I gained was that delivery of FRES by 2012 was a higher priority for the Army than finding funding for a replacement for [soft-skinned] SNATCH [land rovers] from the core equipment budget."[114] In the end, the FRES vehicle class was split into three, whereof some would be bulkier so as to withstand the threats of roadside bombs and rocket-propelled grenades. But given that the program was nonetheless badly delayed and had exceeded its budget, the modification was insufficient in addressing the needs of the soldiers on the ground, with the standard and availability of armored vehicles being one of the recurring complaints from the field.[115] Also, by bulking up the FRES vehicles, the notion of transportability on C-130s was abandoned, which had been one of the system's chief selling points. In the end, lack of strategic thinking had resulted in wasted money, delayed procurement of armored vehicles at a time of two wars, and a final compromise solution that fulfilled neither side's demands.[116]

This backdrop has to be considered when one speaks of the MoD's budgetary crisis. As former chief of the general staff General Sir Michael Jackson has put it, "Large procurement cost overruns in the past have been rather meekly accepted to the detriment of spending on personnel and training."[117] This tendency helps explain the gaps in the preparation and equipping of soldiers detailed throughout this chapter. In late 2009, for example, concerns about the army's manpower budget resulted in cuts to army recruitment and training (saving £2 million in that financial year) and to various upgrades to housing (saving £14 million).[118] In a fiscally restrictive environment, the tendency has been to shuffle or delay funding rather than to reconsider the strategic rationale behind inherited investment patterns. In that regard, as defense analyst Nick Ritchie has put it, the *SDSR* "missed a crucial opportunity to challenge prevailing assumptions about what defence and security mean for British citizens in a post-9/11 era of complex globalization."[119]

A second "solution" for the gap between ambitions and means were the UOR orders of equipment found to be needed in theater. These orders were often presented as indications of institutional flexibility, and they clearly have been critical in bringing weapons systems and protection to the field.[120] Yet on a deeper level the UOR system suffers from the same problems as other ad hoc solutions. Specifically, it illustrates that while the MoD spent its intellectual energy and finite budget on high-tech systems that it had trouble fielding or finding a use for in the modern battlefield, it had underinvested in the basic gear needed for wars as they presented themselves.[121] This is not to deny the point made by Defense Secretary John Hutton in 2010, that "you cannot necessarily plan for all of the detail of the campaign reality . . . as part of your core equipment programme."[122] Nevertheless, not only are the requirements of sustained operations in a hostile environment fairly predictable, but even if prior ignorance can be excused, the lack of a more genuine realignment of priorities once the difficulties had presented themselves is rather surprising. As Lord Drayson explains, the MoD resisted such reprioritization "because the services were concerned that their long term programmes would be cannibalized and lose funding to short term operational needs."[123] Or, in the words of former Chief of Defense Procurement Sir Peter Spencer, there was a fear of the "fratricidal effect" that realignments would have on long-term defense programs.[124]

The UOR system also raises the question of what will happen to the purchased capabilities once the urgency diminishes. Funding that has come through the Treasury must then be integrated as part of MoD expenditures, which produces inevitable trade-offs between competing priorities. The MoD announced it had absorbed about £50 million worth of UOR equipment into the core budget in 2010: what equipment is classified, but it is thought to include vehicles and communications and logistics equipment.[125] Even then, this figure pales in comparison to the £4.2 billion spent on UOR orders by March 2009 alone.[126] Clearly, most of the *urgently needed* equipment bought in this manner will be mothballed or left behind in theater, which places the British military in a precarious position for the future "enduring stabilisation operation" stipulated by the *SDSR*.[127] The manner in which this kit was acquired and now left behind has also done nothing to help finance those conventional combat-oriented platforms for which initial investment in mission-relevant gear was sacrificed.

* * *

Any attempt to assess UK military innovation during the Iraq and Afghan wars will inevitably present a mixed picture. In several areas, the institutional prioritization has changed and come to emphasize the challenges of counter-insurgency operations: doctrine has been published; training exercises have been adapted; and education now focuses more on counterinsurgency than it has for a long time. Yet, in more fundamental ways, ten years of engagement in Afghanistan and Iraq have changed very little: in its structure and resource allocation, the military is still seeking a conventional superiority that provides few advantages in the more complex contemporary operating environment and that ill prepares the armed forces for the types of campaigns that the MoD itself anticipates.

The implication here is that the MoD has wished to retain the foundations of the force but bend it temporarily for the purposes of today's campaigns. This process of bringing new capabilities and skills in from the margins, yet without changing the main text has resulted in unhappy compromises and capability gaps. In many cases, the latter have been addressed through fixes and ad hoc solutions, which, however successful they may be (and the record here is decidedly mixed), do not provide the long-term institutionalization required for learning.

Such institutionalization may just be a matter of time. By 2009, one can see the early signs of a more ambitious reorientation—in the standing up of the FDT Command, the ACC, and the launch of other similarly oriented efforts. At the same time, several factors are militating against longer-term change. First, the MoD has not been open culturally to the need for change, and it will therefore be difficult to sustain the momentum required for longer-term innovation. Second, there is (in part for this reason) still a sense that counter-insurgency and stability operations have been grafted on as added priorities to an institution that still believes conventional primacy will see it through. Absent is the type of reprioritization that would suggest a more deep-rooted effort of change: in how the military structures and educates its forces and prepares them for deployment. Third, the British military is operating with shrinking resources, which will make it more difficult to pursue both new and entrenched priorities simultaneously; in the battle between the two, the latter has so far won, as services seek to defend their highest-profile capabilities regardless of their battlefield relevance and application.

For all of these reasons, it is insufficient to say that if we have not seen a strong institutional reaction to unforeseen challenges to date, we can expect the UK armed services to get there in the end. Instead, it appears more likely that over the long term much of the marginal and incremental progress made to date will be reversed, particularly when the operations galvanizing such change are concluded and the perceived need for the corresponding capabilities disappears. The question is how this reversal will affect the future of the British military as a counterinsurgency force—or as a force able to deploy and sustain a force in the field.

5

WHITHER BRITISH COUNTERINSURGENCY?

LEARNING FROM EXPERIENCE: WHAT WENT WRONG?

D URING THE COURSE of the past ten years, Britain has experienced significant difficulties in conducting counterinsurgency, both in southern Iraq and in Helmand Province, Afghanistan. Though the roots of operational frustration can be traced to deep-running problems at the political–military (or strategic) level, the armed forces have also struggled operationally and tactically to plan and conduct counterinsurgency operations in accordance with the resources provided. The military's ability to understand the local environment and its actors, to train and advise local security forces, and to partner with them on operations have too often been found wanting, as has its capacity for civil–military integration. In other words, few of the enabling factors that underpinned previous, successful British experiences with counterinsurgency still obtain. Lacking local or interagency partners, British forces either did too little and became irrelevant or aimed to do too much, which, when isolated and operating with limited numbers, rarely had the intended effect.

What do these two campaigns say about the British armed forces and their relation to counterinsurgency? What can we learn by studying the campaigns in Iraq and Afghanistan? Based on the analysis in this book, four major findings stand out.

First, the British failure during the early years to understand and adapt to the challenges of counterinsurgency should put to rest the notion of an innate or even particularly British competence in this field. It is not just that this type of "British counterinsurgency legacy" is inaccurate; it is highly unhelpful. Institutionally it created a false sense of confidence that obscured the need for active investment in order to develop and maintain the associated skills, while operationally it bred complacency, which impeded the rate of on-the-ground adaptation. The historical cases upon which the legacy is built are still highly relevant in terms of deriving principles and studying their implementation (particularly where this was done with some degree of success). Yet even when taken as a whole, these past exploits confer no enhanced ability to counter insurgencies across time and space.

This issue goes beyond the atrophy of skill and capability—which should rightly have been expected. As fundamentally, counterinsurgency itself has changed. Counterinsurgency is no longer conducted by an imperial power, in its colonies, and in support of established government, but by a coalition of increasingly cash-strapped states and in countries declared sovereign yet lacking the institutions of state power on which previous counterinsurgency campaigns rested. The counterinsurgency principles derived from past campaigns may still hold true, but their application in the field has, if anything, become more daunting.

Second, it follows that for those powers intent on intervention, the capability to conduct counterinsurgency needs to be carefully nurtured, developed, and sustained through active investment of finite resources. Although counterinsurgencies will always be difficult and no amount of institutional optimization will yield a master key, it should be clear that some level of preparation and readiness, based on the requirements identified in past and current campaigns, increases the likelihood of success. Operational adaptation, on which the British military has tended to rely, is an important means by which techniques and tactics can be developed in theater. Yet as recent history bears out, relying on operational adaptation risks squandering valuable time and opportunities at the early stage of the campaign, a crucial period in which to get things right (or for things to go badly wrong).[1] It is also a precarious form of learning: its distribution across the force is haphazard, and unless it is captured and institutionalized, it is likely to erode or disappear altogether between campaigns.

Third, it is clear from the experiences in Basra and Helmand that even the best military performance on the ground will reap few rewards unless it is complemented and sustained by political support and civilian resources. In Afghanistan, the limited troop numbers and overambitious strategic aims in a far too large an area of responsibility meant that there was never sufficient stability for development, reconstruction, and political reform to take place. In Basra, the British armed forces adapted to the increasingly unstable security environment by ramping up operations and seeking to regain the initiative. Yet without the necessary political support from Whitehall and even from within the MoD, these military operations were strictly limited in what they could achieve. In both campaigns, the lack of in-theater civilian government representatives and expertise undercut the prospect of sustainable progress and denuded the British campaign plan, such as it was, of some of its more critical facets.

Fourth, the British capacity for strategic thinking—its ability to formulate a campaign plan—has proved consistently and fatefully problematic throughout the last decade of operations. Strategy requires a clear alignment of ends, ways and means, prioritization, sequencing, and a theory of victory.[2] In contrast, strategy making for Basra and for Helmand was marked by the failure to grasp the nature of the campaign, to adapt once new realities came to the fore, and to resource these efforts, both politically and financially, to achieve a clearly established objective. To some degree, these shortcomings stemmed from Britain's status as a junior coalition partner, which both restricted its operational autonomy and tied its campaign to broader national-level decisions over which it had only so much control. Even so, there is no fig leaf large enough here to cover the deep flaws in the British government's own approach and conduct in these counterinsurgency campaigns.

THE WAY FORWARD: BEYOND "MUDDLING THROUGH"

Although this list of lessons and implications is sobering, despondency and paralysis are not an option. Instead, it is necessary to ask what the past decade means for the future of British counterinsurgency—and for British military intervention writ large. On the face of it, the notion of simply avoiding future "Iraqs" or "Afghanistans" may strike many observers as a logical reaction to recent operational difficulties. Taking this path acknowledges that although expeditionary counterinsurgency operations may have been historically appropriate during the years of empire, they are strictly ill suited to British society, the British government, and the British armed forces of today.[3] Yet there are three significant difficulties with this course of (non)action. First, it is uncertain whether Britain, given its history and self-perception, would be ready to delimit where and when it is able to deploy its troops. Drawing lines in the sand out of fear of repeating past traumas would reduce Britain's place in the world. It would become a country that stays out of the major campaigns of the day or imposes severe conditions on its participation. "Strategic abstinence" would effectively close the book on Britain's standing as a major world player with global reach as well as undermine its reputation as a reliable and top-tier military partner, both within Europe and the United States. Presented in such stark terms, this course of action is unlikely to be accepted for very long by British politicians or even by its electorate. In the words of Prime Minister David Cameron, "Britain has punched above its weight in the world, and we should have no less ambition for our country in the decades to come."[4]

The next option would be for Britain to retain a global role militarily but simply avoid "counterinsurgency," but here we confront a second problem with the strategy of aversion. This course of action seductively implies that a country can determine the evolution of its foreign military engagements and simply opt out where and whenever its preconditions no longer hold. History has not been kind to this type of interventionism—at the very least, it has jeopardized mission objectives. This lesson was learned most recently by the German troops stationed in northern Afghanistan, whose political constraints made them mere bystanders to the province's gradual destabilization.[5] Britain's own experiences in Basra and Helmand also provide cautionary tales: neither of these engagements was entered into with the intention of conducting counterinsurgency; instead, an environment initially deemed permissive evolved, and British troops adapted by engaging more coercively to ongoing developments. The alternative—not to react—might have protected

British troops in the short term, but it would have led to failure; indeed, this is in part what happened during the initial years in Basra. The broader point is that when the decision is taken to deploy troops to a conflict or "postconflict" environment, it becomes difficult to insist on operational conditions without having these very same prerequisites be manipulated by local actors or constrain the effectiveness of the intervention.[6]

Moreover, as noted in the introduction to this book, the challenges encountered in Iraq and Afghanistan are not unique to counterinsurgencies but are likely to characterize most expeditionary interventions that involve the use of ground forces. War is about politics, and politics is about people; it follows that war is intimately tied to the people over or among whom it is being fought. This relationship is only reinforced by the global trend of urbanization, which suggests that most operations will be conducted in built-up or at least inhabited environments, where the local population cannot be ignored but more often must be co-opted or even protected against attack. Also, although some analysts have declared "the end of expeditionary operations," it seems a safe bet that when Britain's armed forces are deployed, it will more often be abroad than at home.[7] As in Iraq and Afghanistan, this will mean grappling with the society, politics, culture, and languages of a foreign land. In such contexts, it is also likely that the UK military will, despite its recent cuts, nonetheless outgun its would-be adversaries, whose logical response will be to resort to guerrilla tactics and subterfuge—concealment among civilians, hit-and-run attacks, dispersion, and so on—so as to offset their military inferiority. Such adaptation is particularly likely if it is felt that the British forces are unable to respond effectively to insurgent attack, due either to a lack of preparation or to political direction to avoid "another Iraq." Suddenly the key challenges of Iraq of Afghanistan look far less sui generis.

Finally, although the United Kingdom may no longer be in the business of "fixing failed states," it is equally true that most military operations occur in environments where the state's reach and institutions have suffered significant damage: either the lack of state control is what prompts intervention (Sierra Leone, Somalia), or the intervention results in the lack of a state (Afghanistan, Iraq). In either case, Western armed forces will be operating in areas with weak formal structures, where criminality, informal networks of patronage, the proliferation of small arms, and substate politics are common and need to be understood. In other words, in several types of expeditionary operations—even those that are not termed "counterinsurgencies"—there will often be a need for the type of knowledge, skills, and awareness called for and emphasized in counterinsurgency theory: how to engage with a civilian population, how to establish and maintain order, how to collect and process human intelligence, how to operate in a foreign culture, how to provide basic services, and so on. In Michael Howard's words, "The military may protest that this is not the kind of war that they joined up to fight, and taxpayers that they see little return for their money. But . . . this is the only war we are likely to get: it is also the only kind of peace. So let us have no illusions about it."[8]

Howard may be entirely correct, but the apparent inevitability of future counterinsurgency or counterinsurgency-related missions is clearly highly troubling. For the British military, it implies an urgent need to learn from their past wars and to develop the required capabilities for future, nominally similar campaigns—to grapple seriously with the problem of insurgency so as to guard against future upsets. Although such a course of action is for many reasons advisable, it seems financially and politically improbable. Despite continual engagement in counterinsurgency campaigns for more than a decade, only a few steps have so far been taken in this direction. Over the longer term, such an endeavor would be further complicated by the constraints imposed by an economy in decline, an ever-shrinking ground force, and the difficulty of assuring British domestic support for protracted operations. When the defense budget must compete fiercely with other sectors of public spending—health, education, infrastructure—it will be more difficult still to justify military adventures abroad of uncertain duration; indeed, many already see these activities as creating more instability and terrorism at home than they will ever disrupt or as distractions from higher-order priorities.[9] On this last point, developing the capabilities required for counterinsurgency-type operations would also need to overcome the MoD's entrenched prioritization and culture and is therefore doubly unlikely.

For Britain, both the aversion to and the embrace of counterinsurgency are problematic. The ensuing conundrum may help explain Britain's erratic approach to this problem—its unwillingness either to resource or to diminish its ambitions.[10] The contradiction was evident in the *Strategic Defence and Security Review*, which cut capacity all while suggesting that the British armed forces will still be conducting brigade-size stabilization operations, on top of other campaigns.[11] Despite the ten years of experience with stabilization operations of this scale, the MoD does not appear to have grasped their formidable difficulty and requirements. Nor have these experiences informed resource allocation in such a way as to ensure better military preparedness to conduct these types of operations in the future.

In that sense, Britain has not come so far in the past decade: it still purports to be capable of handling operations across the spectrum yet refuses to make the investment necessary to make this possible—a continuation, in some ways, of its "counterinsurgency legacy." As seen in Basra and Helmand, this combination of swagger and unpreparedness risks embroilment in foreign adventures without the necessary strategy, plans, and capabilities. A better approach for the future would be to reassess, on the basis of two operations gone awry, the notion of the United Kingdom as a global expeditionary actor lest dangerous myths are perpetuated, ambitions outgrow capability, and Britain is once again entangled in foreign-policy emprises from which extrication proves difficult, if not impossible.

OPTIONS FOR THE FUTURE: LESS IS MORE

Britons want the rights that come with global leadership, but not necessarily the responsibilities and costs that go with it. A full 54 percent of respondents to a 2010 poll agreed that "Britain is too small a country to be out policing the world," yet 61 percent of the same group nonetheless felt that "Britain should be strong and tough in dealing with other nations" (compared to the 9 percent who disagreed with this assertion).[12] Britain is seen as both strong and too small—as a global player, yet one struggling with shrinking resources. The contradictions have so far led to policy confusion: its government inadvertently signed up for overambitious entanglements for which the British armed forces were inappropriately prepared and that enjoyed only the thinnest of support domestically and therefore had to be downplayed. Rather than learn from this experience by delimiting where and when Britain gets involved, a more promising path would seek to redefine the *role* that Britain can play in future operations.

The point here would be to identify new ways of participating in expeditionary operations and structuring British forces accordingly. The aim is neither to avoid nor to embrace operations like those seen in Afghanistan or Iraq, but to approach future engagements more intelligently and to prepare for what would then be a radically different, and in all likelihood more successful, British role. Whereas Basra and Helmand saw Britain assume responsibility for large areas of operation, there are other alternatives and niche capabilities that can achieve international credibility and be operationally effective. Three options stand out as obvious areas of investment, both intellectually and in terms of capability and resources, though further options can doubtlessly also be explored. Required in each instance, however, is far greater clarity about the nature and requirements of expeditionary operations, their typical duration, and the challenges of operating as one member of a larger team.

DEATH FROM ABOVE

Following a few weeks of civil war in Libya in 2011, pitting a rag-tag resistance movement against the faltering regime of Muammar Gaddafi, it was decided within NATO's North Atlantic Council that some sort of military intervention was needed. On March 19, NATO commenced its Operation Unified Protector by launching Tomahawk missiles and air sorties at government targets. The aims of the operation were officially set by UN Security Council resolutions and included the establishment of a no-fly zone, the protection of civilians, and the enforcement of an arms embargo.[13] The unofficial aim, it was speculated, was regime change in favor of the National Transitional Council (NTC)—the Libyan resistance movement established during the war.

Operating in coordination with the NTC but without ever deploying regular ground forces, NATO and coalition partners assisted in the gradual weakening and defeat of the Libyan government. Most of the support came from above, with aircrafts targeting vital government installations and its forces. The war raged on until October 20, 2011, when during the battle of Sirte NTC forces located Gaddafi and beat him to death. Despite NTC requests that NATO stay on until the end of the year, the death of Gaddafi marked the beginning of the end of NATO's operation in Libya, which was formally terminated the following week. In the campaign's aftermath, the NTC set up a new government, paved the way for elections, and sought to establish and maintain a level of relative security.

The Western intervention in Libya in 2011 has been portrayed as a useful contrast to the costly and drawn-out campaigns in Iraq and Afghanistan. For example, air power expert Christina Goulter argues that

> Operation UNIFIED PROTECTOR was a very clear demonstration of the flexibility and effectiveness of air power as a tool of domestic and international policy. After nearly a decade of counter-insurgency campaigns in Iraq and Afghanistan, it provided a useful corrective to those who have argued that counter-insurgency warfare will be the norm for the foreseeable future. . . . OUP proved that an air campaign, focused and driven by ISR [intelligence, surveillance, reconnaissance], can win a war when combined effectively with irregular ground forces.[14]

Echoing this sentiment, Air Commodore Gary Waterfall, the UK air component commander of British operations in Libya, argued: "The very nature of the Royal Air Force is that we can get in quick, get the job done, and get out quickly, in order to allow us to recuperate to be ready for whenever the Government calls upon us again."[15]

In a powerful sense, the Libya campaign simply repeated and validated the so-called Afghan model, tried and tested during the immediate combat phase of Operation Enduring Freedom and lauded then, too, as a particularly effective means of applying Western military might.[16] Then as now, the model saw Western powers ply their advanced combat capabilities—precision-guided munitions in particular—in support of a local ground force reinforced by a small number of special-operations forces to ensure proper coordination. The prototype for the approach was first tested in the Balkan campaigns of the 1990s, in which NATO conducted precision-guided bombings from a virtually risk-free altitude and let local allies (the Croat forces in Bosnia and the Kosovo Liberation Army in Kosovo) conduct ground operations. When this approach was refined in Afghanistan with the addition of special-operations forces to act as a bridge between land and air, it was met with enthusiasm as a possible way of circumventing the typical pitfalls of "unconventional" or irregular wars.[17] A similar refrain can be heard today, this time with reference to Libya.

The Libya operation clearly presents a number of remarkable advantages to the manner of intervention seen in Iraq and Afghanistan. First, the operation achieved the intended aims within a few months and kept the costs to a fragment of those accrued in Iraq and Afghanistan. Second, as in the NATO-led air campaign over Kosovo, coalition and civilian casualties were kept at a very low minimum; again, NATO was able to intervene without incurring a single fatality. Third, although some ambiguity surrounded the actual aims in Libya, the results of the intervention appear far more promising than those likely to be seen in Afghanistan when British troops withdraw.

Finally, for Britain, the operation strengthened the perception of Britain as still able to play a key military role in maintaining international peace and security. In particular, British commentators have praised the speed of the British response and their "tactical-level excellence" as key factors in the campaign.[18] Closer analysis reveals three ways in which Britain can provide important niche capabilities in these types of campaigns: through its command-and-control capabilities, its air power, and its Special Forces. These are areas of British strength in comparison with many allies, and the smart provision of such capabilities may therefore be one way of maximizing international status and operational effectiveness within the context of expeditionary peace operations. Given the relative success of Operation Unified Protector in Libya, these capabilities are also likely to be in high demand.

Nevertheless, the merits of this mode of intervention notwithstanding, it will also be important to appreciate the preconditions that make it effective or even applicable. Indeed, the campaign in Libya was in many ways exceptional, which undermines its status as a precedent for future wars. First, Col. Muammar Gaddafi's lack of subtlety, in combination with the recent backdrop of democratic revolutions in Northern Africa, provided the campaign with unprecedented international political support as well as a sense of urgency to "do something."[19] From then on, NATO was aided by the simple fact the war was largely fought in the desert, which made targeting from the air relatively easy and effective. There was also a clear opposition to Gaddafi in the NTC and the rebel troops that served as the proxy on the ground. The geographic location, at the very borders of Europe, not only meant a greater sense of urgency but also made the conduct of operations much easier in terms of basing and logistics. In fact, for the first time since the Second World War, Britain was able to launch a bombing strike directly from the British mainland. The broader point is that the conditions that made the emphasis on air power possible and successful in Libya are not always going to present themselves in other contexts. The terrain and geographic location may be more difficult or remote, the coalition's political determination less pronounced, and the existence of a useful proxy on the ground altogether lacking.

Second, although the designated enemy in Libya adapted too late, there were signs even here that "the enemy has a vote" in choosing how the war will be fought—not least by reacting to and exploiting our strategic and tactical preferences. In particular, as seen also in the Balkans and Afghanistan, the obvious response to stand-off weapons (weapons launched from a distance) is concealment. In the early phases of the war in Libya, government forces were operating and moving in large uniformed units across the desert. However, following the initial air attacks, this behavior promptly changed: as Brig. Ben Barry explains, Gaddafi's forces "dispersed heavy weapons in populated areas and made extensive use of armed 4x4 vehicles, similar to those used by the rebels," something that "greatly complicated NATO's ability to identify and attack them."[20]

Third, concealment was not as successful in Libya as it had been in Kosovo more than a decade earlier, but there are good reasons to anticipate more wily adaptation on the part of future adversaries. This more skillful adaptation will also limit the effectiveness of Western air power as a way of winning wars. And, finally, although the initial assessment of the campaign in Libya is difficult to describe as anything but successful, it is much too early to arrive at a final verdict. It is worth remembering that the campaign in Afghanistan is hardly remembered today for the Afghan model used in 2001.

There are clearly cases in which air power can have tremendous strategic effect on its own or in conjunction with special operations forces on the ground. Nevertheless, it is important not to lose sight of the many specific enabling conditions present in Libya that made this model work. Proper analysis of these conditions should also give pause to any hasty conclusions regarding how future wars will and will not be fought.

THE INDIRECT APPROACH

Another way of achieving more with less is through what has come to be termed an "indirect" means of intervention, centered on advising, training, and employing a foreign fighting force rather than on relying primarily on your own troops. The task of raising the number, competence, and legitimacy of local security forces is a key mission component because it allows for a local means of consolidating security gains that can culminate in sustained stability and the gradual withdrawal of foreign forces. Indeed, it has been argued that foreign forces "cannot defeat an insurgency; the best they can hope for is to create the conditions that will enable local forces to win it for them."[21] The successful cooperation between the Iraqi Army and its US and British advisers during Operation Charge of the Knights, which dislodged the militias that had seized control of Basra, is but one case in point. The involvement of Ahmed Wali Karzai and Colonel Raziq during Operation Hamkari in Kandahar, Afghanistan, is an example of how intervening powers can enable local forces to achieve common aims.

As a form of intervention, the "advisory approach" implies other advantages: by putting local forces in the lead, it results in interventions that are more discreet and less politically problematic, for both the intervening force and the host-nation government. It also shields the intervening military from active engagement in complex and difficult operations, which are instead undertaken by local troops who have the required linguistic skills, cultural awareness, and familiarity with the conflict-affected society. The US military's experience in assisting Colombian troops in its campaign against the Fuerzas Armadas Revolucionarias de Colombia (FARC) or its advising of the armed forces of the Philippines in its struggle against the Abu Sayyaf Group stand out as low-profile, relatively successful, and moderately risk-free operations, at least for the United States.

Related to the training and advising of foreign troops is the important task of providing leadership and planning resources for operations. The British Headquarters 6th Division leadership of Operation Moshtarak II in Helmand and Operation Hamkari in Kandahar in 2010 demonstrated the possibility of achieving operational effect and international credibility through the provision of competent command capabilities, but without relying on British ground forces as the primary "doers." Although this option is most likely to require the complementary deployment of ground forces, it might also be possible to provide headquarters functions as a stand-alone capability around which larger multinational operations can be based. This capability is certainly one with which the British armed forces have some experience and that may warrant further investment.

The importance and limited exposure—in terms of risking lives—of training, advising, and commanding are but two reasons why this approach would suit a scaled-down military seeking to retain a global role. This type of work would also offer a means of tying Britain's future to its past: throughout the eras of colonization and decolonization, Britain was crucially concerned with using its small land army to the best possible effect, which commonly meant establishing accountable local forces to whom responsibility could be transferred. The British counterinsurgency campaign in Dhofar from 1962 to 1976 is particularly salient to this point because it was conducted indirectly by relying on the armed forces of the host-nation government along with various substate militias.[22] If Britain were to adopt training and advisory work as a niche, it would make its past meaningful also for the future; its "counterinsurgency legacy" would then live on, yet on a more solid footing than through mere rhetorical invocations and without actually seeking to replicate the larger-scale missions for which it has become most known.

None of this is news to the British Army, which in the aftermath of grueling engagements in Afghanistan and Iraq is looking to boost its forces' advisory and training skills. As part of the reorganization outlined by the modernization plan Army 2020, a new "security assistance group" will be created to centralize British Army advisory assets in one place.[23] Concomitant with this shift in emphasis to indirect engagement, the British campaign in Dhofar has been exhumed to provide a historical precedent for a future capability (much as the campaign in Malaya became the archetypal case for "direct" engagement in counterinsurgency). Yet before going too far in this direction, and certainly before another legacy is spun on the basis of isolated historical experiences, it should be noted that for all its advances, advisory work is rarely easy. Indeed, as a niche, this type of work comes with three critical caveats.

First, recent experience indicates that working with and advising local security forces is an art all in itself, requiring specific instruction and skills. Britain's early setbacks with standing up security forces in Basra compose a cautionary tale about the complexity of this type of work and the futility of simply focusing on numbers. Advisory missions typically struggle with three problems: how to ensure the accountability of the force being trained, whether that force will have the ability to use what it learns, and whether it can do so in ways that are not abusive, corrupt, or otherwise inimical to mission objectives. What the US and UK militaries found in Iraq and Afghanistan is that the effectiveness of the training, the accountability of those trained, and their gradual accumulation of confidence and skills are best guaranteed by "partnering" with the local security forces: to live and operate with them, day and night, from the same base, and on the same streets. Yet the implications of this requirement are significant. It follows, for example, that advisory operations require specific and extensive preparation, including language training and cultural awareness. This was the case also in Oman, as Brig. Ian Gardiner—historian and veteran of the Dhofar campaign—has noted:

> The patience and tolerance to live harmoniously in an unfamiliar culture; the fortitude to be content with less than comfortable circumstances for prolonged periods; an understanding and sympathy for a foreign history and religion; a willingness to learn a new language; the flexibility and imagination and humility necessary to climb into the head of the people who live by a very different set of assumptions; none of these are to be found automatically in our modern developed Euro-Atlantic culture. These attributes, and the attitudes they imply, often have to be taught in addition to purely military skills.[24]

In light of these requirements, it is reassuring to see that the slated security assistance group of Army 2020 will also act "as a repository of reconstruction, language and cultural experts for overseas engagements."[25] But it is questionable whether the British Army has or will invest what is needed to acquire and sustain these skills and capabilities.

On top of these operational and tactical capabilities, advisory work also requires political latitude and buy-in from the political leadership because these types of campaigns are seldom without risk. Nor are these tasks light in terms of force requirements: particularly for those cases where partnering is needed, there must be a sufficient number of advisors to accompany each unit being trained on the operation. These considerations and the other pitfalls of advisory work—most specifically the unhelpful tendency to train foreign security forces for conventional combat operations rather than for the roles and responsibilities they must initially assume—should be carefully assessed before this operational contribution is chosen.

Second, it is also important to acknowledge the circumstances that allow the advisory approach to be effective. In Colombia and the Philippines, the intervening force worked alongside an established government and military, whereas in Iraq, Afghanistan, and other such "postconflict" settings, central institutions are typically weaker or simply nonexistent.[26] In contrast to Afghanistan and Iraq, for example, Colombia has one of the longest records of elected civilian governance. Where a government does not exist or has recently been replaced, it is far more difficult to act as a supporter of host-nation structures, at least on the central level. Meanwhile, partnerships with substate actors require not only their careful identification and location, but an informed political strategy to deal with the consequences of their relative empowerment (note NATO's unpreparedness to deal with the empowerment of the Northern Alliance immediately following the overthrow of the Taliban in 2001).[27] In short, advisory missions have worked best where central structures already are in place, even if they are too weak to manage the problem by themselves. This need for a capable and functioning central government greatly limits the applicability of an exclusively advisory approach, particularly as it is usually host-nation weakness that necessitates foreign assistance in the first place.

Third, even where the central state is extant and somewhat competent, thorny issues of legitimacy and strategy still loom large. It should be obvious that in the quest to defeat insurgency or armed rebellion, the professionalization of a country's armed forces or security sector is but one part of a broader puzzle. Having professional and capable security forces is critical, but not in itself strategically decisive. Even where these forces are rendered more effective, discriminate, and precise than before, questions must still be asked about the political objectives being served by their operations—the broader strategy to which they are contributing. Where this strategy is misguided or altogether absent, security operations have little to no meaning. By analogy, it serves no good having a sharp scalpel if the doctor operating is drunk.

Where the political leadership will not toe the line, there is often a temptation among intervening powers to have it replaced, often with unpredictable results. In Vietnam, American impatience with the Ngo Dinh Diem regime, which was unwilling or unable to implement the reforms recommended to it, resulted in a US-sponsored coup that opened the door to the commitment of American ground troops in 1965. In Oman, too, the British advisory campaign reaped very few rewards under the authoritarian and reactionary leadership of Sultan Said bin Taimur. It took his overthrow by his Sandhurst-educated son, Qaboos bin Said, an act both supported and foreknown by the British government, to see the formulation and execution of an actual campaign plan—a strategy that gave meaning to the military activities on the ground and that was central to the outcome of the war.[28]

The broader point regarding advisory work is that because military effectiveness will often depend on political context, advisers must concern themselves not only with the legitimacy, standing, and effectiveness of the host-nation security forces, but with their political masters as well. This consideration again limits the application of the advisory approach or is at any rate likely to lead to significant frustration because it is not always possible to have the local political leadership replaced and not always desirable to intervene more substantially to compensate for its shortcomings.

The implication of these caveats is that although advisory work can be highly important and help share the burden of intervention with local partners, it should not be seen as a panacea by which to circumvent foreign entanglements or render them "easy."[29] The indirect approach is a model, a template, that must be tailored to specific circumstances and support a sound strategy. Where these conditions have been fulfilled, this approach can play a critical role—one that requires preparation, unique capabilities, and political support, but that may nonetheless be more modest and therefore sustainable a commitment than the wholesale stabilization of entire provinces by an understrength force.

CONTINGENCY OPERATIONS

Another means of burden sharing is by delimiting the role of British forces and ensuring that residual tasks are carried out by international, regional, or local partners. Partnering here might entail the provision of quick-reaction forces to assist a peace operation with force protection or to protect UN missions from sudden deteriorations in security. This role would be similar to that played in Sierra Leone in 2000 as part of Operation Palliser or that played by the French-led European Union force in Operation Artemis in the eastern Democratic Republic of the Congo (DRC) in 2003. The benefit of these types of operations is that by partnering with other institutions, whether it be the UN, regional organizations, or host-nation security forces, the intervening power is able to focus on only one phase of the campaign and thereby limit its exposure, risk, and obligations. Yet by the same token the effectiveness of these interventions relies on the ability to transfer demanding follow-on responsibilities to competent partners with greater staying power.

Operation Artemis is in this sense a cautionary tale. In response to the destabilization of the eastern DRC, a French-led Interim Emergency Multinational Force (IEMF) deployed to Bunia to help shore up security and get the local UN peacekeeping mission back on track. Per the conditions tied to its deployment, the IEMF spent three months in Bunia, during which time it reestablished security in the war-torn city and drove out militia elements. It then handed over responsibility to the newly created "Ituri Brigade," a 5,000-strong unit within the UN force in the DRC. On these merits, the operation was deemed a success, yet the IEMF's limited mandate, temporally and geographically, meant that its effects were transient. As a later UN report found, "The strict insistence on the very limited area of operations—Bunia— merely pushed the problem of violent aggression against civilians beyond the environs of the town, where atrocities continued."[30] Moreover, despite the UN force's expansion, it remained ill equipped and undermanned to sustain the tentative gains of the French intervention, casting doubt on its wider, long-term significance.[31]

The British military have their own experience with a far more successful "contingency operation" that illustrates not only how valuable these types of interventions can be, but also what they often will require. Although British troops were initially deployed to Sierra Leone in 2000 to evacuate British and other European citizens from the war-torn country, the in-country force commander, Gen. David Richards, saw an opportunity to side directly with the government in Freetown against the Revolutionary United Front (RUF). From then on, British forces were involved in a number of decisive confrontations against the RUF; they also helped train Sierra Leone's army and provided assistance to the local UN peacekeeping mission, so that the country's newfound stability could be sustained following the British withdrawal in 2002. By working effectively and helping to strengthen both the host nation and the UN peacekeeping force, and by sustaining its commitment beyond the relatively short duration of military operations, the British government was able to play a key part in helping to stabilize Sierra Leone and lead it toward a period of relative peace.

Key in Sierra Leone was the British military's ability to adapt its mandate, sustain its involvement, and secure a more successful transition. Originally framed as a noncombatant evacuation operation, the British operation in Sierra Leone grew into a much more ambitious effort to support the local UN mission in Sierra Leone, to assist the Sierra Leone Army, and to prepare for humanitarian tasks—all this against British domestic concerns over "mission creep."[32] By extending its mandate and helping to train up the forces that would provide for security following the British withdrawal, the British force helped prevent a return to full-scale war. Even following its withdrawal, Britain maintained a 140-strong force in Sierra Leone to advise the army and has remained one of the country's greatest bilateral donors of aid.[33]

Here, too, however, the results are far from incontestable.[34] Nonetheless, the point is clear: the effectiveness of military force depended on, inter alia, the coordinated and properly resourced follow-up action.[35] To replicate this operation elsewhere would require not only smooth civil–military cooperation, but the ability of British armed forces to work with and raise the competence of local and international peacekeeping forces so as to enable their own eventual withdrawal. In that sense, the use of British troops on contingency operations calls for many of the same skills and capabilities as those needed for advisory and training missions, which again highlights this area as requiring more urgent attention and prioritization.

A NOTE ON STRATEGY

A major enabling factor for the relative level of success in Sierra Leone was the auspicious timing and circumstances of the operation. The role of Guinea and local defense forces in the campaign, the expansion of the UN mission in Sierra Leone, and the war weariness of much of the RUF movement were critical factors behind the success of the British deployment.[36] These factors do not devalue the British military's effort in Sierra Leone but raise an important point about knowing when and where to engage and how to achieve the greatest possible effect. This knowledge is a requirement for all of the modes of engagement discussed here. Simply put, interagency coordination, advisory skills, or carefully crafted military skills will never be sufficient if the strategic plan underlying their deployment and use is unworkable or if the setting provides no entry points for effective intervention.

The implication here is not only that armed forces and civilian agencies must develop the right capabilities, but that policymakers must also know when and how to intervene, a process that requires an in-depth understanding of local context—its politics, structures, hopes, and aspirations—and of the likely unintended consequences of getting involved. This is in part a call for finer strategic thinking—the knowledge of how to use available means in ways so as to reach desired ends, all at an acceptable cost and duration. Yet at a deeper level this requirement also calls for greater understanding and a more sincere interest—across the relevant arms of government—for the lands, people, and context in which military operations are to be launched. All of this will require a greater analytical capacity within government; an interest in area studies, anthropology, and culture; and an ability to integrate such knowledge in military planning. In Sierra Leone, much of this was done on the hoof by the in-country force commander; it would be hopeful to suggest that such improvisation will produce equally promising results next time around.

In recognition of the capability gap for strategic thinking, Prime Minister David Cameron created the United Kingdom's very own National Security Council in May 2010 to "coordinate responses to the dangers we face, integrating at the highest level the work of the foreign, defense, home, energy and international development departments, and all other arms of government contributing to national security."[37] Despite this radical step, it is still uncertain whether another coordinating mechanism or forum in which to meet will help overcome the deep-running deficiencies in strategic thinking and specialist knowledge evidenced in the invasions of both Afghanistan and Iraq.[38]

A NOTE ON BURDEN SHARING

Another common thread running through all of the types of roles discussed here is that they are conducted within a broader, multinational framework in which Britain plays but one part. Simply put, given its resources and political situation, Britain is unlikely to be carrying the load, either chiefly or exclusively, in future campaigns. This is a significant shift from colonial-era counterinsurgency—one that presents new opportunities to a nation facing economic decline, but also one that imposes new requirements and challenges. On the one hand, the synergy of Iraqi, US, and UK troops during and following Operation Charge of the Knights demonstrates the best-case scenario for multinational cooperation in that it allowed British forces to punch above their weight and achieve positive results on the ground. On the other, Charge of the Knights arose because of inadequate UK engagement within its own area of operations. Having entered Iraq as a junior coalition member, Britain was always less interested in seeing the operation through or responding robustly to new challenges.[39] The limited engagement played to domestic political agendas but had crippling effects on the troops in theater and strained the partnership with the United States that British involvement in Iraq was arguably intended to cement.

The implication here is that middle-tier contributors such as Britain must learn how to contribute effectively to operations that it does not fully own, to work better with multinational partners, and to keep the political focus on these operations in spite of its limited commitment. The mere act of sharing the burden by adopting more modest expeditionary roles does not make intervention significantly "easier"—in many ways, it becomes far more complex. Part of the challenge is ensuring not only that British determination, expectations, and roles are reoriented, but also that other coalition members share the necessary vision and commitment. In Afghanistan, for example, part of the problem has been the difficulty to agree to a shared strategic objective. Depending on their national political context and military ability, some contributors to the ISAF are viewed, with some justification, as "there to be seen" rather than to provide a significant contribution as part of a coalition.

This characterization leads to a most fundamental challenge behind effective intervention: How serious are the states involved about these types of undertakings? Certainly, the lack of investment by most governments in the relevant instruments and the lack of strategic thinking going into these endeavors suggest a low overall prioritization. This trend raises the broader question of why modern states engage: To answer to domestic pressures to "do something" in the face of crisis; to establish a higher international profile; to demonstrate commitment to "strategic interests," however defined; or, in fact, to help achieve results on the ground? These motivations augur variable levels of investment, which may explain why commitment has so often fallen short of operational requirements. In turn, it is necessary to ask whether and how convincingly these types of campaigns have been linked to the national interest of the states and governments engaged. Further intellectual investment on this end may be the most useful first step in addressing the downriver problems of commitment, capability, and performance.

THE FUTURE OF BRITISH COUNTERINSURGENCY

The operations in Basra and Helmand have been bruising experiences for the British armed forces. To learn from this experience, the first difficult step will be to acknowledge the military's own role in these campaigns: the negative outcomes were not purely about poor political leadership, unreliable allies, or inadequate resources. If British forces are to maintain their current level of ambition, the second step will involve making counterinsurgency and stabilization greater priorities institutionally rather than relying on an oft-mythologized past. The operations in Helmand and Basra demonstrate the diverse challenges of modern operations: operating in an urban setting, in a foreign language and culture, against or among irregular armed groups, and with the aim of bringing stability to war-torn districts, all while building the local capacity and capability needed to render those security gains permanent. These operations require specific preparation and heavy investment in resources and time; even then, there are clear limits to what exogenous efforts at state building and stabilization can hope to achieve.

To a degree, the British military is trying to meet these challenges: it is releasing new doctrine, reshaping training exercises, and standing up new commands to capture lessons from the field. At the same time, it is uncertain whether the British government can truly muster the level of political and public support needed for these ambitious endeavors. Put more bluntly, the United Kingdom, which has long prided itself on its ability to deploy military force and maintain diplomatic influence internationally, now faces the dilemma of matching this desired role with the required resources and political capital. Given this dilemma, stabilization operations on the brigade scale and higher may now be purposefully avoided; yet, as Basra also illustrates, the desire to shirk specific operational challenges should not be confused with an ability to do so. More generally, "strategic abstinence" and "strategic selectivity" are options fraught with a different type of risk, particularly for a state with global expeditionary ambitions or when alliance commitments come into play.

A more responsible reaction to these recent experiences would be to seek out more modest yet still significant roles to play as part of expeditionary campaigns; to work with partners, both international and local; and to share the burden. Coalitions and partnerships are not without their own problems: as the campaigns in Iraq and Afghanistan demonstrate, coalition counterinsurgency presents both military possibilities and political constraints. In this regard, perhaps the chief lesson from these recent experiences is that when foreign intervention is contemplated, the ensuing operations should be engaged with on their own terms and not artificially simplified to fit domestic or other political agendas.

NOTES

FOREWORD

1. Clausewitz, *On War*, esp. 87.

PREFACE

1. UK MoD, *Strategic Trends Programme: Future Character of Conflict*.

INTRODUCTION

1. Kilcullen, *The Accidental Guerrilla*, 183.
2. British Army, *British Army Field Manual*, vol. 1, part 10: *Countering Insurgency*, 1-6, 1-5.
3. For more on the question of root causes and their importance, see in particular Woodward, "Do the Root Causes of Civil War Matter?"
4. See, among many other sources on the topic, Cohen, "The Myth of a Kinder, Gentler War"; Dunlap, "America's Asymmetric Advantage"; Gentile, "Beneficial War"; Luttwak, "Dead End"; and West, "Counterinsurgency."
5. The framing of this view as a particularly American problem can be found in several tomes and works on the "US way of war." See, inter alia, Buley, *The New American Way of War*; Cassidy, *Peacekeeping in the Abyss*; Echevarria, *Toward an American Way of War*; Kagan, *Finding the Target*; and Weigley, *The American Way of War*.
6. This abbreviated list of principles draws on Mockaitis, *British Counterinsurgency*, 2, and Alderson, "The Validity of British Army Counterinsurgency Doctrine." Alderson's work is

particularly useful because it studies how these principles have evolved over time. See also Rigden, *The British Approach to Counter-insurgency*.

7. For some enumerations of these principles, see Kitson, *Bunch of Five*; Thompson, *Defeating Communist Insurgency*; and, more recently, Cohen et al., "Principles, Imperatives, and Paradoxes."

8. Galula, *Counterinsurgency Warfare*, 63.

9. Mockaitis, *Peace Operations*, 133–134, 136; Cassidy, "The British Army and Counterinsurgency," 56.

10. As is often the case with the British principles of counterinsurgency, it has been argued that the principle of civil–military cooperation, as embodied in the committee system, was refined over many years in Northern Ireland. See Garfield, *Succeeding in Phase IV*.

11. Alderson, "Britain," 29.

12. British Army, *British Army Field Manual*, vol. 1, part 10: *Countering Insurgency*, B-6-2.

13. Garfield, *Succeeding in Phase IV*, 73.

14. Alderson, "Britain," 29. See also Kitson, *Bunch of Five*, 290–291.

15. Quoted in Mockaitis, *British Counterinsurgency*, 18.

16. Quoted in Bulloch, "Military Doctrine and Counterinsurgency," 16. In fact, the phrase precedes Templer, though he has certainly become the one most closely associated with it. See Dixon, "'Hearts and Minds'?" 361–363.

17. Kitson, *Low Intensity Operations*, 84–85, 87.

18. Nagl, *Learning to Eat Soup*, 192, 204.

19. UK War Office, *Keeping the Peace (Duties in Support of the Civil Power)*, 38.

20. Readers will have to excuse this paraphrasing of George Orwell's original formulation. See Orwell, "Politics and the English Language," 265.

21. Kiszely, *Post-modern Challenges for the Modern Warrior*, 8.

22. Written correspondence with the authors, January 2012.

23. Cohen, "Obama's COIN Toss."

24. This point is raised in Mackinlay, "After 2015," 53–54.

25. It is therefore difficult to agree with Gian P. Gentile's assertion that "counterinsurgency operations in Iraq and Afghanistan offer very few strategic guideposts" for how to reform our armed forces and change military policy. Although frustration with the recent campaigns is understandable, even just the negative lessons must be studied and understood, precisely for the guideposts that they provide. See Gentile, "COIN Is Dead."

26. Examples from other countries' experiences would include France in Algeria and the United States in the Philippines, Vietnam, and El Salvador as well as in Iraq and Afghanistan.

27. Frank Hoffman's article "On Adaptation: Innovating During War" captures the breadth and depth of the debate, along with the great fault lines among scholars as to terms and definitions. For some of the core texts on this topic, see Avant, *Political Institutions and Military Change*; Posen, *The Sources of Military Doctrine*; and Rosen, *Winning the Next War*. Or for a newer generation of texts, see Finkel, *On Flexibility*; Murray, *Military Adaptation*; and Russell, *Innovation, Transformation, and War*.

28. See, for example, Knox and Murray, eds., *The Dynamics of Military Revolution 1300–2050*.

29. Cohen, "Change and Transformation in Military Affairs," 400. For an excellent introduction to the topic of "bottom-up innovation," see Grissom, "The Future of Military Innovation Studies," 905–934.

30. As a major project on "the British approach" toward counterinsurgency sponsored by the US Department of Defense and the UK MoD found, "Doctrines and techniques were forgotten as easily as they were gained from experience. The compensation was that doctrine and techniques were re-learned fairly quickly when occasion demanded, thanks to an enduring understanding of [counterinsurgency] in the collective experience." See Eaton et al., *The British Approach to Low-Intensity Operations*, 10.

31. Howard, "Military Science in an Age of Peace," 6, emphasis in original.

32. Stephenson, *Losing the Golden Hour*, 36.

33. Clausewitz, *On War*, 88–89.

34. From an interview on *Charlie Rose*, PBS, broadcast May 30, 2008.

35. This line of argument is most clear in Smith, "A Tradition That Never Was."

36. For a study of these and other factors on political consensus, see Larson, *Casualties and Consensus*.

37. Black, *Rethinking Military History*, 142.

1. UNTANGLING THE BRITISH COUNTERINSURGENCY LEGACY

1. Murray and Scales, *The Iraq War*, 152.

2. HCDC, *Iraq*, Q 361; Chin, "Examining the Application of British Counterinsurgency Doctrine," 8; Murray and Scales, *The Iraq War*, 152; and Keegan, *The Iraq War*, 178.

3. HCDC, *Iraq*, 34–35.

4. Ibid., 4.

5. Quoted in Norton-Taylor, "General Hits Out at US Tactics."

6. *London Sunday Times*, "Confidential Iraq Memo."

7. Chin, "Examining the Application of British Counterinsurgency Doctrine," 9–10.

8. Aylwin-Foster, "Changing the Army for Counterinsurgency Operations." Several newspapers worldwide featured the article, including the *Washington Post*, *The New Yorker*, the *International Herald Tribune*, the *Independent*, and *The Guardian*. See, respectively, *Washington Post*, "Advice from an Ally"; Packer, "The Lessons of Tal Afar; Cohen, "U.S. Army in Iraq Takes a Radical Look at Itself"; Cornwell, "US Army Publishes British Officer's Essay Criticising Its Handling of Iraq"; and Norton-Taylor and Wilson, "US Army in Iraq Institutionally Racist, Claims British Officer."

9. Aylwin-Foster, "Changing the Army for Counterinsurgency Operations," 3.

10. Mockaitis, *British Counterinsurgency in the Post-imperial Era*, 12.

11. See, for instance, Callwell, *Small Wars*; Gwynn, *Imperial Policing*; Kitson, *Low Intensity Conflict*, and *Bunch of Five*; Paget, *Counter Insurgency Campaigning*; Thompson, *Defeating Communist Insurgency*;.

12. This observation of an oral tradition is based on our extensive interviews with serving British military personnel and academics, mostly in the late 1990s and early 2000s.

13. Townshend, *Britain's Civil Wars*, 18.
14. Mackinlay, "War Lords," 24.
15. Mackinlay, "NATO and Bin Laden," 38.
16. British Army, *British Army Field Manual*, vol. 1, part 10: Countering Insurgency, 2-1.
17. British Army, *British Army Field Manual*, vol. 5: *Operations Other Than War*, section B: *Counter Insurgency Operations*, ix.
18. Jackson, "British Counter-insurgency," 347.
19. Another notably successful campaign, the one in Dhofar, has recently begun to receive more attention, but witness the treatment of this campaign in older books on British counterinsurgency, where at best it is discussed under the rubric of "the unknown wars." See Newsinger, *British Counterinsurgency*, chap. 6.
20. Alderson, "Britain," 38.
21. Newsinger, *British Counterinsurgency*, 1. Much as the British legacy with counterinsurgency has been distilled and distorted, many facets of other nations' experiences with counterinsurgency also deserve closer scrutiny. For the development of French theory, which has a substantial effect on modern doctrine, see Rid, "The Nineteenth Century Origins of Counterinsurgency Doctrine."
22. See Strachan, "Introduction," 8.
23. French, *The British Way*, 247.
24. Nagl, *Learning to Eat Soup with a Knife*. Robert Cassidy also helped shape this narrative through his comparison of British and American military cultures and counterinsurgency experiences. See his book *Peacekeeping in the Abyss*.
25. From David H. Ucko's recollection of and personal participation in one such study.
26. In his writing on the use of history, Jeremy Black draws a critical distinction between history as providing "answers" and "history as questions offered by scholars alive to the difficulties and dangers of predicting outcomes." Quoted in Berdal, *Building Peace After War*, 31.
27. Thornton, "Historical Origins of the British Army's Counterinsurgency and Counter-Terrorist Techniques," 26. See also Thornton, "The British Army and the Origins of Its Minimum Force Philosophy," 83.
28. Benest, "Aden to Northern Ireland 1966–1976," 117–118, 141.
29. Hobsbawm, "Introduction," 1.
30. Gumz, "Reframing the Historical Problematic of Insurgency," 581. See also Porch, "The Dangerous Myths and Dubious Promise of COIN."
31. Miller, *Jungle War in Malaya*, 199–208.
32. Elkins, "Royal Screwup."
33. This summary draws on Ucko, "The Malayan Emergency," 29. See also Hack, "The Malayan Emergency as Counter-insurgency Paradigm," 383.
34. As Thomas A. Marks explains, "Two key differences can be seen in the lack of a viable police presence in Vietnam (an efficient, honest force through which to build popular security) and the ample main force component of the adversary in Vietnam, which had been completely lacking in Malaya." Thomas A. Marks, interviewed by David H. Ucko,

Washington, DC, August 1, 2012. For further context, see Beckett, "Robert Thompson and the British Advisory Mission," esp. 49–50. See also Andrade, "Westmoreland Was Right."

35. See Thornton, "Getting It Wrong," 104–105.

36. Black, *Rethinking Military History*, 15.

37. Smith, "A Tradition That Never Was."

38. French, *The British Way in Counter-insurgency*, 247.

39. Dixon, "'Hearts and Minds'?" 366; Mumford, *The Counter-insurgency Myth*.

40. Egnell, "Winning Hearts and Minds?"

41. Strachan, "British Counter-Insurgency from Malaya to Iraq," 8.

42. For these opposing approaches, see, respectively, the US Department of the Army and United States Marine Corps, *Counterinsurgency*, and Elkins, *Imperial Reckoning*.

43. See Jackson, "British Counterinsurgency in History."

44. See Elkins, *Imperial Reckoning*.

45. Many of these squatters were members of the ethnic Chinese community who had been forced out of the villages during the Japanese occupation in the 1940s and had set up settlements in cleared areas of the jungle.

46. Jackson, "British Counterinsurgency in History," 12.

47. See, for example, Gwynn, *Imperial Policing*; Kitson, *Low Intensity Operations*; and Rigden, *The British Approach to Counter-insurgency*, 13;.

48. Thomas A. Marks, interviewed by David H. Ucko, Washington, DC, March 30, 2006.

49. Black, *Rethinking Military History*, 19.

50. John Mackinlay made this very point in 1998, some time before the war in either Afghanistan or Iraq. See Mackinlay, "War Lords," 25. It does not render historical counterinsurgency campaigns entirely irrelevant to the wars of today and tomorrow, however. As David French perceptively argues, the discontinuity, although extant, can easily be exaggerated. See French, *The British Way in Counter-Insurgency*, 252–253.

51. Mackinlay, *The Insurgent Archipelago*, 6.

52. Hoffman, "Neo-classical Counterinsurgency?" 79.

53. See Rid and Hecker, *War 2.0*.

54. UK MoD, *The Strategic Defence Review*, para. 77.

55. Ibid.

56. Forster and Edmunds, *Out of Step*, 24.

57. Krahmann, "United Kingdom," 93.

58. Dannatt, "Transformation in Contact." "The spearhead of our deployable formations in 2003 was our one remaining Armoured Division, still based in Germany and still capable of deploying 3 Armoured Brigades, at readiness, to fight a large scale combat operation—albeit only in an Alliance or Coalition context. Our training depots, Staff Colleges and research and development assets were all focussed on further developing the physical, moral and conceptual components that make up what we term as our 'fighting power,' and doing so in the context of a possible future requirement to fight a large scale battle of this nature."

59. Keaney and Cohen, *Revolution in Warfare?* 199.

60. Gray, "The Revolution in Military Affairs," 58. See also former defense secretary Geoff Hoon's foreword to the 2003 defense White Paper *Delivering Security in a Changing World*, which is indicative of the rhetoric at the time.

61. Brig. Simon Mayall, interviewed by Robert Egnell, MoD, London, November 2004.

62. Alderson, "The Validity of British Army Counterinsurgency Doctrine," 94.

63. UK MoD, *Wider Peacekeeping*.

64. Berdal, "Lessons Not Learned."

65. On this latter point, see Ucko, "Peace-building after Afghanistan."

66. British Army, *British Army Field Manual*, vol. 5: *Operations Other Than War*, section B: *Counter Insurgency Operations*.

67. Alderson, "The Validity of British Army Counterinsurgency Doctrine," 198. See also Marston, "Adaptation in the Field," 72.

68. Alderson, "The Validity of British Army Counterinsurgency Doctrine," 94.

69. McInnes, "The British Army," 66–75.

70. Garfield, *Succeeding in Phase IV*, 32.

71. Ucko, "The Malayan Emergency," 33. See also Cassidy, *Peacekeeping in the Abyss*, 70.

72. Kilcullen, "Counterinsurgency *Redux*," 11. For an authoritative elaboration of other shifts between counterinsurgency then and now, see Hoffman, "Neo-classical Counterinsurgency?"

73. Quoted in *The Economist*, "Britain's Armed Forces."

74. Quoted in ibid.

2. THE BRITISH IN BASRA

1. UK MoD, *Operations in Iraq: First Reflections*, 40. Sections of this chapter draw on an earlier essay published in *Survival* in 2009; see Ucko, "Lessons from Basra."

2. British Army, *British Army Field Manual*, vol. 1, Part 10: *Countering Insurgency*, 1-5.

3. Tony Blair, speech to Chicago Economic Club, April 22, 1999.

4. Tony Blair, speech to Chicago Council on Global Affairs, April 23, 2009.

5. For the view of an uncomplicated occupation, see "Deputy Secretary Wolfowitz Interview with BBC World Service."

6. This chronology draws on two official reports from the British government. See UK MoD, *Operations in Iraq: Lessons for the Future*, 74, and *Operations in Iraq: An Analysis from a Land Perspective*.

7. UN Security Council Resolution 1483, 2.

8. Coalition Provisional Authority (CPA) Regulation Number 1, 1.

9. Ibid.

10. Coalition Provisional Authority, "Achieving the Vision to Restore Full Sovereignty to the Iraqi People (Strategic Plan)," 4.

11. "Military Campaign Objectives," Annex A to UK MoD, *Operations in Iraq: First Reflections*, 40.

12. Ibid., 34.

13. UK MoD, *Operations in Iraq: Lessons for the Future*, 62.

14. UK MoD, *Operations in Iraq: First Reflections*, 34, 40; UK MoD, *Operations in Iraq: Lessons for the Future*, 62; UK MoD, *Stability Operations in Iraq (Op Telic 2-5): An Analysis from a Land Perspective*, 3–4.

15. Cross, evidence submitted to the Iraq Inquiry, December 7, 2009, 17. See also Cross, "Post-invasion Iraq," 14. For details on how US postwar planning progressed, see Gordon and Trainer, *Cobra II*, 138–163.

16. CENTCOM PowerPoint Polo Step Planning Slides briefed to the White House and Secretary of Defense Donald Rumsfeld in 2002, obtained by the National Security Archive through the Freedom of Information Act. See also Chiarelli, with Smith, "Learning from Our Modern Wars," 4.

17. Cross, "Postinvasion Iraq," 6.

18. Ibid., 16.

19. See UK MoD, *Operations in Iraq: An Analysis from a Land Perspective*, 2–6.

20. UK National Audit Office, *Ministry of Defence, Operation TELIC*, 7

21. UK MoD, *Operations in Iraq: First Reflections*, 36

22. Knights and Williams, *The Calm Before the Storm*, 8.

23. Waldman, "British 'Post-conflict' Operations in Iraq," 74.

24. UK National Audit Office, *Ministry of Defence, Operation TELIC*, 32.

25. An MoD report suggested that the lack of postwar planning has squandered "the critical 'exploitation' phase," but that "unit and formation-level experience of peace support operations" meant that this failure had no "undue long-term consequences in the British sector." UK MoD, *Operations in Iraq: An Analysis from a Land Perspective*, 2–6.

26. UK MoD, *Stability Operations in Iraq*, 14.

27. As Frank Ledwidge puts it, "There was undoubtedly a degree of professional smugness on the part of the British. . . . The British knew how to do this; the Americans did not." Ledwidge, *Losing Small Wars*, 24.

28. Peter Mansoor, "The British Army and the Lessons of the Iraq War," *British Army Review*, no. 147 (Summer 2009), 14.

29. See *CNN.com*, "Rampant Looting Across Iraq"; *CNN.com*, "UK Forces Strengthen Grip on Basra"; HCDC, *Lessons of Iraq*, 157.

30. Knights and Williams, *The Calm Before the Storm*, 13; UK MoD, *Stability Operations in Iraq*, 8. See also Rathmell, "Reforming Iraq's Security Sector."

31. Army reforms consisted of mentoring Iraqi National Guardsmen on patrol, integrating six Iraqi National Guard battalions into the Iraqi Army, and establishing a Military Transition Team to help the 10th Iraqi Army Division reach operational readiness. HCDC, *Iraq*, 55.

32. For an exhaustive account of the problems affecting police reform in postwar Iraq, see White, statement made to the Iraq Inquiry, June 20, 2010. Stephen White was the acting deputy chief constable, senior police adviser, and director of law and order for the CPA between July 2003 and January 2004.

33. Knights and Williams, *The Calm Before the Storm*, 15.

34. Mumford, "From Belfast to Basra," 301.

35. Two percent of overall US resources reportedly went into CPA South. See Greenstock, oral evidence given at the Iraq Inquiry, London, December 15, 2009, 94.

36. The only money available, therefore, was from DfID or the "small scale Quick Impact Project funding," which, although used to good effect, was clearly insufficient. UK MoD, *Stability Operations in Iraq*, 33.

37. Chin, "Why Did It All Go Wrong?" 125.

38. UK MoD, *Stability Operations in Iraq*, 45.

39. Synnott, *Bad Days in Basra*, 35. HCDC, *Lessons of Iraq*, 161–162. See also White, statement made at the Iraq Inquiry, 5, 11, 19.

40. Rangwala, "Counter-insurgency Amid Fragmentation," 498.

41. See *BBC News*, "Blair's Address to Troops."

42. UK MoD, *Operations in Iraq: Lessons for the Future*, 70. Nor did coalition deployments offset these cuts.

43. See *BBC News*, "Majar al-Kabir."

44. Mowle, "Iraq's Militia Problem," 47.

45. Rathmell et al., *Developing Iraq's Security Sector*, 66.

46. Knights and Williams, *The Calm Before the Storm*, 14.

47. UK MoD, *Stability Operations in Iraq*, 14.

48. Devenny and McLean, "The Battle for Basra."

49. Mumford, "From Belfast to Basra," 300–302; HCDC, *Lessons of Iraq*, 161–162, 165.

50. Knights and Williams, *The Calm Before the Storm*, 23

51. ICG, *Where Is Iraq Heading?* 12.

52. Finer, "An End to the Soft Sell by the British in Basra."

53. Quoted in ICG, *Where Is Iraq Heading?* 13.

54. UK MoD, *Stability Operations in Iraq*, 14

55. Knights and Williams, *The Calm Before the Storm*, 30.

56. UNHCR, *Basrah Governorate Assessment Report*, 8.

57. Knights and Williams, *The Calm Before the Storm*, 30.

58. See testimony of Sir Suma Chakrabarti, former permanent secretary at the Department for International Development, at the Iraq Inquiry, January 22, 2010.

59. Rangwala, "Counter-insurgency Amid Fragmentation," 495.

60. White House, "President's Address to the Nation," January 10, 2007.

61. See, for example, Biddle, Friedman, and Shapiro, "Testing the Surge"; and Ollivant, *Countering the New Orthodoxy*, 7. See also Ucko, "Counterinsurgency After Afghanistan."

62. See Shirreff, evidence given at Iraq Inquiry, January 11, 2011, 18–19.

63. See Urban, *Task Force Black*, 191.

64. Shirreff, evidence given at the Iraq Inquiry, January 11, 2011, 16.

65. Ibid., 37. Lt. Gen. Sir Richard Shirreff recalls receiving planning instruction for Operation Zenith—the withdrawal from Basra—in November 2006.

66. Based on private correspondence from various government officials to the authors, 2008–2011. See also Marston, "'Smug and Complacent?'" 18.

67. Harding, "British to Evacuate Consulate"; England, "Now Basra Basks."

68. Quoted in UK MoD, "Prime Minister Announces UK Force Reduction in Iraq."

69. Harding, "US 'Delayed the Basra Pull-Out from Basra.'" See also Brown, "The Operation Telic Compendium," n. 28.

70. ICG, *Where Is Iraq Heading?* 17. Gen. Shirreff corroborated this view in his evidence at the Iraq Inquiry: "Once Sinbad had run its course, there was no appetite for any further plan, any further surge, and . . . Op Zenith [the planned withdrawal] was the only show in town." See Shirreff, evidence given at the Iraq Inquiry, January 11, 2011, 39.

71. Stirrup, speech given at the Royal United Services Institute, London, December 1, 2008.

72. See HCDC, *UK Land Operations in Iraq 2007*, 16.

73. Ibid., 17.

74. HCDC, *UK Operations in Iraq and the Gulf*, 10. British military representatives also suggested the Military Transition Teams need not leave the base because the 10th Division was already adequately prepared for its tasks.

75. Haynes, "Once Welcomed, British Troops Are Now the Wrong Tools."

76. The number of prisoners released was actually somewhere near seventy (private correspondence from UK military personnel with the authors).

77. Testimony of Toby Dodge before the HCDC, June 26, 2007, in HCDC, *UK Land Operations in Iraq 2007*, oral evidence, question 46.

78. Quoted in Hanning, "Deal with Shia Prisoner Left Basra at Mercy of Gangs." See also Dodge, "If We Move In."

79. HCDC, *UK Operations in Iraq and the Gulf*, 17.

80. Ibid., 22.

81. HCDC, *UK Land Operations in Iraq 2007*, 22.

82. Translated from an interview on *BBC Panorama*, "The Battle for Basra Palace."

83. HCDC, *UK Land Operations in Iraq 2007*, 17.

84. See Wall, testimony given at the Iraq Inquiry, London, January 6, 2010, 26. As to Maliki's own purported support of the retreat, it may reflect a pragmatic acknowledgment of the status quo or—as Frank Ledwidge suggests—that Maliki had been misled as to the nature and scale of the problem in Basra. See Ledwidge, *Losing Small Wars*, 54.

85. Brown, "Statement on Iraq."

86. Quoted in Coughlin, "New Iraq Receiving Baptism of Fire in Basra."

87. For more details, see ICG, *Iraq's Civil War*, 6–10.

88. Ibid., i.

89. HCDC, *UK Operations in Iraq and the Gulf*, 11. See also Brown, "Government and Security in Iraq," 12.

90. HCDC, *UK Operations in Iraq and the Gulf*, 7. See also US Department of Defense, *Measuring Stability and Security in Iraq*, 25.

91. Most sources cite unemployment figures as high as and sometimes exceeding 70 percent. HCDC, *UK Land Operations in Iraq 2007*, 16.

92. Paley, "On the Sidelines in Basra."

93. As Gen. Shirreff, then the commander of MND-SE, has noted, the prevailing insecurity and the British force's tooth-to-tail ratio meant that even by May 2006 the military could

"put no more than 13 half platoons or multiples on the ground, less than 200 soldiers on the ground, in a city of 1.3 million." See Shirreff, evidence given at the Iraq Inquiry, January 11, 2011, 4.

94. Stirrup, evidence given at the Iraq Inquiry, February 1, 2010, 39–40. It should be noted that the commander of MND-SE at the time characterized matters somewhat differently: "We had a strategy that involved extraction rather than necessarily achieving mission success. It was, in a sense, an exit strategy rather than a winning strategy." See Shirreff, evidence given at the Iraq Inquiry, January 11, 2011, 7.

95. US Department of Defense, *Measuring Stability and Security in Iraq.*

96. ICG, *Where Is Iraq Heading?* i.

97. Mansoor, "The British Army and the Lessons of the Iraq War," 13; HCDC, *UK Operations in Iraq and the Gulf,* 7.

98. Mansoor, "The British Army and the Lessons of the Iraq War," 13.

99. White-Spunner, testimony given at the Iraq Inquiry, January 7, 2010, 14, 32.

100. Ibid., 6. See also Storrie, "'First Do No Harm,'" 30–33.

101. HCDC, *UK Operations in Iraq and the Gulf,* 8.

102. For a detailed table on the civil, military, and police representation at those committees, see Clutterbuck, *The Long Long War,* 58.

103. "Maj.-Gen. Andy Salmon (U.K. Royal Army [*sic*]) Holds a Defense Department News Briefing Via Teleconference from Iraq."

104. Ibid.

105. "DoD News Briefing with Maj. Gen. Salmon from Iraq."

106. Quoted in Haynes, "Major-General Barney White-Spunner."

107. Quoted in UK MoD, "UK Armed Forces Minister Sees a Secure Basra."

108. See part 3 of Smith, *The Utility of Force.*

3. ACT II: BRITISH COUNTERINSURGENCY IN HELMAND

1. The campaign plan in Afghanistan involves three lines of operations: security, governance, and development. See http://smallwarsjournal.com/documents/isafcampaignplansummary .pdf. Sections of this chapter draw on Egnell, "Lessons from Helmand."

2. UK MoD, "Operations in Afghanistan: Background Briefing."

3. Ibid.

4. NATO, *ISAF's Mission in Afghanistan.*

5. For example, the British PRT and later the Swedish PRT in Mazar-e-Sharif, manned by 500–600 soldiers, covered the four northern provinces of Balkh, Samangan, Jowzjan, and Sar-e Pol. It is an area almost as large as England, with a population of roughly 2.5 million people.

6. Dannatt, *Leading from the Front,* 289–291.

7. Troops number had dropped from 8,600 to 7,200 between the end of May 2004 and the end of May 2006, which obviously did not provide a substantial pool of new resources. See *BBC News,* "Iraq War in Figures."

8. Rodwell, "Between Idea and the Reality," 18.

9. Coghlan, "The Taliban in Helmand," 120.

10. Rashid, *Descent Into Chaos*, 259–261.

11. Mantas, "Shafer Revisited."

12. Gordon, *Winning Hearts and Minds?* 31.

13. Marston, "Lessons in 21st-Century Counterinsurgency," 236–237.

14. Clarke, "The Helmand Decision," 17.

15. McCaffrey, "Academic Report," 6.

16. See, for example, UK MoD, "Operations in Afghanistan: Our Strategy."

17. Clarke, "The Helmand Decision," 5–29.

18. Suhrke, "A Contradictory Mission?" 224.

19. Lieven, "Afghanistan," 483–484.

20. UK MoD, "Operations in Afghanistan: Why We Are There."

21. House of Commons Foreign Affairs Committee, *Global Security*, 9.

22. A House of Commons select committee report from 2011 found that "the Government's descriptions of the nature of the mission and its importance to UK interests have varied throughout the campaign, lacking a consistent narrative." See HCDC, *Operations in Afghanistan*, 16.

23. Marston, "Lessons in 21st-Century Counterinsurgency," 237.

24. Clarke, "The Helmand Decision," 17; see also Fergusson, *Taliban*, 133–135.

25. Quoted in HCDC, *Operations in Afghanistan*, 22.

26. Tootal, *Danger Close*, 25–26, 38.

27. See the transcript of the BBC Radio 4 interview with Dr. John Reid, secretary of defense, April 24, 2006, http://www.operations.mod.uk/afghanistan/statements/transcriptjohnreid.doc.

28. Stein and Lang, *The Unexpected War*, 244.

29. HCDC, *Operations in Afghanistan*, 20, 31, 32.

30. As cited in Chin, "Colonial Warfare in a Post-colonial State," 230.

31. Bishop, *3 Para*, 110–111.

32. Clarke, "The Helmand Decision," 25–26.

33. Ibid.

34. HCDC, *Operations in Afghanistan*, 17, 29.

35. Clarke, "The Helmand Decision," 24.

36. Ibid., 27–28.

37. Suhrke, "A Contradictory Mission?" 224; Tootal, *Danger Close*, 58.

38. Tootal, *Danger Close*, 58–59

39. King, "Understanding the Helmand Campaign," 314–315; Marston, "Lessons in 21st-Century Counterinsurgency," 238.

40. Marston, "Lessons in 21st-Century Counterinsurgency," 238; Farrell and Gordon, "COIN Machine," 20.

41. Farrell and Gordon, "COIN Machine," 20.

42. Dressler, *Counterinsurgency in Helmand*, 11.

43. Clarke, "The Helmand Decision," 23.

44. Cited in Chin, "Examining the Application of British Counterinsurgency Doctrine," 234.

45. King, "Understanding the Helmand Campaign," 311.

46. King, "Why We're Getting It Wrong in Afghanistan." See also King, "Understanding the Helmand Campaign," 313.

47. Quoted in Haynes, "They Went Into Helmand with Eyes Shut and Fingers Crossed."

48. Ledwidge, *Losing Small Wars*, 85–86.

49. King, "Understanding the Helmand Campaign," 325.

50. Ibid.; see also Farrell, "Improving in War," 573.

51. Quoted in King, "Understanding the Helmand Campaign," 317.

52. Farrell, "Improving in War," 576; Southby-Tailyour, *Helmand, Afghanistan*, 77–78.

53. Grey, *Operation Snakebite*, 61–65.

54. Clarke, "The Helmand Decision," 28.

55. Quoted in Betz and Cormack, "Iraq, Afghanistan, and British Strategy," 327.

56. HCDC, *Operations in Afghanistan*, 31.

57. Quoted in Betz and Cormack, "Iraq, Afghanistan, and British Strategy," 325.

58. Betz and Cormack, "Iraq, Afghanistan, and British Strategy," 326.

59. Fergusson, *A Million Bullets*, 9.

60. On the international effort to build the Afghan security forces, see Barry, "The ANSF and the Insurgency," 125–126.

61. Clausewitz, *On War*, 75.

62. Thruelsen, "Counterinsurgency and a Comprehensive Approach," 3.

63. Thruelsen, *NATO in Afghanistan*, 11–13.

64. Thruelsen, "Counterinsurgency and a Comprehensive Approach," 7–8.

65. Farrell and Gordon, "COIN Machine," 22.

66. Ibid., 24.

67. Ibid., 22.

68. Troops numbers for the early brigades in Helmand were: 16 Air Assault Brigade (April–October 2006), 3,150; 3 Commando Brigade (October 2006–April 2007), 5,200; 12th Mechanized Brigade (April–October 2007), 6,500; 52 Infantry Brigade (October 2007–April 2008), 6,500.

69. Chin, "Colonial Warfare in a Post-colonial State," 236.

70. Ibid.

71. Dressler, *Counterinsurgency in Helmand*, 11.

72. Dressler, *Securing Helmand*, 39.

73. Dressler, *Counterinsurgency in Helmand*, 11.

74. As Hew Strachan has argued, the British military was not alone in this misstep. See Strachan, "Strategy or Alibi?" 168.

75. The difference between politically led operations and previous work was mainly that clearing operations were not based on intelligence regarding enemy locations but on political aims, such as the establishment of a governor in a district.

76. Farrell, "Appraising Moshtarak," 1.

77. Ibid., 1, 3.

78. Dressler, *Counterinsurgency in Helmand*, 39.

79. LaFranchi, "In Afghanistan War, US Civilian Surge Peaks as Pentagon Begins Pullback."

80. Ibid.

81. Quoted in King, "The Power of Politics," 70.

82. King, "The Power of Politics," 73.

83. Ibid.

84. Although the official ISAF and the MoD webpages are perhaps the more useful sources for this information, a charming addition to the good-news stories is Good News Afghanistan—a website dedicated to the stories that will make you happy. Available at http://www.goodafghannews.com/about/.

85. General John Allen, cited in Ackerman, "What Surge?"

86. Finding accurate and uncontested data from Afghanistan is notoriously difficult. Some of the sources used include: UNAMA, *Afghanistan Annual Report on Protection of Civilians in Armed Conflict 2010*, and iCasualties.org, "Operation Enduring Freedom."

87. Ackerman, "What Surge?" The progress can be described only as tentative at this point because the rate of casualties and other indicators still refuse to point in the right direction. Some of the sources used here include: UNAMA, *Afghanistan Annual Report 2010*, and iCasualties.org, "Operation Enduring Freedom."

88. ICRC, "Afghanistan: Outlook Remains Bleak"; Filkins, "After America"; Bates and Evans, *NATO Strategy in Afghanistan*.

89. This civil war is arguably already decades old, but the fear is that it will enter a new and more violent phase following NATO's withdrawal. For a broader discussion of this point, see Evans, "The Once and Future Civil War in Afghanistan."

90. Lieven, "Insights from the Afghan Field."

4. "A HORSE AND TANK MOMENT"

1. The move toward greater "jointness" in military education in the early 2000s should also be noted. Although well intentioned, this effort robbed the individual services of some of their own infrastructure for analysis and instruction. Within the British Army, it resulted in a reduced focus on counterinsurgency and other "land operations."

2. See, in particular, UK MoD, *Strategic Trends Programme: Future Character of Conflict*.

3. Her Majesty's Government, *Securing Britain in an Age of Uncertainty* (hereafter *SDSR*), 19.

4. UK MoD, *Delivering Security in a Changing World: Future Capabilities*, 2–3.

5. Synnott, *Bad Days in Basra*, 5.

6. Gordon, "Defence Policy and the 'Joined Up Government' Agenda," 127.

7. Ibid.

8. UK MoD, *Stability Operations in Iraq (Op Telic 2–5)*, 21.

9. For details on this lessons-learned mechanism, see Foley, Griffin, and McCartney, "'Transformation in Contact,'" 261.

10. Post-Conflict Reconstruction Unit, "Post Conflict Stabilisation."

11. Secretary of State for International Development Hilary Benn, as cited in House of Commons Commission, "Written Answers to Questions," col. 577W.

12. Gordon, "Defence Policy and the 'Joined Up Government' Agenda," 128.

13. The shift was evident in a 2006 internal MoD review of British operations in Iraq, which made several recommendations on what this experience meant for British counterinsurgency doctrine. See UK MoD, *Stability Operations in Iraq*.

14. Johnson et al., *Preparing and Training for the Full Spectrum of Military Challenges*, 166.

15. This paragraph draws on interviews by the authors with Joint Services Command and Staff College faculty. See also Alderson, *The Validity of British Army Counterinsurgency Doctrine*, 94–95.

16. UK National Audit Office, *Ministry of Defence Battlefield Helicopters*, 4.

17. Quoted in Pengelley, "Reality Check."

18. See UK MoD, *Security and Stabilisation*, part 2, chaps. 6 and 7

19. See, for example, US Under Secretary for Defense, *Instruction 3000.05*, 1.

20. See Griffin, "Iraq, Afghanistan, and the Future of British Military Doctrine," 323–325.

21. *US Fed News*, "British Army Trains at Afghan-Style Village of Hettar."

22. *Telegraph*, "MoD Builds Afghan Village in Norfolk." See also Clapson, "Thetford Theatre," 36.

23. As quality control, OPTAG conducted a one-week confirmatory exercise with the trained units and, if necessary, "retraining at the request of the unit commander." See Johnson et al., *Preparing and Training*, 167, 178, 237.

24. UK National Audit Office, *Support to High Intensity Operations*, 40.

25. Johnson et al., *Preparing and Training*, 159–160.

26. UK National Audit Office, *Support to High Intensity Operations*, 6. Soldiers who deploy as individuals (rather than with a unit) typically receive even less training.

27. See Brown, *Iraqi Study Team Observations*, para. 205–206.

28. A similar argument is made in UK MoD, *Future Land Operational Concept*, 2:3.

29. Brown, "British Army Steps Up Training in Kenya."

30. See Ainsworth, statement, House of Commons, December 15, 2009.

31. Fiddian, "357 UK Training Exercises Axed Since 2003."

32. See Luff, statement, House of Commons, December 16, 2010.

33. Tilney, "Preparing the British Army for Future Warfare," 5–6, passim.

34. See, first, UK MoD, *Future Character of Conflict*, 37, and for the proposal, DCDC, *The Significance of Culture to the Military*, 5:1.

35. *Defence Policy and Business*, "Military Develops Its Cultural Understanding of Afghanistan."

36. Kiszely, *Post-modern Challenges for the Modern Warrior*, 18. Kiszely adds that "important though this [training] is . . . we delude ourselves if we believe that a behavioural checklist and a tourist phrase book do any more than scratch the surface."

37. These arguments draw on extensive written correspondence with a former CULAD, June 2012.

38. The initial plan foresaw the growth of DCSU into the Joint Training Requirements Authority for Cultural Training across the three services—a standing structure responsible for training the military in cultural matters. Progress to date has been slow. Ibid.

39. UK National Audit Office, *Support to High Intensity Operations*, 39. The National Audit Office notes, for example, specific shortages in Mastiff, Jackal, and Bulldog vehicles; equipment to counter improvised explosive devices; night-vision equipment; weapons and ammunition including 60-mm mortar, sniper rifles, heavy and light machine guns, and ammunition; body armor; and communications equipment, such as Bowman radios and satellite communications.

40. *Defence News*, "Virtual Training Prepares Soldiers for Real-Life Operations."

41. Judd, "Welcome to Afghanistan? No, Norfolk."

42. UK MoD, *Strategic Trends Programme*, 4.

43. Ibid., 34.

44. UK MoD, *Future Land Operational Concept*, iii.

45. Dyson, "Organizing for Counter-insurgency," 37.

46. See Foley, Griffin, and McCartney, "'Transformation in Contact,'" 262–265. For the significance of this new command, also in historical terms, see Alderson, "The Army Brain," 10–15.

47. Newton, "The British Vision of Future Commitments and Land Capability Requirements," 5.

48. See slides for the British Army presentation "Agile Warrior," given at the Centre for Defence Enterprise, Cardiff University, September 8, 2011, http://www.scribd.com/doc/84759369/4-Army-Agile-Warrior-8-Sep-2011-Cardiff.

49. *British Forces News*, "Street Fighting Exercise Held in Southampton." See also UK MoD, *Strategic Trends Programme*.

50. Richards, "A Soldier's Perspective," 29.

51. Dyson, "Organizing for Counter-insurgency," 39.

52. Richards, "A Soldier's Perspective," 29.

53. Dando, "The Army Knowledge eXchange," 30.

54. See part 3 of Smith, *The Utility of Force*.

55. Private correspondence to the authors from midranking officer with knowledge of the new organizations, July 2012.

56. See King, "Commentary," 4.

57. Private exchanges between the authors and military officers involved in the ACC's work.

58. DCDC, *The Significance of Culture to the Military*, 5–2

59. Kiszely, "The Educational Upper Hand," 189. See also Mackay and Tatham, *Behavioural Conflict*, 33.

60. Kiszely, "The Educational Upper Hand."

61. See in particular the roles played by Gen. David Petraeus, Gen. H. R. McMaster, Col. (ret.) Peter Mansoor, and Lt. Col. (ret.) John Nagl in the US military, all of whom have doctoral degrees, and most of whom studied topics related to counterinsurgency.

62. Mackay and Tatham, *Behavioural Conflict*, 30.

63. Written correspondence to the authors from David Betz, Department of War Studies, King's College, London, June 2012.

64. UK National Audit Office, *Ministry of Defence: The Major Projects Report 2009*, 4.

65. Pitt, "Decision-Making in the UK MoD," 70.

66. Personal communications from senior British officers to the authors, February 2010.

67. Private exchange between the authors and this two-star general, December 2010.

68. Written correspondence to the authors from David Betz, June 2012.

69. Written correspondence to the authors from senior officer involved in army reforms, June 2012.

70. One exception was MoD's decision to mimic the US method of crowd sourcing a forthcoming capstone concept paper by contacting the UK-based *Kings of War* blog and using it as a platform for discussing the Green Paper of 2010.

71. Communication from Nick Gurr, then the MoD director of media and communication, to Stephen Grey, on the restricted nature of *British Army Review*. See Grey, "Aiding the Enemy."

72. Dannatt, "Transformation in Contact."

73. Richards, "Future Conflict and Its Prevention."

74. See British Army, "Afghanistan," 11.

75. Richards, "Twenty-First Century Armed Forces."

76. Dannatt, "Transformation in Contact."

77. Ibid., emphasis in original.

78. Johnson et al., *Preparing and Training*, 174.

79. Her Majesty's Government, *SDSR*, 19.

80. See statement by the then secretary of state for defense, Hoon, "Delivering Security in a Changing World," col. 343, emphasis added.

81. As one notable transformation enthusiast put it, "Power is increasingly defined not by mass or size, but by mobility and swiftness; influence is measured in information, safety is gained in stealth, and force is projected on the long arc of precision-guided weapons." Bush, "Period of Consequences."

82. UK MoD, *Delivering Security in a Changing World: Defence White Paper*, 11.

83. Rayment, "Army Facing Huge Cuts After Withdrawal from Afghanistan." See also Norton-Taylor, "Liam Fox Announces Army Cuts but Promises Extra Funds in Future."

84. Chalmers, *Unbalancing the Force? Prospects for UK Defence after the SDSR*, 11.

85. *Think Defence*, "Another Look at Balance."

86. *Think Defence*, "Unbalanced—Yes or No?"

87. Johnson et al., *Preparing and Training*, 144.

88. Or as much as 42 percent under strength if "those deemed unfit to deploy (due to, say, battle injuries) are factored out." See *The Economist*, "Britain's Armed Forces"

89. Forster, "New Labour's Governance of the British Army," 154.

90. See comments made by Hew Strachan in his evidence before the House of Commons Defence Committee, March 25, 2008, questions 21–23.

91. This figure is arrived at by dividing the total expenditure of £1.8 by the ten-year period in which this plan is to be implemented. Yet as *Think Defence* adds, "We also assume that this big pot of cash is for the Army exclusively, [but] it is not. The increased RAF [Royal Air Force] and RN/RM [Royal Navy/Royal Marines] reserve (4,900 in total) will also share this money." See *Think Defence*, "#Army2020—a Few Thoughts."

92. See Ledwidge, *Losing Small Wars*, 34–35, 56–57, 85, 133.

93. Marston, "Adaptation in the Field," 84. The issue of extending brigade headquarter tours was raised in the Brown report on lessons from Operation Telic. See Brown, *Iraqi Study Team Observations*, para. 45, 802–805.

94. Gates, address at US Military Academy, Sandhurst.

95. Yet as William Stothard Tee, chief instructor at the Jungle Warfare School from 1948 to 1951, explains, even "two years in Malaya . . . is not really a sufficient time to become acclimatised, to become trained and become used to the circumstances and the enemy." See Stothard Tee, Imperial War Museum Sound Archive.

96. HCDC, *Future Capabilities*.

97. Ibid., 31–32.

98. For the effects of insufficient military police on the ground, see Brown, *Iraqi Study Team Observations*, para. 406(c).

99. HCDC, *Recruiting and Retaining Armed Forces Personnel*, 21; UK National Audit Office, *Ministry of Defence: Recruitment and Retention*, 14.

100. Judd, "MoD Accused of Cover-Up After Troop Data Reclassified."

101. Judd, "What Lies Beneath."

102. Pitt, "Decision-Making," 72 n. 9.

103. Authors' interview with Ryan Evans, former Human Terrain Team social scientist, Task Force Helmand, July 20, 2012.

104. Mackiggan, testimony given at the Iraq Inquiry, January 7, 2010, 52.

105. Ledwidge, *Losing Small Wars*, 35–36.

106. Her Majesty's Government, *SDSR*, 19, emphasis added.

107. Who does what is also a matter of approach because DFiD tends to operate through the center, whereas the military deploys on the periphery, often with few partners around. See Gordon, "Defence Policy and the 'Joined Up Government' Agenda," 135.

108. See, respectively, UK MoD, *Delivering Security in a Changing World: Defence White Paper*, 6, and Hoon, "Introduction by the Secretary of State for Defence," 5.

109. By contrast, US defense spending over the same period rose both in real terms and as a proportion of GDP, increasing from 3.15 percent of GDP in 1998 to 4.28 percent in 2008. See Petri, *Britain's Expeditionary Approach 1997–2010*, 3.

110. Forster, "New Labour's Governance," 155.

111. Gray, *Review of Acquisition for the Secretary of State for Defence*, 16.

112. Haynes and Robertson, "Scandal of £6 billion wasted by the MOD."

113. See testimony of Chief of Defense Procurement Sir Peter Spencer before the HCDC, December 12, 2006, as included in HCDC, *The Army's Requirement for Armoured Vehicles*, 5.

114. Drayson, written statement submitted to the Iraq Inquiry, December 15, 2010. Drayson also noted that "the Army's difficulty in deciding upon a replacement to SNATCH was in part caused by their [*sic*] concern over the likelihood of FRES budgets being cut to fund a SNATCH replacement vehicle."

115. As a result, "about 50% of the UORs have been spent on force protection of ground manoeuvre capability." Figgures, oral evidence given to the Iraq Inquiry, July 27, 2010, 22.

116. Felstead, "UK MoD Concedes FRES Frustrations."

117. *London Sunday Times*, "Sir Mike Jackson."

118. Kirkup, "British Army Recruitment Reduced in £97 Million Cuts Package."

119. Ritchie, "Rethinking Security," 355.

120. Brown, "The Operation Telic Compendium," para. 807.

121. Gen. Dannatt makes a similar point in "Transformation in Contact."

122. As transcribed in HCDC, *Readiness and Recuperation of the Armed Forces*, 43.

123. Drayson, written statement, 7. In Lord Drayson's words, such reprioritizations were therefore "quite unusual."

124. Spencer, evidence given to the Iraq Inquiry, July 26, 2010, 49. On the topic of helicopters, Sir Peter Spencer commented: "Clearly having enough money to buy helicopters would have been extremely useful, but the [MoD] decided to spend its capital programme elsewhere. [It] goes back to the fundamental issue . . . , which is being more realistic about what money would actually buy you and to just accept that you can't have every toy in the shop" (60–61).

125. Hoon, as transcribed in HCDC, *Readiness and Recuperation*.

126. UK National Audit Office, *Support to High Intensity Operations*, 5.

127. Her Majesty's Government, *SDSR*, 19.

5. WHITHER BRITISH COUNTERINSURGENCY?

1. Berdal, *Building Peace After War*, 21.

2. Cohen, "Obama's COIN Toss."

3. This is more or less the line advanced by John Mackinlay in, for example, "After 2015," 53–54.

4. Cameron, "Statement on Strategic Defence and Security Review."

5. Rid and Noetzel, "Germany's Options in Afghanistan."

6. This is true also of the seemingly "benign" or "permissive" peace-support operations of the 1990s. See Ucko, "Peace-building After Afghanistan."

7. Mackinlay, "After 2015," 59.

8. Howard, "A Long War?" 14.

9. See, for example, Blagden, "Strategic Thinking for the Age of Austerity," 60–66.

10. As Paul Cornish also notes, there is a "British inclination to 'muddle through' in matters of security and defense; a tendency towards procrastination in which ever more operational commitments are undertaken with ever-diminishing resources." Cornish, *Strategy in Austerity*, 3.

11. Her Majesty's Government, *Securing Britain in an Age of Uncertainty*, 19.

12. YouGov, Universities of Strathclyde and Leeds Survey Results, February 5, 2010, , http://www.yougov.co.uk/extranets/ygarchives/content/pdf/UniversityofStrathclyde_05-Feb-2010.pdf, 4–5.

13. UN Security Council Resolution 1973, March 17, 2011.

14. Goulter, "Ellamy," 139.

15. Quoted in UK MoD, "Parliament Honours UK Troops for Libya Operations."

16. The original formulation of the "Afghan model" can be found in Biddle, "Allies, Airpower, and Modern Warfare," 161–176. For the Libyan revival of this model, see, for example, Farley, "Over the Horizon."

17. To George W. Bush, OEF offered a "proving ground," showcasing how "innovative doctrine and high-tech weaponry can shape and then dominate in an unconventional conflict." See White House, "President Speaks on War Effort to Citadel Cadets."

18. Goulter, "Ellamy," 164.

19. Particularly after Gaddafi's speech in which he invoked the Rwandan genocide by referring to the opposition and rebels in Libya as "rats" and "cockroaches." See BBC News, "Libya Protests."

20. Barry, "Libya's Lessons," 6.

21. Nagl, Learning to Eat Soup with a Knife, xiv.

22. For more on the Dhofar campaign, see Beckett, "The British Counterinsurgency Campaign in Dhofar," 175–190. For a firsthand account, see Gardiner, In the Service of the Sultan. For a revisionist take on the conflict, see Devore, "A More Complex and Conventional Victory."

23. Army, "Army 2020 Structure Explained."

24. Gardiner, In the Service of the Sultan, 174.

25. Barry, "Army 2020."

26. Particularly in Colombia, the successes against the Fuerzas Armadas Revolucionarias de Colombia and the demobilization of paramilitary formations must be seen primarily as the result of the Colombian government's own strategy, which, although funded by the United States, is a function of its government and military's own cohesiveness and functionality. See Marks, "Colombian Military Support for 'Democratic Security.'" For more detail, see also Rabasa et al., From Insurgency to Stability, 41–73.

27. For a historical perspective on these difficulties, see Hughes and Tripodi, "Anatomy of a Surrogate."

28. Beckett, "The British Counterinsurgency Campaign in Dhofar," 178–182.

29. This point, along with several other difficulties with the indirect approach, are discussed in Burton, "The Promise and Peril of the Indirect Approach."

30. Peacekeeping Best Practices Unit (Military Division), Operation Artemis, 14.

31. UN Security Council Resolution 1484, May 30, 2003; Berdal, Building Peace After War, 112.

32. Dorman, "Sierra Leone (2000)," 181. See also Hoon, "Statement on Sierra Leone," col. 863.

33. Berdal, Building Peace After War, 120.

34. Mitton, "Engaging with Disengagement."

35. Berdal, Building Peace After War, 120.

36. Keen, Conflict & Collusion in Sierra Leone, 267–273.

37. Number 10, "Establishment of a National Security Council."

38. For one early (possibly too early) critique of the UK National Security Council, see Prins, The British Way of Strategy-Making.

39. See Betz and Cormack, "Iraq, Afghanistan, and British Strategy," 324.

BIBLIOGRAPHY

Ackerman, Spencer. "What Surge? Afghanistan's Most Violent Places Stay Bad, Despite Extra Troops." *The Wired*, August 23, 2012, http://www.wired.com/dangerroom/2012/08/afghanistan-violence-helmand/.

Ainsworth, Secretary of State for Defense Bob. Statement, House of Commons, December 15, 2009, http://www.publications.parliament.uk/pa/cm200910/cmhansrd/cm091215/debtext/91215-0004.htm.

Alderson, Alexander. "The Army Brain." *RUSI Journal* 155, no. 3 (2010): 10–15.

——. "Britain." In Thomas Rid and Thomas A. Kearney, eds., *Understanding Counterinsurgency: Doctrine, Operations, Challenges*, 28–45. London: Routledge, 2010.

——. "The Validity of British Army Counterinsurgency Doctrine After the War in Iraq 2003–2009." PhD diss., University of Cranfield, 2009.

Andrade, Dale. "Westmoreland Was Right: Learning the Wrong Lessons from the Vietnam War." *Small Wars and Insurgencies* 19, no. 2 (2008): 145–181.

Army. "Army 2020 Structure Explained." July 6, 2012, http://www.army.mod.uk/news/24272.aspx.

Avant, Deborah D. *Political Institutions and Military Change: Lessons from Peripheral Wars*. Ithaca, NY: Cornell University Press, 1994.

Aylwin-Foster, Nigel. "Changing the Army for Counterinsurgency Operations." *Military Review* 85, no. 6 (November–December 2005): 2–15.

Barry, Ben. "The ANSF and the Insurgency." In Toby Dodge and Nicholas Redman, eds., *Afghanistan to 2015 and Beyond*, 121–140. Abingdon, UK: Routledge for International Institute for Strategic Studies, 2011.

——. "Army 2020: Fighting for the Future." *The Guardian*, July 5, 2012.

——. "Libya's Lessons." *Survival* 53, no. 5 (2011): 5–14.

Bates, Scott and Ryan Evans. *NATO Strategy in Afghanistan: A New Way Forward.* Washington, DC: Center for National Policy, May 2012.

BBC News. "Blair's Address to Troops." May 29, 2003, http://news.bbc.co.uk/2/hi/uk_news/politics/2946644.stm.

——. "Iraq War in Figures." December 14, 2011, http://www.bbc.co.uk/news/world-middle-east-11107739.

——. "Libya Protests: Defiant Gaddafi Refuses to Quit." February 22, 2011, http://www.bbc.co.uk/news/world-middle-east-12544624.

——. "Majar al-Kabir: From Quiet to Carnage." June 26, 2003.

BBC Panorama. "The Battle for Basra Palace." Aired December 10, 2007.

Beckett, Ian F. W. "The British Counterinsurgency Campaign in Dhofar 1965–1975." In Daniel Marston and Carter Malkasian, eds., *Counterinsurgency in Modern Warfare*, 175–190. Oxford: Osprey, 2008.

——. "Robert Thompson and the British Advisory Mission to South Vietnam, 1961–1965." *Small Wars & Insurgencies* 8, no. 3 (1997): 41–63.

Benest, David. "Aden to Northern Ireland 1966–1976." In Hew Strachan, ed., *Big Wars and Small Wars: The British Army and the Lessons of War in the 20th Century*, 115–144. Abingdon, UK: Routledge, 2006.

Berdal, Mats. *Building Peace After War.* Abingdon, UK: Routledge for International Institute for Strategic Studies, 2009.

——. "Lessons Not Learned: The Use of Force in Peace Operations in the 1990s." *International Peacekeeping* 7, no. 4 (Winter 2000): 55–74.

Betz, David and Anthony Cormack. "Iraq, Afghanistan, and British Strategy." *Orbis* 53, no. 2 (Spring 2009): 319–336.

Biddle, Stephen. "Allies, Airpower, and Modern Warfare: The Afghan Model in Afghanistan and Iraq." *International Security* 30, no. 3 (Winter 2005–2006): 161–176.

Biddle, Stephen, Jeffrey A. Friedman, and Jacob N. Shapiro. "Testing the Surge: Why Did Violence Decline in Iraq in 2007?" *International Security* 37, no. 1 (Summer 2012): 7–40.

Bishop, Patrick. *3 Para.* London: Harper Press, 2007.

Black, Jeremy. *Rethinking Military History.* New York: Routledge, 2004.

Blagden, David. "Strategic Thinking for the Age of Austerity." *RUSI Journal* 154, no. 6 (December 2009): 60–66.

Blair, Tony. Speech to Chicago Council on Global Affairs, April 23, 2009, http://www.tonyblairoffice.org/speeches/entry/tony-blair-speech-to-chicago-council-on-global-affairs/.

——. Speech to Chicago Economic Club, April 22, 1999, http://www.pbs.org/newshour/bb/international/jan-june99/blair_doctrine4-23.html.

British Army. "Afghanistan: In Pursuit of Security and Stabilisation." In *British Army*, 11–12. London: Public Relations Army, 2010.

——. *Army Field Manual.* Vol. 1, part 10: *Counter Insurgency Operations.* Army Code 71749. London: Ministry of Defence, October 2009.

——. *British Army Field Manual.* Vol. 1, part 10: *Countering Insurgency.* Army Code 71876. London: Ministry of Defence, October 2001.

——. *British Army Field Manual.* Vol. 5: *Operations Other Than War,* section B: *Counter Insurgency Operations.* Army Code 71596 (Pt. 1). London: Ministry of Defence, 1995.

British Forces News. "Street Fighting Exercise Held in Southampton." October 21, 2011, http://bfbs.com/news/england/street-fighting-exercise-held-southampton-52722.html.

Brown, Lt. Gen. Christopher. *Iraqi Study Team Observations.* May 28, 2010. Internal report, https://www.gov.uk/government/uploads/system/uploads/attachment_data/file/16787/operation_telic_lessons_compendium.pdf.

——. "The Operation Telic Compendium." Unpublished manuscript.

Brown, Des. "Government and Security in Iraq: The Evolving Challenge." *RUSI Journal* 151, no. 3 (June 2006): 10–13.

Brown, Gordon. "Statement on Iraq." House of Commons, London, October 8, 2007, http://www.labourfriendsofiraq.org.uk/archives/001179.html.

Brown, Nick. "British Army Steps Up Training in Kenya." *Jane's Defence Weekly,* October 17, 2008.

Buley, Benjamin. *The New American Way of War: Military Culture and the Political Utility of Force.* New York: Routledge, 2007.

Bulloch, Gavin. "Military Doctrine and Counterinsurgency: A British Perspective." *Parameters* 26, no. 2 (Summer 1996): 4–16.

Burton, Brian. "The Promise and Peril of the Indirect Approach." *Prism* 3, no. 1 (2012): 47–62.

Bush, President George W. "Period of Consequences." Address given at the Citadel, South Carolina, September 23, 2003.

Callwell, Charles E. *Small Wars: Their Principles and Practice.* New York: Cosimo Classics, 2010.

Cameron, Prime Minister David. "Statement on Strategic Defence and Security Review." October 19, 2010, http://www.number10.gov.uk/news/sdsr/.

Cassidy, Robert M. "The British Army and Counterinsurgency: The Salience of Military Culture." *Military Review* 85, no. 3 (May–June 2005): 53–59.

——. *Peacekeeping in the Abyss: British and American Peacekeeping Doctrine and Practice After the Cold War.* Westport, CT: Praeger, 2004.

Chakrabarti, Sir Suma, former permanent secretary at the Department for International Development. Testimony at the Iraq Inquiry, January 22, 2010, http://www.iraqinquiry.org.uk/.

Chalmers, Malcolm. *Unbalancing the Force? Prospects for UK Defence After the SDSR.* Future Defence Review Working Paper no. 9. London: Royal United Services Institute, November 2010.

Chiarelli, Lt. Gen. Peter W., with Maj. Stephen M. Smith. "Learning from Our Modern Wars: The Imperatives of Preparing for a Dangerous Future." *Military Review* 87, no. 5 (September–October 2007): 2–15.

Chin, Warren. "Colonial Warfare in a Post-colonial State: British Operations in Helmand Province Afghanistan." *Defence Studies* 10, nos. 1–2 (March–June 2010): 215–247.

——. "Examining the Application of British Counterinsurgency Doctrine by the American Army in Iraq." *Small Wars and Insurgencies* 18, no. 1 (March 2007): 1–26.

——. "Why Did It All Go Wrong? Reassessing British Counterinsurgency in Iraq." *Strategic Studies Quarterly* (Winter 2008): 119–135.

Clapson, Joe. "Thetford Theatre: OPTAG Transforms Rural Pastures Into War Zone." *Soldier* (August 2010): 35–37.

Clarke, Michael. "The Helmand Decision." *Whitehall Papers* 77, no. 1 (2011): 5–29.

Clausewitz, Carl von. *On War*. Ed. and trans. Michael Howard and Peter Paret. Princeton, NJ: Princeton University Press, 1976.

Clutterbuck, Richard. *The Long Long War: The Emergency in Malaya 1948–1960*. London: Cassell, 1967.

CNN.com. "Rampant Looting Across Iraq." April 8, 2003.

——. "UK Forces Strengthen Grip on Basra." April 9, 2003.

Coalition Provisional Authority. "Achieving the Vision to Restore Full Sovereignty to the Iraqi People (Strategic Plan)." Baghdad, Iraq. Working document as of October 1, 2003, http://www.globalsecurity.org/military/library/congress/2003_hr/03-10-08strategicplan.pdf.

Coghlan, Tom. "The Taliban in Helmand: An Oral History." In Antonio Giustozzi, ed., *Decoding the New Taliban: Insights from the Afghan Field*, 119–154. New York: Columbia University Press, 2009.

Cohen, Eliot A. "Change and Transformation in Military Affairs." *Journal of Strategic Studies* 27, no. 3 (September 2004): 395–407.

——. "Obama's COIN Toss." *Washington Post*, December 6, 2009.

Cohen, Eliot, Conrad Crane, Jan Horvath, and John Nagl. "Principles, Imperatives, and Paradoxes of Counterinsurgency." *Military Review* 86, no. 2 (2006): 49–53.

Cohen, Michael A. "The Myth of a Kinder, Gentler War." *World Policy Journal* 27, no. 1 (2010): 75–86.

Cohen, Roger. "U.S. Army in Iraq Takes a Radical Look at Itself." *International Herald Tribune*, February 1, 2006.

Cornish, Paul. *Strategy in Austerity: The Security and Defence of the United Kingdom*. A Chatham House Report. London: Chatham House, October 2010.

Cornwell, Rupert. "US Army Publishes British Officer's Essay Criticising Its Handling of Iraq." *Independent*, January 12, 2006.

Coughlin, Con. "New Iraq Receiving Baptism of Fire in Basra." *Telegraph*, March 30, 2008.

Cross, Maj. Gen Tim. "Postinvasion Iraq: The Planning and the Reality After the Invasion from Mid 2002 to the End of August 2003." Written evidence submitted to the Iraq Inquiry, December 7, 2009, http://www.iraqinquiry.org.uk/media/39160/timcross-statement.pdf.

Dando, Lt. Col. Judith. "The Army Knowledge eXchange (AKX)—One Year On." *The Sapper* 36, no. 1 (February 2011): 30.

Dannatt, Richard. "Transformation in Contact." Address given at the Institute for Public Policy Research (IPPR). London, January 19, 2009,http://www.ippr.org.uk/events/54/6394/transformation-in-contact-with-general-sir-richard-dannatt-chief-of-the-general-staff.

——. *Leading from the Front: The Autobiography*. London: Transworld, 2010.

Defence News. "Virtual Training Prepares Soldiers for Real-Life Operations." March 16, 2010.

Defence Policy and Business. "Military Develops Its Cultural Understanding of Afghanistan." February 24, 2010.

"Deputy Secretary Wolfowitz Interview with BBC World Service." US Department of Defense News Transcript, March 24, 2003, http://www.defense.gov/Transcripts/Transcript.aspx?TranscriptID=2139.

Development, Concept, Doctrine Centre (DCDC). *The Significance of Culture to the Military*. Joint Doctrine Note 1/09. Shrivenham, UK: DCDC, 2009.

Devenny, Patrick and Robert T. McLean. "The Battle for Basra." *American Spectator*, November 1, 2005.

Devore, Mark R. "A More Complex and Conventional Victory: Revisiting the Dhofar Counter-insurgency, 1963–1975." *Small Wars & Insurgencies* 23, no. 1 (2012): 144–173.

Dixon, Paul. "'Hearts and Minds'? British Counter-insurgency from Malaya to Iraq." *Journal of Strategic Studies* 32, no. 3 (2009): 353–381.

"DoD News Briefing with Maj. Gen. Salmon from Iraq." US Department of Defense News Transcript, February 2, 2009.

Dodge, Toby. "If We Move In, We Have to Stay Committed." *Independent*, May 3, 2009.

Dorman, Andy. "Sierra Leone (2000)." In Hugh Eaton, Greg Boehmer, Eric Rambo, Lana Oh, Jeremy Works, Michael Clarke, Warren Chin, et al., *The British Approach to Low-Intensity Operations*, Technical Report, Part II, Network-Centric Operations Case Study, 173–206. Washington, DC: Office of Force Transformation, 2007.

Drayson, Paul, Lord of Kensington. Written statement submitted to the Iraq Inquiry, December 15, 2010, http://www.iraqinquiry.org.uk/media/50260/LordDraysonofKensington-statement.pdf.

Dressler, Jeffrey. *Counterinsurgency in Helmand: Progress and Remaining Challenges*. Afghanistan Report no. 8. Washington, DC: Institute for the Study of War, January 2011.

———. *Securing Helmand: Understanding and Responding to the Enemy*. Afghanistan Report no. 2. Washington, DC: Institute for the Study of War, September 2009.

Dunlap, Maj. Gen. Charles J., Jr. "America's Asymmetric Advantage." *Armed Forces Journal* (September 2006), http://www.armedforcesjournal.com/2006/09/2009013/.

Dyson, Tom. "Organizing for Counter-insurgency: Explaining Doctrinal Adaptation in Britain and Germany." *Contemporary Security Policy* 33, no. 1 (2012): 27–58.

Eaton, Hugh, Greg Boehmer, Eric Rambo, Lana Oh, Jeremy Works, Michael Clarke, Warren Chin, et al. *The British Approach to Low-Intensity Operations*. Technical Report, Part I. Network-Centric Operations Case Study. Washington, DC: Office of Force Transformation, 2007.

Echevarria, Antulio J., II. *Toward an American Way of War*. Carlisle, PA: Strategic Studies Institute, US Army War College, 2004.

The Economist. "Britain's Armed Forces: Losing Their Way?" January 29, 2009.

Egnell, Robert. "Lessons from Helmand, Afghanistan: What Now for British Counterinsurgency?" *International Affairs* 87, no. 2 (2011): 297–315.

———. "Winning Hearts and Minds? Legitimacy and the Challenge of Counterinsurgency Operations in Afghanistan." *Civil Wars* 12, no. 3 (September 2010): 282–303.

Elkins, Caroline. *Imperial Reckoning: The Untold Story of Britain's Gulag in Kenya*. New York: Henry Holt, 2005.

———. "Royal Screwup: Why Malaya Is No Model for Iraq." *New Republic*, December 19, 2005.

England, Andrew. "Now Basra Basks." *Financial Times*, September 1, 2008.

Evans, Ryan. "The Once and Future Civil War in Afghanistan." *AfPak Channel*, July 26, 2012, http://afpak.foreignpolicy.com/posts/2012/07/26/the_once_and_future_civil_war_in_afghanistan.

Farley, Robert. "Over the Horizon: Libya and the Afghan Model Revisited." *World Politics Review*, August 24, 2011, http://www.worldpoliticsreview.com/articles/9870/over-the-horizon-libya-and-the-afghan-model-revisited.

Farrell, Theo. "Appraising Moshtarak: The Campaign in Nad-e-Ali District, Helmand." Royal United Services Institute briefing note, June 2010, http://www.rusi.org/downloads/assets/Appraising_Moshtarak.pdf.

——. "Improving in War: Military Adaptation and the British in Helmand Province, Afghanistan, 2006–2009." *Journal of Strategic Studies* 33, no. 4 (September 2010): 567–594.

Farrell, Theo and Stuart Gordon. "COIN Machine: The British Military in Afghanistan." *RUSI Journal* 154, no. 3 (March 2010): 18–25.

Felstead, Peter. "UK MoD Concedes FRES Frustrations." *Jane's Defence Weekly*, May 23, 2007.

Fergusson, James. *A Million Bullets: The Real Story of the British Army in Afghanistan*. London: Bantam Press, 2008.

——. *Taliban: The True Story of the World's Fiercest Guerrilla Fighters*. London: Bantam Press, 2010.

Fiddian, Paul. "357 UK Training Exercises Axed Since 2003." *Armed Forces International News* (October 2007), http://www.armedforces-int.com/news/357-uk-military-training-exercises-axed-since-2003.html.

Figgures, Lt. Gen. Andrew. Oral evidence given to the Iraq Inquiry, July 27, 2010, http://www.iraqinquiry.org.uk/media/49817/20100727-figgures-fulton-final.pdf.

Filkins, Dexter. "After America: Will Civil War Hit Afghanistan When the U.S. Leaves?" *The New Yorker*, July 9, 2012.

Finer, Jonathan. "An End to the Soft Sell by the British in Basra." *Washington Post*, February 26, 2006.

Finkel, Meir. *On Flexibility: Recovery from Technological and Doctrinal Surprise on the Battlefield*. Stanford, CA: Stanford Security Studies, 2011.

Foley, Robert T., Stuart Griffin, and Helen McCartney. "'Transformation in Contact': Learning the Lessons of Modern War." *International Affairs* 87, no. 2 (2011): 253–270.

Forster, Anthony. "New Labour's Governance of the British Army." In David Brown, ed., *The Development of British Defence Policy: Blair, Brown, and Beyond*, 153–168. Farnham, UK: Ashgate, 2010.

Forster, Anthony and Tim Edmunds. *Out of Step: The Case for Change in British Armed Forces*. London: Demos, 2007.

French, David. *The British Way in Counter-insurgency 1945–1967*. Oxford: Oxford University Press, 2011.

Galula, David. *Counterinsurgency Warfare: Theory and Practice*. 1964. Reprint. Westport, CT: Praeger, 2006.

Gardiner, Ian. *In the Service of the Sultan*. Barnsley, UK: Pen and Sword, 2006.

Garfield, Andrew. *Succeeding in Phase IV: British Perspectives on the U.S. to Stabilize and Reconstruct Iraq*. Philadelphia: Foreign Policy Research Institute, 2006.

Gates, US Secretary of Defense Robert M. Address at the US Military Academy, Sandhurst, West Point, NY, February 25, 2011.

Gentile, Gian P. "Beneficial War." *Harvard International Review* 32, no. 4 (December 24, 2011), http://hir.harvard.edu/india-in-transition/beneficial-war-o.

——. "COIN Is Dead: U.S. Army Must Put Strategy Over Tactics." *World Politics Review*, November 22, 2011, http://www.worldpoliticsreview.com/articles/10731/coin-is-dead-u-s-army-must-put-strategy-over-tactics.

Gordon, Michael R. and Gen. Bernard E. Trainer. *Cobra II: The Inside Story of the Invasion and Occupation of Iraq*. New York: Pantheon Books, 2006.

Gordon, Stuart. "Defence Policy and the 'Joined Up Government' Agenda: Defining the Limits of the 'Comprehensive Approach.'" In David Brown, ed., *The Development of British Defence Policy: Blair, Brown, and Beyond*, 121–137. Farnham, UK: Ashgate, 2010.

——. *Winning Hearts and Minds? Examining the Relationship Between Aid and Security in Afghanistan's Helmand Province*. Boston: Feinstein International Center, Tufts University, April 2011.

Goulter, Christina. "Ellamy: The UK Air Power Contribution to Operation Unified Protector." Draft paper in RAND study on Operation Unified Protector, Santa Monica, CA, forthcoming.

Gray, Bernard. *Review of Acquisition for the Secretary of State for Defence*. London: Ministry of Defence, October 2009.

Gray, Colin S. "The Revolution in Military Affairs." In Brian Bond and Mungo Melvin, eds., *The Nature of Future Conflict: Implications for Force Development*, 58–65. Camberley, UK: Strategic and Combat Studies Institute, 1998.

Greenstock, Sir Jeremy. Oral evidence given at the Iraq Inquiry, London, December 15, 2009, http://www.iraqinquiry.org.uk/transcripts/oralevidence-bydate/091215.aspx.

Grey, Stephen. "Aiding the Enemy." *StephenGrey.com*, September 8, 2009, http://www.stephengrey.com/2009/09/aiding-the-enemy/.

——. *Operation Snakebite: The Explosive True Story of an Afghan Desert Siege*. London: Viking, 2009.

Griffin, Stuart. "Iraq, Afghanistan, and the Future of British Military Doctrine: From Counterinsurgency to Stabilization." *International Affairs* 82, no. 2 (2011): 317–333.

Grissom, Adam. "The Future of Military Innovation Studies." *Journal of Strategic Studies* 29, no. 5 (October 2006): 905–934.

Gumz, Jonathan E. "Reframing the Historical Problematic of Insurgency: How the Professional Military Literature Created a New History and Missed the Past." *Journal of Strategic Studies* 32, no. 4 (2009): 553–588.

Gwynn, Charles W. *Imperial Policing*. London: MacMillan, 1939.

Hack, Karl. "The Malayan Emergency as Counter-insurgency Paradigm." *Journal of Strategic Studies* 32, no. 3 (June 2009): 383–414.

Hanning, James. "Deal with Shia Prisoner Left Basra at Mercy of Gangs, Colonel Admits." *Independent*, August 3, 2008.

Harding, Thomas. "British to Evacuate Consulate in Basra After Mortar Attacks." *Telegraph*, October 30, 2006.

——. "US 'Delayed the Basra Pull-Out from Basra.'" *Telegraph*, September 10, 2007.

Haynes, Deborah. "Major-General Barney White-Spunner: Troops to Have Long-Term Iraq Role." *London Times*, July 14, 2008.

——. "Once Welcomed, British Troops Are Now the Wrong Tools for the Job." *London Times*, August 4, 2007.

——. "They Went Into Helmand with Eyes Shut and Fingers Crossed." *London Times*, June 9, 2010.

Haynes, Deborah and David Robertson. "Scandal of £6 billion Wasted by the MOD." *London Times*, December 14, 2010.

Her Majesty's Government. *Securing Britain in an Age of Uncertainty: The Strategic Defence and Security Review*. London: TSO Limited, 2010.

Hobsbawm, Eric. "Introduction: Investing Traditions." In Eric Hobsbawm and Terence Ranger, eds., *The Invention of Tradition*, Canto Edition, 1–14. Cambridge: Cambridge University Press, 1992.

Hoffman, Frank G. "Neo-classical Counterinsurgency?" *Parameters: U.S. Army War College Quarterly* 37, no. 2 (2007): 71–87.

——. "On Adaptation: Innovating During War." *Proceedings* (forthcoming).

Hoon, Geoffrey. "Delivering Security in a Changing World: Future Capabilities." *Commons Hansard Debates* 424, part. 24 (July 21, 2004): cols. 344–349.

——. "Introduction by the Secretary of State for Defence." In UK Ministry of Defence, *The Strategic Defence Review: A New Chapter*, 4–5. London: Ministry of Defence, July 2002.

——. "Statement on Sierra Leone." *House of Commons Parliamentary Debates* 350, May 15–25, 2000 (May 23, 2000): 15–25.

House of Commons Commission. "Written Answers to Questions." July 20, 2006, http://www.publications.parliament.uk/pa/cm200506/cmhansrd/vo060720/index/60720-x.htm.

House of Commons Defence Committee (HCDC). *The Army's Requirement for Armoured Vehicles: The FRES Programme* (oral evidence). Seventh Report. London: TSO, February 6, 2007.

——. *Future Capabilities*. Fourth Report. London: TSO, March 2005.

——. *Iraq: An Initial Assessment of Post Conflict Operations*. HC 65-I, 2004–2005. London: HMSO, 2005.

——. *Lessons of Iraq*. Vol. 1. London: HMSO, March 16, 2004.

——. *Operations in Afghanistan: Fourth Report of Session 2010–12*. Vol. 1. London: TSO , 2011.

——. *Readiness and Recuperation of the Armed Forces: Looking Towards the Strategic Defence Review* (oral evidence). Fourth Report. London: TSO, 2010.

——. *Recruiting and Retaining Armed Forces Personnel*. Fourteenth Report of 2007–2008. London: HMSO, July 15, 2008.

——. *UK Land Operations in Iraq 2007*. London: HMSO, December 3, 2007.

——. *UK Operations in Iraq and the Gulf*. London: HMSO, July 22, 2008.

House of Commons Foreign Affairs Committee. *Global Security: Afghanistan and Pakistan*. Eighth Report of Session 2008–2009. London: HMSO, February 2, 2009.

Howard, Michael. "A Long War?" *Survival* 48, no. 4 (Winter 2006–2007): 7–14.

——. "Military Science in an Age of Peace." *RUSI Journal* 119, no. 1 (February 1974): 3–11.

Hughes, Geraint and Christian Tripodi. "Anatomy of a Surrogate: Historical Precedents and Implications for Contemporary Counter-insurgency and Counter-terrorism." *Small Wars & Insurgencies* 20, no. 1 (2009): 1–35.

iCasualties.org. "Operation Enduring Freedom." September 2011, http://icasualties.org/oef/.

International Committee of the Red Cross (ICRC). "Afghanistan: Outlook Remains Bleak Despite Progress in Some Areas." Operational Update, January 16, 2012, http://www.icrc.org/eng/resources/documents/update/2012/afghanistan-update-2012-01-16.htm.

International Crisis Group (ICG). *Iraq's Civil War: The Sadrists and the Surge*. Middle East Report no. 72. Brussels: ICG, February 2008.

——. *Where Is Iraq Heading? Lessons from Basra*. Middle East Report no. 67. Brussels: ICG, 2007.

Jackson, Ashley. "British Counterinsurgency in History: A Useful Precedent?" *British Army Review* 139 (Spring 2006): 12–22.

Jackson, Mike. "British Counter-insurgency." *Journal of Strategic Studies* 32, no. 3 (2009): 347–348.

Johnson, David E., Jennifer D. P. Moroney, Roger Cliff, M. Wade Markel, Laurence Smallman, and Michael Spirtas. *Preparing and Training for the Full Spectrum of Military Challenges: Insights from the Experiences of China, France, the United Kingdom, India, and Israel*. Santa Monica, CA: RAND Corporation, 2009.

Judd, Terri. "MoD Accused of Cover-Up After Troop Data Reclassified." *Independent*, February 26, 2010.

——. "Welcome to Afghanistan? No, Norfolk." *Independent*, March 11, 2010.

——. "What Lies Beneath: Army's Bomb-Disposal Teams in Training." *Independent*, April 9, 2010.

Kagan, Frederick W. *Finding the Target: The Transformation of American Military Policy*. New York: Encounter Books, 2006.

Keaney, Thomas A. and Eliot A. Cohen. *Revolution in Warfare? Air Power in the Persian Gulf*. Annapolis, MD: Naval Institute Press, 1995.

Keegan, John. *The Iraq War*. London: Hutchinson, 2004.

Keen, David. *Conflict & Collusion in Sierra Leone*. New York: Palgrave, 2005.

Kilcullen, David. *The Accidental Guerrilla: Fighting Small Wars in the Midst of a Big One*. New York: Oxford University Press, 2009.

——. "Counter-insurgency *Redux*." *Survival* 48, no. 4 (2006): 111–130.

King, Anthony. "Commentary." Submitted to "The Changing Face of War" online conference, November 14–20, 2011, http://wileyblackwellwar.files.wordpress.com/2011/11/foley_et_al_commentary1_anthony_king.pdf.

——. "The Power of Politics." *RUSI Journal* 155, no. 6 (December 2010): 68–74.

——. "Understanding the Helmand Campaign: British Military Operations in Afghanistan." *International Affairs* 86, no. 2 (2010): 311–332.

——. "Why We're Getting It Wrong in Afghanistan." *Prospect*, September 4, 2009.

Kirkup, James. "British Army Recruitment Reduced in £97 Million Cuts Package." *Telegraph*, October 16, 2009.

Kiszely, John. "The Educational Upper Hand." *Defence Management Journal* 46 (Autumn 2009): 188–191.

——. *Post-modern Challenges for the Modern Warrior*. Cranfield, UK: Defence Academy, 2007.

Kitson, Frank. *Bunch of Five*. London: Faber and Faber, 1977.

——. *Low Intensity Operations: Subversion, Insurgency, Peace-keeping*. London: Frank Cass, 1971.

Knights, Michael and Ed Williams. *The Calm Before the Storm*. Policy Focus no. 66. Washington, DC: Washington Institute for Near Eastern Policy, 2007.

Knox, MacGregor and Williamson Murray, eds. *The Dynamics of Military Revolution 1300–2050*. Cambridge: Cambridge University Press, 2001.

Krahmann, Elke. "United Kingdom: Punching Above Its Weight." In Emil J. Kirchner and James Sperling, eds., *Global Security Governance: Competing Perceptions of Security in the 21st Century*, 93–112. London: Routledge, 2007.

Lafranchi, Howard. "In Afghanistan War, US Civilian Surge Peaks as Pentagon Begins Pullback." *Christian Science Monitor*, June 23, 2011.

Larson, Eric V. *Casualties and Consensus: The Historical Role of Casualties in Domestic Support for U.S. Military Operations*. Santa Monica, CA: RAND Corporation, 1996.

Ledwidge, Frank. *Losing Small Wars: British Military Failure in Iraq and Afghanistan*. New Haven, CT: Yale University Press, 2011.

Lieven, Anatol. "Afghanistan: An Unsuitable Candidate for State Building." *Conflict, Security & Development* 7, no. 3 (October 2007): 483–489.

——. "Insights from the Afghan Field." *Current Intelligence*, September 6, 2010, http://www.currentintelligence.net/reviews/2010/9/6/insights-from-the-afghan-field.html.

London Sunday Times. "Confidential Iraq Memo," May 23, 2004.

——. "Sir Mike Jackson: Dimbleby Lecture Full Text." December 7, 2006.

Luff, Undersecretary of State Peter. Statement, House of Commons, December 16, 2010, http://www.publications.parliament.uk/pa/cm201011/cmhansrd/cm101216/text/101216w0002.htm.

Luttwak, Edward N. "Dead End: Counterinsurgency Warfare as Military Malpractice." *Harpers* (February 2007): 33–42.

Mackay, Andrew and Steve Tatham. *Behavioural Conflict: From General to Strategic Corporal: Complexity, Adaptation, and Influence*. Shrivenham Papers no. 9. London: Defence Academy of the United Kingdom, December 2009.

Mackiggan, Keith. Oral testimony given at the Iraq Inquiry, January 7, 2010, http://www.iraqinquiry.org.uk/transcripts/oralevidence-bydate/100107.aspx.

Mackinlay, John. "After 2015: The Next Security Era for Britain." *Prism* 3, no. 2 (2012): 51–60.

——. *The Insurgent Archipelago*. London: Hurst, 2009.

——. "NATO and Bin Laden." *RUSI Journal* 146, no. 6 (2001): 36–40.

——. "War Lords." *RUSI Journal* 143, no. 2 (1998): 24–32.

"Maj.-Gen. Andy Salmon (U.K. Royal Army [*sic*]) Holds a Defense Department News Briefing Via Teleconference from Iraq." *CQ Transcriptions*, October 15, 2008.

Mansoor, Peter. "The British Army and the Lessons of the Iraq War." *British Army Review*, no. 147 (Summer 2009): 11–15.

Mantas, Mirjam Grandia. "Shafer Revisited: The Three Great Oughts of Winning the Hearts and Minds: Analysing the Assumptions Underpinning the British and Dutch COIN Approach in Helmand and Uruzgan." Paper presented at the Society for Military History Conference, Washington, DC, May 2012.

Marks, Thomas A. "Colombian Military Support for 'Democratic Security.'" *Small Wars and Insurgencies* 17, no. 2 (June 2006): 197–220.

Marston, Daniel. "Adaptation in the Field: The British Army's Difficult Campaign in Iraq." *Security Challenges* 6, no. 1 (Autumn 2010): 71–84.

——. "Lessons in 21st-Century Counterinsurgency: Afghanistan 2001–2007." In Daniel Marston and Carter Malkasian, eds., *Counterinsurgency in Modern Warfare*, 220–240. Oxford: Osprey, 2008.

——. "'Smug and Complacent?' Operation TELIC: The Need for Critical Analysis." *British Army Review*, no. 147 (Summer 2009): 16–23.

McCaffrey, Gen. Barry R. "Academic Report—Trip to Afghanistan and Pakistan, Friday 19 May Through Friday 26 May." Memo to Col. Mike Meese, Department of Social Sciences, US Military Academy, June 3, 2006, http://www.mccaffreyassociates.com/wp-content/uploads/2012/05/AfghanAAR-052006.pdf.

McInnes, Colin. "The British Army: Adapting to Change in the 1990s and Beyond." In Brian Bond and Mungo Melvin, eds., *The Nature of Future Conflict: Implications for Force Development*, 66–75. Camberley, UK: Strategic and Combat Studies Institute, 1998.

Miller, Harry. *Jungle War in Malaya: The Campaign Against Communism 1948–60*. London: Arthur Barker, 1972.

Mitton, Kieran. "Engaging with Disengagement." In Mats Berdal and David H. Ucko, eds., *Reintegrating Armed Groups After Conflict: Politics, Violence, and Transition*, 172–198. Abingdon, UK: Routledge, 2009.

Mockaitis, Thomas R. *British Counterinsurgency in the Post-imperial Era*. Manchester, UK: Manchester University Press, 1995.

——. *Peace Operations and Intrastate Conflict: The Sword or the Olive Branch*. Westport, CT: Praeger, 1999.

Mowle, Thomas. "Iraq's Militia Problem." *Survival* 48, no. 3 (2006): 41–58.

Mumford, Andrew. *The Counter-insurgency Myth: The British Experience of Irregular Warfare*. London: Routledge, 2011.

——. "From Belfast to Basra: Britain and the 'Tripartite Counter-insurgency Model.'" PhD diss., University of Warwick, 2009.

Murray, Williamson, *Military Adaptation: The Fear of Change*. New York: Cambridge University Press, 2012.

Murray, Williamson and Robert H. Scales. *The Iraq War: A Military History*. London: Belknap Press, 2003.

Nagl, John A. *Counterinsurgency Lessons from Malaya and Vietnam: Learning to Eat Soup with a Knife*. Westport, CT: Praeger, 2002.

——. *Learning to Eat Soup with a Knife: Counterinsurgency Lessons from Malaya and Vietnam*. Chicago: University of Chicago Press, 2005.

Newsinger, John. *British Counter-insurgency: From Palestine to Northern Ireland*. New York: Palgrave, 2002.

Newton, Lt. Gen. Paul. "The British Vision of Future Commitments and Land Capability Requirements." Unpublished report, December 12, 2011.

North Atlantic Treaty Organization (NATO). *ISAF's Mission in Afghanistan*. December 2, 2012, http://www.nato.int/cps/en/SID-F112BA9A-8DFC140A/natolive/topics_69366.htm.

Norton-Taylor, Richard. "General Hits Out at US Tactics." *The Guardian*, April 20, 2004.

——. "Liam Fox Announces Army Cuts but Promises Extra Funds in Future." *The Guardian*, July 18, 2011.

Norton-Taylor, Richard and Jamie Wilson. "US Army in Iraq Institutionally Racist, Claims British Officer." *The Guardian*, January 12, 2006.

Number 10. "Establishment of a National Security Council." May 12, 2010, http://www.number10.gov.uk/news/establishment-of-a-national-security-council/.

Ollivant, Douglas. *Countering the New Orthodoxy: Reinterpreting Counterinsurgency in Iraq*. Policy Paper. Washington, DC: National Security Studies Program, June 2011.

Orwell, George. "Politics and the English Language." *Harpers* 13, no. 76 (1946): 252–265.

Packer, George. "The Lessons of Tal Afar: Is It Too Late for the Administration to Correct Its Course in Iraq?" *The New Yorker* (April 2006).

Paget, Julian. *Counter-insurgency Campaigning*. London: Faber and Faber, 1967.

Paley, Amit. "On the Sidelines in Basra: British Tackle a New Role." *Washington Post*, December 17, 2007.

Peacekeeping Best Practices Unit (Military Division). *Operation Artemis: The Lessons of the Interim Emergency Multinational Force*. New York: United Nations Department for Peace Keeping Operations, October 2004.

Pengelley, Rupert. "Reality Check: Learning the Art of War in an Age of Diverse Threats." *Jane's International Defence Review*, October 10, 2006.

Petri, Stephen. *Britain's Expeditionary Approach 1997–2010: The Failure to Maintain Pocket Superpower Status*. Seaford House Papers. London: Royal College of Defence Studies, July 2010.

Pitt, Maj. A. R. "Decision-Making in the UK MoD." *British Army Review* 150, no. 2 (Winter 2010–2011): 68–72.

Porch, Douglas. "The Dangerous Myths and Dubious Promise of COIN." *Small Wars & Insurgencies* 22, no. 2 (2011): 239–257.

Posen, Barry R. *The Sources of Military Doctrine: France, Britain, and Germany Between the World Wars*. Ithaca, NY: Cornell University Press, 1984.

Post-Conflict Reconstruction Unit. "Post Conflict Stabilisation: Improving the United Kingdom's Contribution." Consultation on United Kingdom strategy and practice and establishment of a Post-Conflict Reconstruction Unit, Autumn 2004, http://www.niwep.org.uk/id108.htm.

Prins, Gwyn. *The British Way of Strategy-Making: Vital Lessons for Our Times*. Occasional Paper. London: Royal United Services Institute, October 2011.

Rabasa, Angel, John Gordon IV, Peter Chalk, Audra K. Grant, K. Scott McMahon, Stephanie Pezard, Caroline Reilly, David Ucko, and S. Rebecca Zimmerman. *From Insurgency to Stability*. Vol. 2: *Insights from Selected Case Studies*. Santa Monica, CA: RAND Corporation, 2011.

Rangwala, Glen. "Counter-insurgency Amid Fragmentation: The British in Southern Iraq." *Journal of Strategic Studies* 32, no. 3 (June 2009): 495–513.

Rashid, Ahmed. *Descent Into Chaos: The United States and the Failure of Nation Building in Pakistan, Afghanistan, and Central Asia*. New York: Viking Adult, 2008.

Rathmell, Andrew. "Reforming Iraq's Security Sector." *RUSI Journal* 50, no. 1 (February 2005): 8–11.

Rathmell, Andrew, Olga Oliker, Terrence K. Kelly, David Brannan, and Keith Crane. *Developing Iraq's Security Sector: The Coalition Provisional Authority's Experience*. Santa Monica, CA: RAND Corporation, 2005.

Rayment, Sean. "Army Facing Huge Cuts After Withdrawal from Afghanistan." *Telegraph*, February 19, 2011.

Richards, David. "Future Conflict and Its Prevention: People and the Information Age." Address given at the International Institute for Strategic Studies, London, January 18, 2010.

——. "A Soldier's Perspective on Countering Insurgency." In David Richards and Greg Mills, eds., *Victory Among People: Lessons from Countering Insurgency and Stabilising Fragile States*, 15–34. London: Royal United Services Institute, 2011.

——. "Twenty-First Century Armed Forces: Agile, Useable, Relevant." Address given at the Royal United Services Institute Land Warfare Conference, London, June 23–25, 2009.

Rid, Thomas. "The Nineteenth Century Origins of Counterinsurgency Doctrine." *Journal of Strategic Studies* 33, no. 5 (2010): 727–758.

Rid, Thomas and Marc Hecker. *War 2.0: Irregular Warfare in the Information Age*. Westport, CT: Praeger Security International, 2009.

Rid, Thomas and Timo Noetzel. "Germany's Options in Afghanistan." *Survival* 51, no. 5 (2009): 71–90.

Rigden, I. A. *The British Approach to Counter-insurgency: Myths, Realities, and Strategic Challenges*. Strategy Research Report. Carlisle, PA: US Army War College, 2008.

Ritchie, Nick. "Rethinking Security: A Critical Analysis of the Strategic Defence and Security Review." *International Affairs* 87, no. 2 (2011): 355–376.

Rodwell, Tom. "Between Idea and the Reality: The Evolution of an Application of the Comprehensive Approach. Hollow Men and Doctrine in Helmand?" Master's thesis, King's College, London, 2010.

Rosen, Steven Peter. *Winning the Next War: Innovation and the Modern Military*. Ithaca, NY: Cornell University Press, 1991.

Russell, James A. *Innovation, Transformation, and War: Counterinsurgency Operations in Anbar and Ninewa Provinces, Iraq, 2005–2007*. Stanford, CA: Stanford Security Studies, 2011.

Shirreff, Lt. Gen. Sir Richard. Evidence given at the Iraq Inquiry, January 11, 2011, http://www.iraqinquiry.org.uk/media/44178/20100111am-shirreff-final.pdf.

Smith, M. L. R. "A Tradition That Never Was: Critiquing the Critique of British COIN." *Small Wars Journal*, August 9, 2012, http://smallwarsjournal.com/jrnl/art/a-tradition-that-never-was.

Smith, Gen. Rupert. *The Utility of Force: The Art of War in the Modern World*. New York: Knopf, 2005.

Southby-Tailyour, Ewen. *Helmand, Afghanistan*. London: Ebury, 2008.

Spencer, Sir Peter. Evidence given to the Iraq Inquiry, July 26, 2010, http://www.iraqinquiry.org.uk/media/48689/20100726pm-spencer.pdf.

Stein, Janice and Eugene Lang. *The Unexpected War*. Toronto: Viking, 2007.

Stephenson, James. *Losing the Golden Hour: An Insider's View of Iraq's Reconstruction*. Washington, DC: Potomac Books, 2007.

Stirrup, Air Chief Marshal Sir Jock. Evidence given at the Iraq Inquiry, February 1, 2010, http://www.iraqinquiry.org.uk/media/45320/20100201am-stirrup-final.pdf.

——. Speech given at the Royal United Services Institute, London, December 1, 2008.

Storrie, Brig. Sandy. "'First Do No Harm': 7 Armoured Brigade in Southern Iraq." *British Army Review*, no. 147 (Summer 2009): 29–34.

Stothard Tee, William. Imperial War Museum Sound Archive, Accession no. 16397, January 6, 1996.

Strachan, Hew. "British Counter-insurgency from Malaya to Iraq." *RUSI Journal* 152, no. 6 (December 2007): 8–11.

——. Evidence before the House of Commons Defence Committee, March 25, 2008, http://www.publications.parliament.uk/pa/cm200708/cmselect/cmdfence/424/8032503.htm.

——. "Introduction." In Hew Strachan, ed., *Big Wars and Small Wars: The British Army and the Lessons of War in the 20th Century*, 1–20. Abingdon, UK: Routledge, 2006.

——. "Strategy or Alibi? Obama, McChrystal, and the Operational Level of War." *Survival* 52, no. 5 (2010): 157–182.

Suhrke, Astri. "A Contradictory Mission? NATO from Stabilization to Combat in Afghanistan." *International Peacekeeping* 15, no. 2 (2008): 214–236.

Synnott, Hilary. *Bad Days in Basra*. London: I. B. Taurus, 2008.

Telegraph. "MoD Builds Afghan Village in Norfolk." May 1, 2009.

Think Defence. "Another Look at Balance." March 13, 2011, http://www.thinkdefence.co.uk/2011/03/another-look-at-balance/.

——. "#Army2020—a Few Thoughts." July 12, 2012, http://www.thinkdefence.co.uk/2012/07/army2020-a-few-thoughts.

——. "Unbalanced—Yes or No?" February 27, 2011, http://www.thinkdefence.co.uk/2011/02/unbalanced-yes-or-no/.

Thompson, Robert. *Defeating Communist Insurgency: The Lessons of Malaya and Vietnam*. New York: Praeger, 1966.

Thornton, Rod. "The British Army and the Origins of Its Minimum Force Philosophy." *Small Wars & Insurgencies* 15, no. 1 (2004): 83–106.

——. "Getting It Wrong: The Crucial Mistakes Made in the Early Stages of the British Army's Deployment to Northern Ireland (August 1969 to March 1972)." *Journal of Strategic Studies* 30, no. 1 (2007): 73–107.

——. "Historical Origins of the British Army's Counterinsurgency and Counter-terrorist Techniques." In Theodor Winkler, Anja Ebnöther, and Mats Hansson, eds., *Combating Terrorism and Its Implications for the Security Sector*, 24–49. Stockholm: Swedish National Defence College, 2005.

Thruelsen, Peter Dahl. "Counterinsurgency and a Comprehensive Approach: Helmand Province, Afghanistan." *Small Wars Journal* 4, no. 9 (September 2008), http://smallwarsjournal.com/jrnl/art/counterinsurgency-and-a-comprehensive-approach.

——. *NATO in Afghanistan: What Lessons Are We Learning and Are We Willing to Adjust?* Copenhagen: Danish Institute for International Studies, 2007.

Tilney, Angus M. A. "Preparing the British Army for Future Warfare." Master's thesis, US Army Command and General Staff College, Fort Leavenworth, KS, 2011, http://www.dtic.mil/dtic/tr/fulltext/u2/a556554.pdf.

Tootal, Stuart. *Danger Close: Commanding 3 Para in Afghanistan*. London: John Murray, 2009.

Townshend, Charles. *Britain's Civil Wars: Counterinsurgency in the Twentieth Century*. London: Faber and Faber, 1986.

Ucko, David H. "Counterinsurgency After Afghanistan: A Concept in Crisis." *Prism* 3, no. 1 (December 2011): 3–20.

——. "Lessons from Basra: The Future of British Counter-insurgency." *Survival* 52, no. 4 (2010): 131–158.

——. "The Malayan Emergency: The Legacy and Relevance of a Counter-insurgency Success Story." *Defence Studies* 10, no. 1 (2010): 13–39.

——. "Peace-building after Afghanistan: Between Promise and Peril." *Contemporary Security Policy* 31, no. 3 (2010): 465–485.

UK Ministry of Defence (MoD). *Delivering Security in a Changing World: Defence White Paper*. London: TSO, 2003.

——. *Delivering Security in a Changing World: Future Capabilities*. London: MoD, 2004.

——. *Future Land Operational Concept*. Shrivenham: Development, Concept, Doctrine Centre, 2008.

——. "Operations in Afghanistan: Background Briefing." Undated factsheet,https://www.gov.uk/uk-forces-operations-in-afghanistan.

——. "Operations in Afghanistan: Our Strategy." Undated factsheet,https://www.gov.uk/uk-forces-operations-in-afghanistan.

——. "Operations in Afghanistan: Why We Are There."Undated factsheet,https://www.gov.uk/uk-forces-operations-in-afghanistan.

——. *Operations in Iraq: An Analysis from a Land Perspective*. London: MoD, February 2005.

——. *Operations in Iraq: First Reflections*. London: Director General Corporate Communication, July 2003.

——. *Operations in Iraq: Lessons for the Future*. London: Director General Corporate Communication, December 2003.

——. "Parliament Honours UK Troops for Libya Operations." *Defence News*, April 25, 2012, https://www.gov.uk/government/news/parliament-honours-uk-troops-for-libya-operations.

——. "Prime Minister Announces UK Force Reduction in Iraq." *Defence Policy and Business*, February 21, 2007.

——. *Security and Stabilisation: The Military Contribution*. Joint Doctrine Publication 3-40. Shrivenham: Development, Concept, Doctrine Centre, 2009.

——. *Stability Operations in Iraq (Op Telic 2-5): An Analysis from a Land Perspective*. London: MoD, July 2006.

——. *The Strategic Defence Review*. Norwich: TSO, 1998.

——. *The Strategic Defence Review: A New Chapter*. London: MoD, July 2002.

——. *Strategic Trends Programme: Future Character of Conflict*. Shrivenham: Development, Concepts, Doctrine Centre, 2010.

——. "UK Armed Forces Minister Sees a Secure Basra." *Defence Policy and Business*, February 9, 2009.

——. *Wider Peacekeeping*. London: HMSO, 1995.

UK National Audit Office. *Ministry of Defence, Battlefield Helicopters.* Report by the Comptroller and Auditor General, HC 486, Session 2003–2004. London: TSO, April 7, 2004.

——. *Ministry of Defence: The Major Projects Report 2009.* Report by the Comptroller and Auditor General, HC 85-i, Session 2009–2010. London: TSO, December 15, 2009.

——. *Ministry of Defence, Operation TELIC: United Kingdom Military Operations in Iraq.* London: TSO, December 11, 2003.

——. *Ministry of Defence: Recruitment and Retention in the Armed Forces.* HC 1633-I. London: TSO, November 3, 2006.

——. *Support to High Intensity Operations.* HC 508, Session 2008–2009. London: TSO, 2009.

UK War Office. *Keeping the Peace (Duties in Support of the Civil Power).* Code 9455. London: War Office, April 10, 1957.

United Nations Assistance Mission in Afghanistan (UNAMA). *Afghanistan Annual Report on Protection of Civilians in Armed Conflict 2010.* Jalalabad, Afghanistan: UNAMA, March 2011, http://unama.unmissions.org/Portals/UNAMA/human%20rights/March%20PoC%20Annual%20Report%20Final.pdf.

United Nations High Commissioner for Refugees (UNHCR). *Basrah Governorate Assessment Report.* Geneva: UNHCR, August 2006.

Urban, Mark. *Task Force Black: The Explosive True Story of the Secret Special Forces War in Iraq.* New York: St. Martin's Press, 2011.

US Department of the Army and United States Marine Corps. *Counterinsurgency.* , FM 3-24 MCWP 3-33.5. Washington, DC: Department of the Army, December 2006.

US Department of Defense. *Measuring Stability and Security in Iraq.* Washington, DC: Department of Defense, December 2007.

——. *Measuring Stability and Security in Iraq.* Washington, DC: Department of Defense, March 2008.

US Fed News. "British Army Trains at Afghan-Style Village of Hettar." November 19, 2009.

US Under Secretary for Defense. *Instruction 3000.05: Stability Operations.* Washington, DC: Department of Defense, September 16, 2009.

Waldman, Thomas. "British 'Post-conflict' Operations in Iraq: Into the Heart of Strategic Darkness." *Civil Wars* 9, no. 1 (March 2007): 61–86.

Wall, General Sir Peter. Testimony given at the Iraq Inquiry, London, January 6, 2010, http://www.iraqinquiry.org.uk/media/49687/20100106-wall-day-final.pdf.

Washington Post. "Advice from an Ally: Get Past the Warrior Ethos." January 15, 2006.

Weigley, Russell F. *The American Way of War: A History of United States Military Strategy and Policy.* Bloomington: Indiana University Press, 1973.

West, Bing. "Counterinsurgency: A New Doctrine's Fading Allure." *Counterinsurgency in the Post COIN Era.* N.p.: World Politics Review Feature, 2012, http://www.worldpoliticsreview.com/articles/11249/counterinsurgency-a-new-doctrines-fading-allure.

White, Stephen, OBE. Statement made at the Iraq Inquiry. June 20, 2010, http://www.iraqinquiry.org.uk/media/46537/white-statement.pdf.

White House. "President's Address to the Nation." January 10, 2007.

——. "President Speaks on War Effort to Citadel Cadets, South Carolina." December 11, 2001.

White-Spunner, Lt. Gen. Barney. Testimony given at the Iraq Inquiry, January 7, 2010, http://www.iraqinquiry.org.uk/.

Woodward, Susan L. "Do the Root Causes of Civil War Matter? On Using Knowledge to Improve Peacebuilding Interventions." *Journal of Intervention and Statebuilding* 1, no. 2 (June 2007): 143–170.

INDEX

Abdel-Latif, Wael, 58

Abu Sayyaf Group, 156

ACC. *See* Afghan COIN Centre

accommodation: of Basra militias, 57, 65; in British counterinsurgency legacy, 32, 43

adaptation: bottom-up, 13–15; relationship of learning to, 13–15; tactical, in British operations in Helmand, 75, 90–91. *See also* operational adaptation

Adaptive Foundation, 118–19

Aden (Yemen), 19, 29

Advanced Command and Staff Course, 40

Advanced Research and Assessment Group (ARAG), 126

advisory approach to intervention, 156–61

aerial warfare. *See* air power

Afghan COIN Centre (ACC), 124–25, 126, 143

Afghan Development Zones, 95, 96, 100

Afghanistan: civil war in, potential escalation of, 106, 179n89; future of, after transition, 105–6; presidential elections in, 97

"Afghanistan good enough," 104, 105

Afghan model, 153–54, 155, 185n16

Afghan National Army, 76, 87

Afghan National Security Forces (ANSF), 100, 101

Afghan Transitional Authority, 76

Afghan War (2001–): as aberration, perception of, 131, 138; British participation in initial phase of, 76; campaign plan in, pillars of, 75, 88, 176n1; expansion of British role in, 77; expansion of scope of, 75, 76–77; future of Afghanistan after, 105–6; German participation in, constraints on, 148; vs. Libyan intervention, 153, 154; Northern Alliance in, 159; number of British troops in, 76, 77; Operation Enduring Freedom in, 76, 77, 83, 153–54, 184n17; Operation Herrick in, 76; Operation Mountain Thrust in, 86–87, 108; politically led operations in, switch to, 100, 178n75; purpose of, confusion over, 80–82, 83, 106, 165; recent levels of violence in, 105; relevance of British counterinsurgency legacy in, 36–37; search for way of ending, 81–82; start of, 76; surge of 2010 in, 100, 101, 105; as third-party intervention, 4, 36;

US strategic evolution in, 81; US troop sizing in, 133. *See also* Helmand

Agile Warrior exercise, 124

Ainsworth, Bob, 72

Air Force, Royal, 77, 153

Air–Land Battle, US doctrine of, 39

air power: in future of counterinsurgency, 152–56; in Libyan intervention, 152–56

Akhundzada, Sher Mohammed, 78–79, 103–4

AKX. *See* Army Knowledge Exchange

Alderson, Alexander, 23–24, 41, 127, 167n7

Allen, John, 105

ambitions vs. means, of British military, 138–42, 150–51

analytical capabilities, reform of, 122–28

Anbar Province (Iraq), 61, 98

ANSF. *See* Afghan National Security Forces

ARAG. *See* Advanced Research and Assessment Group

armored vehicles, 114, 140–41

arms embargo, in Libya, 152

Army, Afghan National, 76, 87

Army, British: Army 2020 plan for, 134–35, 157, 158–59; after Cold War, lack of changes in, 38–39; conventional warfare as focus of, 40–41, 89, 109–10, 115, 118; on definition of counterinsurgency, 5; exaggeration of role in counterinsurgency, 34–35; as learning institution, 13, 124; postgraduate education in, 127; reform of (*See* institutional reform); regimental system of, 41–42, 89; size of, 132–35; structure of, 131–38. *See also* Basra; counterinsurgency; Helmand

Army, Iraqi: British collaboration with, expansion of, 69–70; British withdrawal from Basra and, 64, 67; in Operation Charge of the Knights, 69, 156, 164

Army, US: in Basra, 71; Future Combat System of, 132–33; postgraduate education in, 127, 181n61; rediscovery of counterinsurgency in, 113

Army Knowledge Exchange (AKX), 124–25

Army Reserve, British, 135, 182n91

Army 2020, 134–35, 157, 158–59

Artemis, Operation, 161–62

assassinations, 59

Aylwin-Foster, Nigel, 20

Az Zubayr (Iraq), 47, 48

Badr Brigade, 56, 57

Badr Organisation for Reconstruction, 57, 66

Baghdad (Iraq), US surge of 2007 in, 61, 98

Balkan campaigns of 1990s, 139, 153–54, 155

Barry, Ben, 155

bases: in Afghanistan, British establishment of, 79; in Iraq, British withdrawal from, 63, 64

Basra (Iraq): fall of (2003), 19, 48; location of, 47; militias in (*See* militias); opposition to Hussein in, 47, 52; population of, 47; provincial council of, 60, 63, 67; revolts of 1991 and 1999 in, 47

Basra, British operations in, xv, 45–74; avoidance of counterinsurgency in, 148–49; casualties in, 57, 60, 65–66; civilian agencies in, 54–55, 60, 70, 112; in creation of insurgency, 45–46; end of, 71; expectations about benefits of counterinsurgency legacy in, 2, 25–26, 52–53, 73; extrinsic vs. intrinsic factors in outcome of, 2–3, 91; funding for, 54, 173nn35–36; initial missteps in, 52–57, 72; and institutional reform, recognition of need for, 112, 113; and institutional reform, resistance to, 128, 129–30; length of tours in, 135; lessons learned from, 4, 73–74, 147; lessons learned from, application in Helmand, 92–94, 107; local opposition to, rise of, 59–60; local security forces in (*See* security forces); normalization after invasion, 35, 51–52, 53; number of British troops in, 48, 56, 60, 67, 77, 132, 175n93, 176n7; operational adaptation in, 57–58, 69–72; Operation Charge of

the Knights, 68–72, 74, 93, 128, 156, 164;
Operation Salamanca, 61–63; Operation
Sinbad, 62–63, 174n70; Operation Zenith,
174n65, 174n70; origins of, 47–49; as
peace operation vs. counterinsurgency,
52–57; political control in, British transfer
of, 51, 55, 63–68; political control in,
struggle for, 56–57, 58–59, 61; and postwar
planning, lack of, 51–52, 72–73, 173n25;
strategic inertia in, 57–62, 73; strategic
miscalculations in, 55–57, 72–74, 147; study
of, need for, 16–18; success in, perception
of, 57, 128; as target and cause of violence,
64–65; transition from major combat
to postconflict operations in, 19, 48;
typical counterinsurgency tasks in, 1; UN
on security climate of, 51; use of term
"counterinsurgency" for, 1, 4; US forces
supporting, 68–71; withdrawal of forces
in 2003, 55–56; withdrawal of forces in
2006–2007, 62–68; withdrawal of forces
in 2009, 70–71
Basra Investment Commission, 70
Basra Operational Command, 65
Bastion, Camp (Afghanistan), 79, 117
Batang Kali massacre of 1948, 32
Belize, British military training in, 118
Betz, David, 129
Black, Jeremy, 16, 35, 170n26
Blair, Tony: in British entry into Iraq War,
45, 46; on deployments to Helmand,
113; on equipment shortages, 114; on
expansion of British role in Afghanistan,
77; international community doctrine of,
46; strategic inertia in Basra under, 61;
strategic objectives for Basra under, 55;
withdrawal of forces from Basra in 2006
by, 63
bottom-up adaptation, 13–15
Britain: international community doctrine of,
46, 139–40; US "special relationship" with,
viii, 82. See also government; military

British Army Field Manual, 8–9
British Army Field Manual: Counter Insurgency
Operations, 116–17
British Army Review (journal), 129–30, 137
Brown, Christopher, 182n93
Brown, Gordon, 61, 66
Browne, Des, 86
brutality, in counterinsurgency practice,
31–32
budget, British defense: ambitions vs. means
in, 138–42, 150–51; Basra operations in, 54,
173nn35–36; financial crisis and, 115–16;
flawed perception of, 138–42; gap in,
estimates of, 127; institutional reform
affected by, 111, 115–16, 126, 127–28; as
proportion of GDP, 140, 183n109; recent
cuts to, 16, 111
budget, US defense, 183n109
burden sharing, future of, 164–65
bureaucracy, in resistance to institutional
reform, 128, 129
Bush, George W.: on end of combat phase
of Iraq War, 48; on force transformation,
182n81; on Operation Enduring Freedom,
184n17; surge in Iraq under, 61, 104
Butler, Ed, 83, 84, 87, 92, 93

Cameron, David, 148, 164
Canada: British military training in, 113, 117;
on mission in Afghanistan, 83
Carter, Nick, 103
Cassidy, Robert, 170n24
casualties: in air campaigns, 154; in Basra, 57,
60, 65–66; in Helmand, 80, 88, 137
cease-fires, in Iraq, 66, 69
censorship, within military, 128–30
Central Command, US, planning for Iraq
War by, 50
Chalmers, Malcolm, 134
Charge of the Knights, Operation, 68–72, 74,
93, 128, 156, 164
Chin, Warren, 55

Chinese population, in Malayan Emergency, 35, 171n45
cholera, 55
Churchill, Winston, viii
CIMIC. *See* civil–military cooperation
civilian agencies: in Basra operations, increase in, 60, 70; in Basra operations, lack of, 54–55, 112; downplaying of role in counterinsurgency campaigns, 34–35; in Helmand operations, increase in, 95–96, 101; in Helmand operations, lack of, 88, 93; in institutional reform of military, 112–13, 116, 137–38; shortfall in capacity of, 137
civil–military cooperation (CIMIC): as counterinsurgency principle, 8; in Helmand, establishment of, 95; in Helmand, lack of, 86, 93; in institutional reform, 112–13, 137–38
civil war, Afghan, potential escalation in, 106, 179n89
Clarke, Michael, 91–92
Clausewitz, Carl von, ix, x, 94
clearing operations, in Helmand, 91, 96, 97, 100, 103, 104
coalition, Iraq War: Britain as junior partner in, 2, 49, 72–73, 147, 164; UN resolution on legal status of, 48; US responsibility for planning in, 49–50
coalition(s), challenge of organizational learning in, 15
Coalition Provision Authority (CPA): in Basra operations, role of, 54–55, 173n35; creation of, 48; on local political control, 56, 57; on militias, 56; mission of, 48–49; Regulation Number 1 of, 48
coercion: in British counterinsurgency practice, 30–34; co-option combined with, 31, 33, 43
Coghlan, Tom, 78
Cohen, Eliot, 12
COIN. *See* counterinsurgency

Cold War: changes in military after, 38–39; conventional view of war during, 38
Colombia, advisory approach in, 156, 159, 185n26
colonialism, British: and advisory approach to intervention, 157; counterinsurgency legacy based on, 1, 23; and relevance of counterinsurgency legacy, 36, 37–38, 43. *See also specific colonies*
combat operations, major: in Basra, end of, 19, 48; in British military ethos, 89; in Helmand, 89, 99
Combined Arms Tactical Trainer, 121
command, unity of, as counterinsurgency principle, 8, 60, 86
command-and-control capabilities, British strength in, 154, 157
communication technology, in changes to nature of insurgency, 37
complacency, 43, 52, 146
computer simulations, 121
concealment, 155
concept of operations (CONOPS), 90–91
Congo, Democratic Republic of the (DRC), 161–62
CONOPS. *See* concept of operations
contingency operations, 161–63
conventional warfare: as focus of British military, 38–41, 109–10; in institutional reform, 118–22; in military education, 40–41, 89, 109–10, 115, 118; in revolution in military affairs, 39–40; use of term, 7
co-option, coercion combined with, 31, 33, 43
Cornish, Paul, 184n10
counterguerrilla wars, 7
counterinsurgency: attempts to avoid, xv, 12, 148–51; challenges of, 10–12, 17; characteristics of, 6–7; criteria for undertaking, 12–13; definitions of, 5–6, 98; as failed doctrine, 11–12; fluidity of concept, 5; fundamental changes to nature of, 146; modern applicability of concept

of, 3; vs. peacekeeping operations, 7, 40, 110; political will in outcome of, 15–16; primary goal of, 8; principles of (*See* counterinsurgency principles); rediscovery and reintroduction of, 2, 12, 113; root causes of insurgency in, 5–6; as strategy vs. operational approach, 98; study of, need for, 12, 16–18, 168n26; tasks associated with, 1; vs. third-party intervention, 4; traditional categories of war challenged by, 7, 10; unique nature of each operation, 11–12, 41

counterinsurgency, British, future of, xv–xvi, 145–66; air power in, 152–56; avoidance as approach to, 148–51, 166; burden sharing in, 164–65; contingency operations in, 161–63; indirect (advisory) approach to intervention in, 156–61; inevitability of missions in, 148–51; institutional recognition of, 110–11; Operation Charge of the Knights as indication of, 74, 156, 164; strategic thinking in, role of, 163–64

counterinsurgency, British, legacy of, xiv, 19–44; accuracy of, 21, 26–35, 146; in advisory approach to intervention, 157; claims about usefulness of, 1–2, 22–26; in education and training, 40–41; exaggeration of role of military in, 34–35; expectations about application of, in Basra, 2, 25–26, 52–53, 73; expectations about application of, in Helmand, 2; historical cases cited as bases for, 1–2, 19, 23–24, 25; historiography of, xiv, 22–24; origin and nature of, 22–26; principles derived from, 21, 24; problems with common understanding of, xiv, 3, 21, 24, 32, 43–44; relevance of, 3, 21, 26–27, 35–42, 146; US embrace of, 24–25

counterinsurgency, British, recent experience with. *See* Basra; Helmand

counterinsurgency, US: British counter-insurgency legacy in, 24–25; British

influence on, 3, 24–25; open discussions of, vs. British self-censorship, 130; rediscovery of, 113; after Vietnam War, xv

Counterinsurgency Lessons from Malaya and Vietnam (Nagl), 25

Counter Insurgency Operations (Strategic and Operational Guidelines), 113–14, 115, 116

counterinsurgency principles: derived from counterinsurgency legacy, 21, 24; knowledge vs. practice of, 42, 43; overview of, 7–13; relevance of, 42, 146

counternarcotics, in Afghanistan, 81, 82

counterterrorism, in Afghanistan, 81–82, 83

CPA. *See* Coalition Provision Authority

Cranfield University, 120

Cross, Tim, 50

crowd sourcing, 182n70

cultural advisors (CULADs), 120

cultural education, 112, 119–20

Cultural Institute, 126

culture, organizational, of British military, 89–90, 128–30

Dannatt, Richard, 77, 130, 131, 171n58

Daoud, Mohammad, 78, 85, 86

DCSU. *See* Defence Cultural Specialist Unit

Defeating Communist Insurgency (Thompson), 24

Defence, Ministry of. *See* Ministry of Defence

Defence Academy, 126–27

Defence Academy Reserve Cadre, 126

Defence Attaché posts, 127

Defence Cultural Specialist Unit (DCSU), 120, 180n38

Defence Fellowships program, 127

Defence Intelligence Staff, 127

defense budget. *See* budget

democracy: in Afghanistan, as goal of intervention, 81; in Iraq, as goal of CPA, 49

Democratic Republic of the Congo (DRC), 161–62

Denmark, in Afghan War, 87

Department for International Development (DfID): in Basra, return of, 70; funding for Basra operations from, 173n36; in planning for Iraq War, 50; in Post-Conflict Reconstruction Unit, 112–13

Development, Concepts, Doctrine Centre, MoD, 119

development activities: in Basra, 54–55, 64, 70; in campaign plan for Afghanistan, 75, 176n1; in Helmand, 88, 95–97. *See also* reconstruction

DfID. *See* Department for International Development

Dhi Qar (Iraq), 48

Dhofar, British counterinsurgency in, 157–58, 160, 170n19

district war executive committees, 70

Dixon, Paul, 30

dominant battle-space knowledge, 39

Drayson, Paul, 141, 142, 183n114, 184n123

DRC. *See* Democratic Republic of the Congo

drug lords, Afghan, 78

Duties in Aid of Civil Power (1923 manual), 9

dwell time, 131, 134

education. *See* military education; training

effects-based operations, 110, 139

elections: Afghan, 97; Iraqi, 58

Elkins, Caroline, 27–28

Emergency Infrastructure Plan, in Basra, 54

empire. *See* colonialism

Enduring Freedom, Operation (OEF), 76, 77, 83, 153–54, 184n17

Entirety, Operation, 130

EOD. *See* explosive ordnance disposal

equipment: cost of, 140–41; shortages in, 114, 121, 141–42, 180n39

Etherington, Mark, 89

ethnic conflict, in Malayan Emergency, 35

ethos, of British military, 89–90

European Union (EU), in Operation Artemis in DRC, 161

expeditionary operations: changes to, after colonialism, 37–38; future of, 106, 149–50; non-counterinsurgency, challenges of, 149, 150. *See also specific operations*

explosive ordnance disposal (EOD) technicians, 136–37

Facilities Protection Service, 58

failing states: future of interventions in, 149–50; as national-security threats, 111

Fallujah (Iraq), 20

Farrell, Theo, 96, 100

Fartusi, Ahmed al-, 64–65

FDT. *See* Force Development and Training

Ferguson, James, 93

V Corps (U.S.), 47

52 Infantry Brigade (British), 94–96, 107

Figgures, Andrew, 183n115

financial crisis: competition for funding in, 115–16; and force sizing, 133

1st Armoured Division (British), 47, 51

1st Marine Expeditionary Force (U.S.), 47

flexibility, operational, as counterinsurgency principle, 8, 9–10

food-denial operations, 32, 33

force, use of minimum: as counterinsurgency principle, 8, 9; in winning hearts and minds, 9, 30

Force Development and Training (FDT) Command, 123–24, 125–26, 128, 143

forced relocation, 32–33, 171n45

force sizing: in advisory approach to intervention, 159; in Basra, 48, 56, 60, 67, 77, 132, 175n93, 176n7; British reform of, 132–35, 182n88; in Helmand, 79, 80, 84, 85, 94, 96, 132, 178n68; US increases in, 133

force structure, British reform of, 131–38

force transformation, 110, 132, 182n81

Foreign Affairs Select Committee, 136

Foreign and Commonwealth Office, UK:
in planning for Iraq War, 50; in Post-
Conflict Reconstruction Unit, 112–13; on
US postconflict operations, 20
foreign policy, British, international
community doctrine in, 46, 139–40
Forster, Anthony, 140
Fort Leavenworth, Counterinsurgency
Center at, 124
foundational training, reform of, 118–19
14th Division (Iraq), 67, 68, 70–71
France: counterinsurgency legacy of, 24, 170n21;
in Operation Artemis in DRC, 161, 162
French, David, 24, 30, 171n50
FRES. See Future Rapid Effects System
Fuerzas Armadas Revolucionarias de
Colombia, 156, 185n26
funding. See budget
Furayji, Mohan al-, 65, 66, 68
Future Army Structure program, 132, 133
Future Combat System, US, 132–33
Future Land Operational Concept (MoD),
121–22
Future Rapid Effects System (FRES), 132–33,
140–41

Gaddafi, Muammar, 152, 153, 154–55, 185n19
Galula, David, 8
Gardiner, Ian, 158
Gates, Robert, 133, 135
GDP. See gross domestic product
genocide, Rwandan, 185n19
Gentile, Gian P., 168n26
Germany, in Afghan War, 148
Good News Afghanistan, 179n84
Gordon, Stuart, 96
Goulter, Christina, 153
governance: in campaign plan for
Afghanistan, 75, 88, 176n1; in Helmand,
improvements to, 95–97, 101
government, British: in planning for Iraq
War, 50; politics of, in resistance to

institutional reform, 128–30; response to
counterinsurgency failures, xv; role in
counterinsurgency failures, 2–3. See also
House of Commons; Ministry of Defence
governorships: Afghan, 78–79, 85, 86, 101;
Iraqi, 57, 58, 60
Gray, Bernard, 140
gross domestic product (GDP), defense
budgets as proportion of, 140, 183n109
ground forces: in advisory approach to
intervention, 157; air power combined
with, 153; as proportion of total personnel,
134
Guinea, 163
Gulf War (1991), 39, 139
Gumz, Jonathan, 27

Hakim, Abdul Aziz al-, 56
Hamkari, Operation, 102, 103, 104, 156, 157
Harmony Guidelines, 134
Headquarters 6th Division (British), 102–3,
157
hearts and minds. See winning hearts and
minds
helicopters, 114, 184n124
Helmand (Afghanistan): before British
deployment, 75, 77–78; governorship of,
78–79; recent levels of violence in, 105;
Taliban in (See Taliban)
Helmand, British operations in, xv, 75–108;
avoidance of counterinsurgency in,
148–49; casualties in, 80, 88, 137; civilian
agencies in, 88, 93, 95–96, 101; decision
to undertake, 80; expectations about
benefits of counterinsurgency legacy
in, 2; extrinsic vs. intrinsic factors in
outcome of, 2–3, 91; initial missteps in,
75, 78–80, 107; "ink spot" strategy in, 79,
88, 95, 100, 105; intelligence gaps in, 77,
79, 80, 82–83, 94; length of tours in, 135;
lessons from Basra applied to, 92–94,
107; lessons learned from, 4, 92, 99, 106,

107–8, 147; local security forces in (*See* security forces); NATO's plan for, 75; in northern parts of province, 80, 85–86, 87, 90, 99; number of British troops in, 79, 80, 84, 85, 94, 96, 132, 178n68; operational adaptation in, 88–92, 94–99, 107; operational mistakes in, 84–92; Operation Moshtarak II, 100–101, 102, 104, 157; Operation Panther's Claw, 97; Operation Strike of the Sword, 97; organizational culture in, influence of, 89–90; origins of, 75–80; as peacekeeping operation, 82, 83, 88–89; planning for, 78–79, 83, 93; platoon-house strategy of, 85, 87–88, 90; purpose of, confusion over, 75, 80–82, 83, 106; resources provided for, 84–85, 96, 99, 101; security status of region before, 75, 77–78; strategic evolution of, 95–96; strategic inertia in, 96–99, 107; strategic miscalculations in, 79–86, 91–92, 147; study of, need for, 16–18; success of, lack of indicators of, 105, 106, 179n87; theory vs. application of counterinsurgency in, 96–99; transition process in, 102–6; typical counterinsurgency tasks in, 1; use of term "counterinsurgency" for, 1; US Operation Mountain Thrust and, 86–87, 108; US reinforcements in, 75, 97, 99–102, 107

Helmand Road Map, 95

Herrick, Operation, 76

Higher Command and Staff Course, 114

Hizb al-Fadhila al-Islamiya, 58

Hizbullah, 58

Hobsbawn, Eric, 26

Hoffman, Frank G., 11, 168n28

Hoon, Geoff, 140

"horse and tank moment," 130

House of Commons, British: on deployment in northern Helmand, 86; Foreign Affairs Select Committee of, 136; on mission in Afghanistan, 82, 177n22; on number of troops in Helmand, 84; on postconflict operations in Basra, 19–20

Howard, Michael, 14, 150

human intelligence, crucial role of, as counterinsurgency principle, 9

human rights violations, 32, 46

Hussein, Saddam: Basra's opposition to, 47, 52; Iraqi response to overthrow of, 50. *See also* Iraq War

Hutton, John, 142

Hybrid Foundational Training, 119

Iban Scouts, 34

IEMF. *See* Interim Emergency Multinational Force

Independent (newspaper), 136

India, 29

indigenous forces. *See* security forces

influence operations, in Helmand, 95–96

information superiority, 110. *See also* technological superiority

information technology revolution, 37

infrastructure, of Basra, 51, 54–55, 70. *See also* reconstruction

Ingram, Adam, 114

"ink spot" strategy, 79, 88, 95, 100, 105

innovation: in learning and adaptation, 13; in principles of counterinsurgency, 9–10

institutionalization, of bottom-up adaptation, 14

institutional reform, xv, 109–44; ambitions vs. means in, 138–42; analytical and intellectual capabilities in, 122–28; civilian agencies in, 112–13, 116, 137–38; conservatism in organizational culture and, 128–30; cost of, 115–22; cultural awareness in, 112, 119–20; doctrine revision in, 113–14, 116–17; equipment shortages and, 114, 121; financial crisis and, 115–16; flawed premises guiding optimism about, 138–42; force structure in, 131–38; foundational training in, 118–19; impetus for, 109–13; predeployment training in, 110, 112, 113, 117–21; recognition of need for, 109–13; resistance to, 111, 128–30; reversal of, potential for, 111, 122, 144; slow pace of, 112–15, 130

insurgency: in Basra, British role in creation of, 45–46; changes in nature of, 37; definitions of, 5–6, 46; goals of, 5–6; root causes of, 5; simplistic views of, 21

intellectual capabilities, reform of, 122–28

intelligence: crucial role of, as counterinsurgency principle, 8–9, 10; on Helmand, gaps in, 77, 79, 80, 82–83, 94

Interim Emergency Multinational Force (IEMF), 161

Interim Governing Council, of Iraq, 56

international community, doctrine of, 46, 139–40

International Crisis Group, 68

International Development, Department for. See Department for International Development

International Security Assistance Force (ISAF): British leadership of, 76; burden sharing in, 165; campaign plan of, 75, 88, 176n1; establishment of, 76; mission of, 76–77, 81; number of British troops in, 76; Taliban opposition to, 78; Turkish leadership of, 76; US leadership of, 100

intervention, third-party: Afghan War as, 4, 36; indirect (advisory) approach to, 156–61; Iraq War as, 4; motivations for participating in, 165; in weak or failing states, 111, 149–50. See also specific interventions

invented traditions, 26

Iran, influence in Basra, 64, 69

Iraq Inquiry (2009–2011), 45, 50, 62, 137, 141

Iraq War (1991), 39, 139

Iraq War (2003–2011): as aberration, perception of, 131, 133, 138; Britain as junior coalition partner in, 2, 49, 72–73, 147, 164;

British decision to participate in, 45, 46, 80; initial plan for transition to peace in, 49; invasion of 2003 in, 47–48; vs. Libyan intervention, 154; postwar planning for, lack of, 49–52, 72–73; relevance of British counterinsurgency legacy in, 36–37, 41; as third-party intervention, 4; UN resolution on legal status of postconflict operations in, 48; US embrace of British counterinsurgency legacy in, 24–25; US strategic evolution in, 61; US surge of 2007 in, 61, 98, 104–5; US troop sizing in, 133; US vs. British postconflict operations in, 19–20. See also Basra

Iraq War coalition. See coalition, Iraq War

Ireland. See Northern Ireland

Irish Republican Army Council, 28

Iron, Richard, 65, 68, 127

irregular war. See unconventional war

ISAF. See International Security Assistance Force

Ituri Brigade, 161

Jacana, Task Force, 76

Jackson, Michael, 20, 23, 141

Jaish al-Mahdi (JAM): Iranian influence on, 69; members in prison, 65, 175n76; renegade units of, 66; response to British withdrawal, 64–65, 66; in struggle for political control, 56, 58

Joint Combat Operation Virtual Environment program, 121

joint operations, in military education, 179n1

joint security stations, in Basra, 70

Joint Services Command and Staff College, 40, 114, 115, 116

Joint Training Requirements Authority for Cultural Training, 180n38

Joint UK Plan for Helmand, 93

journals, military, 129–30, 137

Jund al-Samaa, 68

Kabul (Afghanistan), British contributions to security in, 76

Kandahar (Afghanistan): coalition operations in, 86–87, 100–101; Operation Hamkari in, 102, 103, 104, 156, 157; recent levels of violence in, 105; Taliban strongholds in, 77

Karzai, Ahmed Wali, 103, 156

Karzai, Hamid, 78–79, 85

Keeping the Peace (Duties in Support of Civil Power) (War Office), 10

Kennett, Andrew, 123

Kenya, British military training in, 118

Kilcullen, David, 5, 42

"kill zones," 91

King, Anthony, 89, 125

Kings of War blog, 182n70

Kiszely, John, 10–11, 120, 180n36

Kitson, Frank, 9, 34

Kosovo, 46, 154, 155

land forces. *See* ground forces

Land Forces Standing Order 1118, 112

Land Warfare Centre (LWC), 123, 124–25

Land Warfare Collective Training Group, 115

Land Warfare Development Group, of LWC, 124–25

Lashkar Gah (Afghanistan), 102, 105

learning, individual. *See* military education and training

learning, organizational, 13–15; challenge of, 14–15, 168n31; as counterinsurgency principle, 13; definitions of, 13; gaps in scholarship on, 17–18; in institutional reform, 122–28; mechanisms of, 13; relationship of adaptation to, 13–15; top-down, 13–15

Ledwidge, Frank, 89, 135, 173n27, 175n84

legacy. *See* counterinsurgency, British, legacy of

legitimacy of operations: in advisory approach to intervention, 159–60; need for perception of, 9, 10

Lesson Exploitation Centre (LXC), 123

Libya, Western intervention in, 152–56

Lieven, Anatol, 81, 107

Logistics Corps, Royal, 121

looting, in Basra, 53

LWC. *See* Land Warfare Centre

LXC. *See* Lesson Exploitation Centre

Mackiggan, Keith, 137

Mackinlay, John, 37, 171n50, 184n3

Mahdi Army, 61–62, 66

Majar al-Kabir (Iraq), 56

major combat operations. *See* combat operations

Malayan Emergency of 1948–1960: accuracy of historical accounts of, 27–28, 30, 32–35; vs. Basra operations, 60–61; British counterinsurgency legacy based on, 19, 20, 23–24, 25; coercive techniques used in, 32–34; district war executive committees in, 70; ethnic Chinese population in, 35, 171n45; initial missteps in, 13, 58; length of tours in, 135–36, 183n95; nonmilitary actors in, 34; outcome of, 27–28, 29; principles of counterinsurgency used in, 8, 9

Malayan National Liberation Army, 28, 33

Maliki, Nuri al-: on British withdrawal, 175n84; Operation Charge of the Knights under, 68–69, 72; on Operation Salamanca, 61–62; on Operation Sinbad, 63; on state of emergency in Basra, 60

Mansoor, Peter, 181n61

manuals, counterinsurgency: 2001 version of, 113, 115; 2007 update of, 113–14, 115, 116; 2009 update of, 116–17; influence of British legacy on, 2; principles of counterinsurgency in, 7, 8–9. *See also* *specific manuals*

Marines, Royal, in Afghanistan, 76, 90–91

Marines, US: in Afghanistan, 75, 97, 99, 100, 101; rediscovery of counterinsurgency in, 113

Marjah (Afghanistan), 100, 101, 102

Marks, Thomas A., 170n34
Master's Programme, Modular, 127
Mastiff vehicles, 114
Mayall, Simon, 40
Maymana (Afghanistan), 77
Maysan (Iraq), 48
Mazar-e-Sharif (Afghanistan), 77, 176n5
McCaffrey, Barry, 80
McChrystal, Stanley, 100
McMaster, H. R., 15, 181n61
media coverage: of British entry into Iraq War,
    45; in changes to nature of insurgency, 37;
    and demand for progress, 14
Medicine Man exercises, 117
mentoring, of Afghan security forces, 93–94,
    101–2
military, Afghan. *See* Army, Afghan National
military, British: ambitions vs. means of,
    138–42, 150–51; changes in, and relevance
    of counterinsurgency legacy, 38–42; after
    Cold War, 38–39; conventional view of
    war in, 38–41, 109–10, 115; exaggeration
    of role in counterinsurgency campaigns,
    34–35; organizational culture of, 89–90,
    128–30; reasons for lack of preparedness
    for counterinsurgency, 109–10; reform
    of (*See* institutional reform); response to
    counterinsurgency failures, xv; revolution
    in military affairs in, 39–40, 139; role
    in counterinsurgency failures, 3, 165;
    self-censorship by, 128–30; size of, 132–35;
    structure of, 131–38. *See also* Afghan War;
    counterinsurgency; Iraq War; *specific
    branches and operations*
military, Iraqi. *See* Army, Iraqi
military, US: advisory approach used by, 156,
    159, 185n26; Air–Land Battle doctrine
    of, 39; force transformation in, 110, 132,
    182n81; length of tours in, 135; revolution
    in military affairs in, 39, 139; size of, 133.
    See also Afghan War; counterinsurgency;
    Iraq War; *specific branches and operations*

military education and training, British:
    counterinsurgency in, 40–41, 110–11,
    113–15; cultural awareness in, 112, 119–20;
    focus on conventional warfare in, 40–41,
    89, 109–10, 115, 118; joint operations in,
    179n1; for "operations other than war,"
    40–41; for peacekeeping operations, 40;
    postgraduate, 127; predeployment, 110,
    112, 113, 117–21; reform of (*See* institutional
    reform); in regimental system, 41–42
military reform. *See* institutional reform
Military Review (journal), 20, 130
Military Transition Teams, British, in Basra,
    64, 69, 175n74
militias, Afghan, 79, 103
militias, Iraqi: infiltration of security forces
    by, 54, 57, 59, 67; Operation Charge of the
    Knights against, 68–69, 156; Operation
    Sinbad against, 63; response to British
    withdrawal, 64–67; rise in power of, 58–60;
    struggle for political control among,
    56–57, 58–59, 61; US strategic evolution in
    response to, 61
Ministry of Defence (MoD), UK: budget
    of (*See* budget); on civilian agencies in
    Basra, 55; on cultural education, 119; on
    future character of conflict, xv, 110–11, 121,
    124, 125; *Future Land Operational Concept*,
    121–22; Harmony Guidelines of, 134; on
    mission in Afghanistan, 82; and planning
    for Iraq War, 50, 173n25; in Post-Conflict
    Reconstruction Unit, 112–13; recognition
    of need for institutional reform in, 179n13;
    response to counterinsurgency failures,
    xv; *Security and Stabilisation*, 116–17; self-
    censorship in, 129–30, 182n70; *Strategic
    Defence Review*, 38–39; *Strategic Trends
    Programme*, 121, 124; *Wider Peacekeeping*,
    40; on withdrawal from Basra, 65–66, 67
mission creep, 162
mission exploitation, 124, 125
mission-specific training, 118–19

MND-SE. *See* Multinational Division–Southeast

MND-South. *See* Multinational Division–South

Mobile Operations Groups (MOGs), 90–91

Mockaitis, Thomas, 21

Modular Master's Programme, 127

MOGs. *See* Mobile Operations Groups

Moshtarak II, Operation, 100–101, 102, 104, 157

Moshtarak III, Operation, 103

Mountain Thrust, Operation, 86–87, 108

Multinational Division–South (MND-South), 71

Multinational Division–Southeast (MND-SE): number of British troops in, 56; Operation Charge of the Knights and, 68; in Operation Salamanca, 61; transfer from British to US command, 71. *See also* Basra

Mumford, Andrew, 30

Musa Qaleh (Afghanistan), 87, 97

Muslims, Shia, in Basra, 47

Muthanna, al- (Iraq), 48

Nad-e-Ali (Afghanistan), 100, 101, 102, 105

Nagl, John, 25, 181n61

Nahr-e Saraj (Afghanistan), 105

Najaf (Iraq), 20

National Audit Office, 121, 127, 136, 180n39

national security, weak and failing states as threats to, 111

National Security Council, UK, 164

National Transitional Council (NTC), 152–53, 155

NATO: in Balkan campaigns, 153–54; on expansion of British role in Afghanistan, 77; in Libyan intervention, 152–55. *See also* Afghan War; International Security Assistance Force

NATO Training Mission–Afghanistan, 93–94, 104

networked-enabled operations, 110, 132–33, 139

Newton, Paul, 124, 126

"New Villages," in Malayan Emergency, 33, 79

Ngo Dinh Diem, 160

niche capabilities, British, 152, 154, 157–58

no-fly zones, in Libya, 152

Nonkinetic Effects Teams, 95

normalization, in Basra, 35, 51–52, 53

Northern Alliance, 159

Northern Ireland: accuracy of historical accounts of, 27–28; British counterinsurgency legacy based on experience in, 1–2, 19, 23–24; civil–military cooperation in, 168n11; initial missteps in, 13, 58; outcome of conflict in, 28–29

NTC. *See* National Transitional Council

Oates, Michael, 71

Obama, Barack, 81

OEF. *See* Enduring Freedom, Operation

Office of Reconstruction and Humanitarian Assistance (ORHA), 48

Oil Protection Force, 58

oil resources, in Basra, 47, 58

Oman. *See* Dhofar

OMLTs. *See* Operational Mentoring and Liaison Teams

operation(s). *See specific names and types of operations*

operational adaptation: in British operations in Basra, 57–58, 69–72; in British operations in Helmand, 88–92, 94–99, 107; as counterinsurgency principle, 9–10, 13; limitations of, 146

operational flexibility, as counterinsurgency principle, 8, 9–10

Operational Mentoring and Liaison Teams (OMLTs), 93, 101–2

operational mistakes, in British operations in Helmand, 84–92

Operational Training and Advisory Group (OPTAG), 112, 117, 180n23

Operational Training Equipment Pool, 121

OPTAG. *See* Operational Training and Advisory Group

Options for Change review (1991), 38

organizational culture, of British military, 89–90, 128–30

organizational learning. *See* learning, organizational

ORHA. *See* Office of Reconstruction and Humanitarian Assistance

overstretch, 91, 94

Palestine, 29

Palliser, Operation, 161

Panther's Claw, Operation, 97

Parameters (journal), 130

partnering, with local security forces: in advisory approach to intervention, 158; in Afghanistan, lack of, 97, 102, 108

PCRU. *See* Post-Conflict Reconstruction Unit

peacekeeping operations: Basra as, 52–57; vs. counterinsurgency, 7, 40, 110; in Democratic Republic of the Congo, 161–62; education and training for, 40; Helmand as, 82, 83, 88–89; historical experience with, 23, 39, 139–40; misguided optimism based on experience in, 139–40; principles of, 53; in Sierra Leone, 162

Petraeus, David, 104, 181n61

Philippines, advisory approach in, 156, 159

pinch points, 136

Pitt, A. R., 137

planning: for British operations in Helmand, 78–79, 83, 93; for Iraq War, 49–52, 72–73

platoon-house strategy, 85, 87–88, 90

police, in counterinsurgency campaigns, 34. *See also* security forces

Police Service, Iraqi, 67

Police Staff College, 40

political control, in Basra: British transfer of, 51, 55, 63–68; local struggle for, 56–57, 58–59, 61

political control, in Helmand: before British operations, 78; British transfer of, 103–4; local struggle for, 78, 105

politically led operations, in Afghanistan, switch to, 100, 178n75

political primacy, as counterinsurgency principle, 7–8

political strategy, in Malayan Emergency, 35

political support: in advisory approach to intervention, 159–60; for British operations in Basra, 46, 58; for future counterinsurgency operations, 147, 166; for institutional reform, 128–30; for Libyan intervention, 154–55; as limiting factor for operations, 147; in outcome of counterinsurgency, 15–16

political will, 15–16

politics, in resistance to institutional reform, 128–30

poppy eradication, 78

postconflict operations: British recognition of need for preparedness for, 111; demand for demonstration of progress in, 14; in Iraq, 19–20, 48; US vs. British, 19–20

Post-Conflict Reconstruction Unit (PCRU), 93, 96, 112–13, 137

postgraduate education, 127

presidential elections, Afghan, 97

Price, Camp (Afghanistan), 79

priorities, in strategy, 12, 147. *See also* institutional reform

prisoners, Jaish al-Mahdi, 65, 175n76

progress, modern demand for timely demonstration of, 14

provincial council, of Basra, 60, 63, 67

Provincial Reconstruction Teams (PRTs), in Afghanistan: force structure and, 137, 138; in Helmand, 75, 83, 95–96, 138; limitations of, 77; in Maymana, 77; in Mazar-e-Sharif, 77, 176n5

Provincial Reconstruction Teams (PRTs), in Iraq, 60, 137

Provisional Irish Republican Army, 28
PRTs. *See* Provincial Reconstruction Teams

Qaboos bin Said, 160
Qaeda, al-: British contributions to campaign
    against, 76; in Helmand, 78; in mission of
    Afghan War, 81–82

RAND Corporation, 134
Rangwala, Glen, 61
Rashid, Hasan al-, 58
Raziq, Abdul, 103, 156
reconstruction activities: in Basra, 54–55, 60,
    63, 64, 70; in Helmand, 83, 96. *See also*
    Provincial Reconstruction Teams
reform. *See* institutional reform
regime change: in advisory approach to
    intervention, 160; in Libya, 152
regimental system, 41–42, 89
Regional Command South (Afghanistan),
    102–3
Reid, John, 83, 86
relocation, forced, 32–33, 171n45
reserve forces, reform of, 135, 182n91
resource allocation: for British operations
    in Helmand, 84–85, 96, 99, 101; and
    equipment shortages, 114, 121
Review of Acquisition (Gray), 140
Revolutionary United Front (RUF), 162, 163
revolution in military affairs (RMA), 39–40, 139
Richards, David, 88, 130, 162
Rigden, I. A., 34
Ritchie, Nick, 141
RMA. *See* revolution in military affairs
Robinson, Camp (Afghanistan), 79
robust peacekeeping, vs. counterinsurgency, 7
rotational policy, 135, 136
RUF. *See* Revolutionary United Front
Rwandan genocide, 185n19

Sadr, Moqtada al-: cease-fire called by, 66;
    Coalition Provision Authority and, 57;

Operation Salamanca and, 61–62; in
    struggle for political control, 56, 58
Said bin Taimur, 160
Salamanca, Operation, 61–63
Salmon, Andy, 71
Sandhurst, 116, 123
Schoomaker, Peter J., 25
SCIRI. *See* Supreme Council for the Islamic
    Revolution in Iraq
SCU. *See* Serious Crimes Unit
*SDSR. See Strategic Defence and Security
    Review*
security, in campaign plan for Afghanistan,
    176n1
*Security and Stabilisation: The Military
    Contribution* (MoD), 116–17
security assistance group, in British Army,
    157, 158–59
security forces, Afghan: British transfer of
    control to, 104; lack of partnering with,
    97, 102, 108; in surge of 2010, 100; training
    and mentoring of, 93–94, 101–2, 104
security forces, in advisory approach to
    intervention, 156–61
security forces, Iraqi: British attempts
    at reform of, 54, 59, 173n32; British
    collaboration with, expansion of, 70;
    British transfer of control to, 63–68;
    establishment of, 36; militias' infiltration
    of, 54, 57, 59, 67; mission of, 54; in
    Operation Charge of the Knights, 68–71,
    93, 156, 164; in Operation Salamanca,
    61–62; in Operation Sinbad, 63; in US
    surge of 2007, 61, 98
security stations, joint, in Basra, 70
self-censorship, by military, 128–30
September 11, 2001, terrorist attacks, 76, 81, 82
sequencing, in strategy, 12, 147
Serious Crimes Unit (SCU), 59
Shia Muslims, in Basra, 47
Shirreff, Richard, 61–62, 174n65, 174n70,
    175nn93–94

Sierra Leone, British operations in, 139, 161, 162–64
simulations, computer, 121
Sinbad, Operation, 62–63, 174n70
Sirte, battle of, 153
16 Air Assault Brigade (British), 79, 83, 87–90, 93, 96, 99
small wars, British experience with, 22–23
"smile, shoot, smile" approach, 51, 53
Smith, Rupert, 73, 125
Snatch land rovers, 114, 141, 183n114
social media, in changes to nature of insurgency, 37
Special Forces, British, 154
Special Forces, US, 78
special-operations forces, air power combined with, 153, 154, 155–56
Spencer, Peter, 142, 184n124
squatters, in Malayan Emergency, 33, 171n45
Stabilisation Unit, UK, 60, 96, 137
stability operations: ambitions vs. means in, 151; in Basra, 49; British experience with, 23; vs. counterinsurgency, 7; force sizing and, 132, 133. *See also* peacekeeping operations
stand-off weapons, concealment in response to, 155
Stanford Training Area (Stanta), 117, 118
state building: in Afghanistan, 81, 82; gaps in British understanding of, 46
state-on-state warfare: as focus of British military, 38, 40, 109; preconceptions about, 7. *See also* conventional warfare
Stirrup, Jock, 44, 64, 68
Stothard Tee, William, 183n95
Strachan, Hew, 24, 178n74
strategic abstinence, 148, 166
Strategic Defence and Security Review (SDSR), 132, 133, 138, 141, 142, 151
Strategic Defence Review (MoD), 38–39
strategic evolution: in British operations in Afghanistan, 95–96; in US operations

in Afghanistan, 81; in US operations in Iraq, 61
strategic inertia: in British operations in Basra, 57–62, 73; in British operations in Helmand, 96–99, 107
strategic miscalculations: in British operations in Basra, 55–57, 72–74, 147; in British operations in Helmand, 79–86, 91–92, 147; in planning of Iraq War, 49–52
strategic objectives: of British operations in Basra, 55; use of force as contribution to, 33–34
strategic selectivity, 166
strategic thinking: British capacity for, 4, 141, 147, 163–64; definition of, 163; preconceptions of war in, 7; vital role of, 163–64
Strategic Trends Programme: Future Character of Conflict (MoD), 121, 124
strategy: in advisory approach to intervention, 159–60; components of, 12, 147; vs. counterinsurgency, 98; definition of, 12, 147; lessons learned about counterinsurgency in absence of, 46; principles of counterinsurgency in, 11–12
Strike of the Sword, Operation, 97
success: in Basra, perception of, 57, 128; in counterinsurgency, political will in, 15–16; in Helmand, lack of indicators of, 105, 106, 179n87; institutional reform inhibited by need to promote image of, 128–30
Suffield (Canada), training site in, 113, 117
Suhrke, Astri, 80
Supreme Council for the Islamic Revolution in Iraq (SCIRI), 56–57, 58
surge: in Afghan War, 100, 101, 105; in Iraq War, 61, 98, 104–5
Sweden, in Afghan War, 176n5

tactical adaptation, in British operations in Helmand, 75, 90–91
Tactical Conflict Assessment Framework, 95

Taliban: Afghan militias in fight against, 79; attacks in response to British deployment, 79–80, 83, 87; British contributions to campaign against, 76; local services provided by, 78; in mission of Afghan War, 76, 81–82; need for British operations against, 75, 77, 78; operational mistakes and, 90–91; Operation Panther's Claw against, 97; removal from power as goal, 76, 81–82; rise of power after 2001, 78, 81; underestimation of capabilities of, 80, 82–83

Tamimi, Muzahim al-, 51, 55

Task Force Jacana, 76

technological superiority: force sizing based on, 132–33; in force transformation, 110, 132; revolution in military affairs based on, 39–40, 139

Telic, Operation, 182n93

Templer, Gerald, 8, 9, 28, 168n17

10th Division (Iraq), 65, 67, 175n74

Thetford (England), Stanford Training Area in, 117, 118

Think Defence blog, 134, 135, 182n91

third-party intervention. *See* intervention, third-party

Thompson, Robert, 22–23, 24, 28, 30

3 Battalion Parachute Regiment (British), 83

3 Commando Brigade (British), 87, 90–91, 96, 99

Tootal, Stuart, 83

top-down learning, 13–15

tours: dwell time between, 131, 134; length of, 135–36, 182n93

traditional war, use of term, 7. *See also* conventional war

training, of British military. *See* military education

training, of local security forces: in advisory approach to intervention, 156–61; in Afghanistan, 93–94, 101–2, 104

Training and Doctrine Command, US, 123

Transforming to Contact initiative, 131

Troubles. *See* Northern Ireland

Turkey: in invasion of Iraq, 51; in ISAF, 76

12th Mechanized Brigade (British), 91

UK. *See* Britain

UN. *See* United Nations

unconventional (irregular) war: air power in, 154, 184n17; preparedness for, in institutional reform, 121–22; use of term, 7

unemployment, in Basra, 67, 70

Unified Protector, Operation, 152–53, 154

United Kingdom (UK). *See* Britain

United Nations (UN): in Afghanistan, mission of, 81; on Basra security climate after invasion, 51; in Democratic Republic of the Congo, 161–62; in establishment of ISAF, 76; in political transition of Iraq, coalition assumptions about, 49; in Sierra Leone, 162, 163

United Nations Security Council: on invasion of Iraq, 49; on Libyan intervention, 152; Resolution 1483, 48; Resolution 1510, 77

United States: British colonial rule of, 29; British "special relationship" with, viii, 82. *See also* military, US

unity of command, as counterinsurgency principle, 8, 60, 86

UOR. *See* Urgent Operational Requirements

urban operations, 113, 124, 149

Urban Warrior exercises, 124

Urgent Operational Requirements (UOR), 114, 121, 141–42, 183n115

victory, theory of, in strategy, 12, 147

Vietnam War, xv, 25, 28, 160, 170n34

virtual training, 121

Waeli, Muhammad al-, 58

war(s): counterinsurgency as corrective to traditional views of, 7, 10; political will in outcome of, 15–16. *See also specific wars and types of wars*

warlords, Afghan, 78

Waterfall, Gary, 153

weak states: future of interventions in, 149–50; as national-security threats, 111

Wesa, Tooryalai, 103

White, Stephen, 173n31

White Paper of 2003, 132–33

White-Spunner, Barney, 71–72

Wider Peacekeeping (MoD), 40

winning hearts and minds: activities used for, 9, 30; in British counterinsurgency legacy, 30–32; humanitarian vs. utilitarian understanding of, 30–31; origins of phrase, 9, 168n17; in simplistic views of insurgency, 21

Zenith, Operation, 174n65, 174n70